THE DUDE DIET DINNERTIME

ALSO BY SERENA WOLF

THE DUDE DIET:
Clean(ish) Food for People Who Like to Eat Dirty

THE
DUDE DIET
DINNERTIME

125 Clean(ish) Recipes for Weeknight Winners and Fancypants Dinners

Serena Wolf

Photographs by Matt Armendariz

Harper Wave

An Imprint of HarperCollinsPublishers

HarperCollins books may be purchased for educational, business, or sales promotional use. For information, please email the Special Markets Department at SPsales@harpercollins.com.

FIRST EDITION

Designed by Bonni Leon-Berman

Photographs copyright © by Matt Armendariz

Library of Congress Cataloging-in-Publication Data has been applied for.
ISBN 978-0-06-285470-4

19 20 21 22 23   LSC   10 9 8 7 6 5 4 3 2 1

FOR LOGAN,
the dinner date
of my dreams.
Especially on
Sundays.

CONTENTS

If I ever die eating,
at least I died doing
something happy.

—LOGAN SMITH UNLAND
(after almost choking to
death on a sandwich)

INTRODUCTION

Eight years ago, I fell madly in love with a wonderful and hilarious food-loving dude named Logan. I recently married him, mostly for his hot body, but we'll come back to that.

Before we go any further, I need you to understand a few things about Logan Smith Unland and his unparalleled obsession with "dank eats." This is the type of man who discusses a favorite sandwich or pizza in the same giddy, adoring way that most adults gush about their child or pet, right down to showing unsolicited photos on his phone. When attending a party, he immediately zeroes in on servers, becomes their best friend, and then enlists their help in procuring the freshest finger food throughout the night. (Hugs and high fives are not unusual upon leaving.) He comes close to hyperventilating in the vicinity of melted cheese, hasn't missed our local barbecue festival in over a decade, and braves ailments ranging from cayenne-induced rashes to somewhat alarming meat sweats in his relentless pursuit of deliciousness. I'd go on, but you catch my drift.

When we first met, I was a culinary student at Le Cordon Bleu Paris, and Logan's die-hard passion for food was one of the many things that piqued my interest in him. And since the first few months of our courtship were long-distance between Paris and New York City, I chalked up his decadent meal choices on dates to special-occasion eating. He definitely ate some nutritious stuff on his own time, right?

WRONG. Upon cohabiting, I quickly realized that Logan's day-to-day diet was, in a word, *terrifying*. Scarier still was the fact that he thought he

ate "pretty healthy." Given that Logan's primary food groups were meat, cheese, white bread, and Coors Light (all of which were consumed with flagrant disregard for normal human portion sizes), this belief only served to highlight his nutritional confusion. The more we talked about nutrition, the more I began to worry about Logan's long-term health. If the iceberg lettuce and carrot shavings beneath his daily serving of chicken tenders— aka Buffalo chicken salad—remained his primary source of vegetables, he certainly wasn't going to win any longevity contests. I was actually rather surprised he'd made it to the ripe old age of twenty-eight without falling victim to anything more serious than a raging Zantac habit.

Desperate to help my new roommate avoid an early, and likely deep-fried, grave, I'd occasionally suggest that Logan consider cleaning up his diet, only to be met with anti-kale rants and refusals to eat "weird vegan things" like me. (I found the latter a particularly interesting rebuff, as I am not vegan, nor do I enjoy eating weird things.) He blanketly condemned all health food as "boring and gross," repeatedly scoffing at my claims that nutritionally sound meals could taste just as awesome as his beloved Chinese takeout or football-size burritos . . .

CHALLENGE ACCEPTED

Motivated by love (and my competitive nature), I committed myself to overhauling Logan's perspective on eating well. Fully aware that he would never restrict himself to a life of steamed chicken breasts and broccoli, and not wanting him to, I decided to re-create his favorite comfort foods—I'm talking everything from lasagna and cheesesteaks to cocktails and cupcakes—using nutrient-dense whole foods. My mission wasn't to create recipes that were "good for being healthy," but rather ones that were straight-up delicious and elicited the same excitement freak-outs associated with more fattening fare. It wouldn't be easy, but I knew that if I could pull it off, Logan might just come to see the healthy eating light.

And he did! The Dude inhaled my cleaner creations without question, happily eating more lean meats, whole grains, vegetables, and, eventually, his words. Slowly but surely, he dropped his post-college fun pounds, felt more energized, and began making smarter food choices and exercising respectable portion control *on his own*, which was downright inspiring to witness. If I could get Logan psyched about nutritious food, I knew I had a shot at converting other skeptics. And thus, The Dude Diet was born.

The early Dude Diet gospel was spread via my blog (domesticate-me .com), where I posted a regular column featuring slimmed-down comfort food recipes along with nuggets of nutritional wisdom and realistic healthy eating tips that didn't involve counting calories, cutting out entire food groups, or purchasing obscure ingredients from eighteen different specialty stores. The series struck a chord with so many more people than I ever could have anticipated and set a pretty amazing chain of events in motion—starting with the emergence of a fledgling Dude Diet community, then landing me a job as the private chef for a couple of players on the New York Giants, and ultimately spawning my first book.

The Dude Diet: Clean(ish) Food for People Who Like to Eat Dirty was my Buffalo-scented love letter to Logan and his nutritionally confused peers the world over. It provided the building blocks for a healthy lifestyle—from kicking cravings and developing portion control to responsible boozing and the concept of No-Calorie Sunday—as well as an arsenal of foolproof recipes, all of which could be accomplished with minimal kitchen equipment and culinary skill. The goal? Help people get their shit together on the nutrition and cooking fronts, and make it as fun and tasty as humanly possible.

Since the book's release in the fall of 2016, hordes of men, women, and children alike have enthusiastically embraced The Dude Diet, which truly warms my heart. As I've maintained since writing the inaugural blog post more than six years ago, The Dude Diet may have been inspired by a nutritionally confused dude and conceptualized with his beer-guzzling, finger-food-crushing, meat-sweat-suffering brethren in mind, but its core philosophy and flavor-packed recipes have universal appeal. The Dude Diet is a lifestyle for *anyone*—regardless of gender, age, and nutritional understanding—who wants to grab health by the proverbial balls, get busy in the kitchen, and eat drool-worthy nutritious food sans deprivation. In a time when everyone and their mom seems to be promoting a new diet with a laundry list of restrictions (Paleo, and Keto, and Whole30, oh my!), The Dude Diet offers an accessible alternative for those looking to live well without sacrificing the foods they love. As one Dude Dieter so eloquently stated: *The Dude Diet is a lifestyle for the rest of us.*

In the wake of *The Dude Diet*'s release, I've been lucky enough to meet countless Dude Dieters both in real life and online. And while our discussions have covered every topic from Logan's impressive chest hair to successfully foisting quinoa bakes on toddlers, most convos typically end with the same request:

GIMME MORE DUDE DIET DINNERS!

I get it. Breakfast may be the most important meal of the day, but when it comes to staying on the nutritional straight and narrow, *dinner* is where people fall down the most. You're tired, you've had a long day at home, work, or school, and the temptation to call a favorite deliveryman or self-soothe with a couch meal of Hot Pockets and Ben & Jerry's can be strong. However, armed with a well-stocked pantry, a little motivation, and a book of recipes for easy evening feasts, a healthy homemade dinner suddenly becomes a lot less daunting. And that, friends, is why I wrote this book.

The following pages are filled with crave-worthy dinnertime recipes made with mostly good-for-you ingredients, and there's a little something for every type of occasion and Dude Diet chef. You'll find bomb burgers and sandwiches for times when you need classic comfort; an entire chapter devoted to fingers, wings, and other things perfect for game day (and everyday) celebrations; and plenty of cozy, crowd-pleasing casseroles. There are fuss-free one-pot recipes to minimize mess, hearty dinner salads made with leafy green haters in mind, and some egg-y options for nights when you're feeling breakfast more than dinner. Hosting a dinner party or got a hot date? Put on your fancy pants and flip to the "black tie optional" recipes for slightly elevated Dude Diet fare. I've also labeled recipes that take thirty minutes or less with a *Quick + Dirty* stamp should you be pressed for time. Many recipes are complete meals in and of themselves, but there's also an arsenal of sexy sides that you can mix and match with your favorite meat and seafood mains to create an endless variety of epic spreads. God knows I love it when you get creative.

Now that we've covered the important stuff, let's circle back to the beginning where I mentioned marrying my muse, which was a significant event in The Dude Diet's ongoing story. Logan and I tied the knot in October 2017, and this entire collection of recipes was tested and written during our newlywed year. Not to be a total sap, but sharing these dinners with Logan was a life highlight, and I like to think that this book is a reflection of the extreme happiness and excitement I felt about hitching my wagon to the Dude's star. Don't worry, Logan didn't go easy on his critiques given our upgraded marital status. If anything, he took his duties as the arbiter of Dude Diet taste that much more seriously. Lucky for you, Logan is exactly the type of detail-oriented critic you want vetting your healthier mac and cheese and taquitos.

So, whether you're a longtime Dude Diet devotee, a new disciple looking to turn your body into a wonderland, or someone standing in a library or bookstore deciding what to make for dinner, I'm pumped that this book is currently in your hands. I hope it provides some pearls of nutritional wisdom, plenty of laughs, and countless cleanish feasts. (Or at the very least supplies some high-quality bathroom reading material.) Let's have some fun, shall we?

THE DUDE DIET COMMANDMENTS

1 I resolve to be less of a nutritional idiot. I shall think before I put things in my mouth, especially pizza, burritos, and other foods that are larger than my head.

2 I shall eat more fish, poultry, and lean pork. Red meat is an indulgence, not a diet staple.

3 Excluding my birthday and barbecue festivals to which I have purchased a ticket, I shall not eat any type of meat in quantities large enough to give me the meat sweats. Not even on No-Calorie Sunday.

4 If it's white, I shall always think twice. I will limit my consumption of white bread, rice, and pasta, and eat more whole grains, which are surprisingly delicious.

5 I shall curb my refined sugar habit because it makes me fat, sick, and unhappy.

6 I shall crush less dairy. Cream, butter, cheese, and ice cream will be eaten sparingly.

7 I shall not clog my arteries with large quantities of fried food. There are many healthier cooking methods, and I will learn to appreciate them.

8 I shall make an effort to consume at least five servings of vegetables a day and three servings of fruit. This will provide me with essential nutrients and leave me too full to eat junk.

9 I shall pay attention to sauces, dressings, and condiments, many of which are filled with a shocking amount of calories, sugar, fat, and scary additives. I will eat fresh, flavor-packed foods so that I'm not tempted to douse them in ranch.

10 I shall exercise portion control. I will not eat to the point where I feel ill, require medication, or am unable to move.

11 I shall eat at a reasonable pace. Eating more slowly will give my body a chance to recognize when it's full. It is also more civilized.

12 I shall exercise on a regular basis. Such exercise will break a sweat. Sitting in a steam room or sauna does not count.

13 I shall drink alcohol responsibly (most of the time) and keep my beer belly in check.

14 My body is a wonderland. I commit myself to The Dude Diet in the hope that other people will agree with this statement.

1

STEP UP TO THE DINNER PLATE

I'm about to hit you with my top tips for dinnertime domination, and they're important, but the true key to establishing and maintaining a healthy cooking routine is a well-stocked kitchen. Having a variety of versatile ingredients, cookware, and tools on hand mitigates shopping lists and stress levels while boosting day-to-day Dude Diet morale. Longtime Dude Dieters and/or enthusiastic home cooks, I assume you already have a handle on your culinary setup—go ahead and get cooking! As for the rest of you, let's quickly run down The Dude Diet's kitchen essentials.

The following pages contain a list of the ingredients and equipment used over and over again throughout this book. It may seem long, but don't panic. The food items are widely available (if not at your local market, definitely on a little site called Amazon.com), and you obviously don't need to buy every single one right away. Start with the basics: extra-virgin olive oil, kosher salt, black pepper, and a few of your favorite flavors—i.e., low-sodium soy sauce and sriracha if you're into Asian food, chipotles in adobo and cumin for the Mexican enthusiasts, etc.—and then snag a few more staples every time you hit the grocery store.

KITCHEN ESSENTIALS

Oils
Avocado oil
Extra-virgin coconut oil
Extra-virgin olive oil
Light sesame oil
Dark (aka toasted) sesame oil

Vinegars
Apple cider vinegar
Balsamic vinegar
Distilled white vinegar
Red wine vinegar
Unseasoned rice vinegar

Whole-Grain Goods
Old-fashioned rolled oats (not quick-cooking!)
Brown rice
Quinoa
Farro
Whole-grain or grain-free pasta (I recommend Barilla whole-grain pasta, Jovial brown rice pasta, and Banza chickpea flour pasta.)
Whole-wheat panko bread crumbs (I love Kikkoman brand, which I order on the cheap from Amazon.com.)

Fridge Favorites
Baby spinach
Barbecue sauce (Choose something with pronounceable ingredients and minimal added sugar.)
Bread-and-butter pickles
Chicken or turkey sausage links
Dijon mustard
Eggs
Lemons
Low-sodium soy sauce
Marinara sauce (I like Rao's brand.)
Milk (dairy or non-dairy)
Nonfat plain Greek yogurt
Parmesan cheese (Buy a wedge and grate it as needed.)
Salad greens (such as arugula or mesclun)
Sharp cheddar cheese
Sriracha sauce/hot sauce of your choice
Whole-grain tortillas (whole-wheat, sprouted grain, or brown rice)
Worcestershire sauce
Fresh herbs (Basil, cilantro, parsley, and chives will get the most action.)

Pantry Staples
Canned beans (I recommend black, cannellini, chickpeas, great northern, and kidney, but you do you.)
Canned tomatoes (crushed, diced, and pureed)
Chia seeds
Canned chipotles in adobo sauce
Cornstarch
Fresh garlic (Make sure to store it in a cool, dry place.)
Honey
Low-sodium broths (beef, chicken, and vegetable)
Nonstick cooking spray
No-sugar-added nut butters (Almond and peanut will likely get the most use.)
Onions (red and yellow)
Pure maple syrup
Raw nuts (such as almonds, cashews, and walnuts)
Shallots
Tomato paste
Tahini

Spice Cabinet Essentials

Kosher salt

Black pepper (I recommend purchasing a small grinder with whole peppercorns.)

Cayenne pepper

Chili powder

Crushed red pepper flakes (aka red chile flakes)

Dried oregano

Garlic powder

Ground cinnamon

Ground cumin

Onion powder

Paprika

Smoked paprika

    Adventurous folks should also consider: chipotle chile powder, curry powder, dried parsley, dried rosemary, dried thyme, garam masala, and ground ginger.

Cookware

Large (12- to 14-inch) ovenproof skillet

True nonstick skillet (for delicate foods like fish and eggs)

Dutch oven or heavy-bottomed soup pot

Small and medium saucepans

Grill pan (Not required but very handy. Especially if you don't have a real grill.)

Bakeware

9 × 13-inch baking dish (ceramic or glass)

9 × 9-inch baking dish (ceramic or glass)

2 large, rimmed baking sheets

2 wire baking racks

Tools

Chef's knife

Serrated knife

Cutting board

Mixing bowls

Measuring cups and spoons

Colander

Silicone spatula

Flexible thin metal spatula (Very helpful for fish.)

Whisk

Kitchen tongs

Vegetable peeler

Coarse grater (box grater)

Microplane grater/zester (This is essential for grating garlic, ginger, and Parmesan cheese.)

Can opener

Electronics

High-speed blender (preferably with a personal cup attachment)

Food processor (I recommend a 6- to 8-cup model for most of your basic needs.)

Instant-read meat thermometer

Other Helpful Things

Parchment paper

Aluminum foil

Plastic wrap

Glass or plastic containers in various sizes (for storing prepped ingredients and leftovers)

TIPS FOR DUDE DIET DINNER DOMINATION

1. BE A PLANNER. The simple action of sitting down on a Sunday or Monday and choosing dinners for the upcoming week will streamline your shopping, reduce daily dinnertime stress, and bolster your overall Dude Dieting efforts in a big way. Once you've picked out your recipes, make a master list of all the ingredients you'll need to purchase and do a single big shop or online order. (You can then supplement the initial haul with fresh meat or fish later in the week.) Armed with a plan and the goods to execute it, tackling dinner after a long day feels far less daunting.

2. READ THE ENTIRE RECIPE, DAMMIT! Don't fight me on this. Reading an entire recipe from start to finish *before* shopping or cooking is critical to its success. Figure out the ingredients and tools needed, the prep work required, and the timing for each step of the process. Spending a few extra minutes up front to get your dinnertime ducks in a row sets you up for success and helps prevent all manner of culinary disasters. There's nothing more annoying than starting a recipe and realizing that you forgot a key ingredient, didn't factor in marinating time, or can't find the colander needed to strain the pasta that's rapidly turning to mush on the stove. Oh, and do NOT skip steps. I know waiting for meat to rest or "flavors to marry" may seem like time wasted, but these things have a big impact on a recipe's deliciousness. Trust.

3. MEAL PREP FOR SUCCESS. Relax, I'm not suggesting you re-create the notorious Instagram tableau of endless Tupperware containers filled with steamed chicken, broccoli, and sweet potatoes. That's not The Dude Diet way. All I'm asking is that you make your life easier by working in some strategic meal prep when you can. Tackling a recipe that calls for a whole grain like farro or quinoa? Cook double or

triple what you need so that you can have a prepared grain on hand for salads, sides, and bowls throughout the week. Same goes for cooked vegetables. When making a soup or chili, consider doubling down and freezing the extra batch for future busy weeknights. If a recipe requires some hands-off time on the stovetop or in the oven whip up a batch of Idiotproof Chicken Breasts (page 136) or another *Quick + Dirty* recipe while you wait. You get the picture. Knocking out a little extra prep on the nights you have free time will save your ass on the nights you don't.

4. PORTION CONTROL IS KEY. Unfortunately, eating well is only one part of the health and weight-loss puzzle. In order to achieve and maintain a wonderland body, you not only need to eat nutritious food, you also need to eat said food in **reasonable quantities!** Please respect the serving sizes indicated for the recipes in this book. They're there for a reason. The servings may seem smaller than you're used to at first—most Americans suffer from portion distortion—but I promise that once you embrace proper portions, your body will adjust its "appetite thermostat" pretty quickly. For the record, The Dude Diet's servings are actually much more generous than those dictated by the American Heart Association. (I'm all too aware that hangry dudes would punt this book out the window after being told to eat four bites of chicken for dinner.)

5. SIDELINE THE "CHEF'S SNACKS." Speaking of portion control, let's talk about the "invisible snacks" many chefs consume while they cook. I understand that a nutritious dinner can sometimes take a bit of time, and you may feel peckish while you wait. However, mindlessly consuming the rest of the block of cheese you grated for chili, or "tasting" the guacamole for tacos with a bag of tortilla chips will severely diminish your Dude Diet returns. Resist the urge. (If you're actually starving—not just bored—and can't hold out, reach for some raw vegetables with a little bit of hummus, a handful of raw nuts, or Greek yogurt to tide you over.)

6. EAT YOUR VEGETABLES. Every single dinner should involve one serving of vegetables at *minimum*, but two are ideal. To state the obvious, vegetables are really, really, ridiculously good for you and contain the fiber and essential vitamins and minerals you need to feel and look your best. Many recipes in this book will meet your dinnertime veggie quota as written, but in certain cases (i.e. burgers, sandwiches, and stand-alone recipes for meat and fish), you'll need to incorporate a vegetable. You'll find an array of sexy sides to choose from in Chapter 10, but a roasted vegetable or green salad is always an excellent option when you want to keep things simple.

7. BEWARE THE BOOZE. Making smarter solid food choices is the focus of this book, but regulating your liquid consumption is equally important to your Dude Dieting success. In addition to being highly caloric, alcohol distracts your liver from one of its most important jobs: burning fat. When your liver is busy ridding itself of boozy toxins, it can't torch fat as effectively, which is counterintuitive for anyone hoping to shed some extra lbs. With the exception of special occasions and truly terrible days, limit yourself to one portion-controlled alcoholic beverage with dinner. (For the record, there are 12 ounces of beer, 5 ounces of wine, and 1.5 ounces of hard liquor in a single serving.) Dedicated Dude Dieters

should consider drying out completely during the workweek. You'll be surprised how quickly the pounds fall off when you kick casual drinks to the curb.

8. TAKE ADVANTAGE OF NO-CALORIE SUNDAY. Whether it's your mom's meatloaf with buttery mashed potatoes or the supreme pie from

your favorite pizza place, there are some wildly indulgent dinners that you just can't imagine life without. The best part about The Dude Diet is that you don't have to. No-Calorie Sunday is the one day a week when you can abandon your healthy eating habits and get weird on the food front without derailing your Dude Diet progress. You'll find that celebrating this weekly "holiday" satisfies your crazier cravings, cuts you some psychological slack, and helps you stay on the nutritional straight and narrow the rest of the week. (FYI, No-Calorie Sunday doesn't have to fall on a Sunday, but the concept works best when celebrated on the same day each week.)

9. YOU DO YOU. The epic evening feasts in this book can and should be adapted to your personal preferences and the ingredients you have on hand. I often suggest substitutions and alternative serving options in the "You Do You" sidebars throughout this book, but don't hesitate to unleash your creativity within the realm of common sense (no, the meatloaf won't work if you sub peanut butter for avocado, skip the glaze, and bake it for only twenty minutes).

10. HAVE FUN!!! Not everyone loves cooking, and that's cool. But if you look at making dinner as a chore or a punishment, you're unlikely to commit to it on the reg. So pump some jams, listen to a podcast, watch sports or your favorite TV show, call a friend on speaker, get family and friends involved, or enjoy your portion-controlled evening cocktail. Do whatever you need to do in order to make the time spent in your kitchen less work and more play. You'll settle into a solid cooking groove in no time.

A LITTLE PEP TALK

Before you run off to make dinner, I'd like to quickly remind you that The Dude Diet is a lifestyle and should be treated as such. It's not a crash diet or a get thin quick fix. You won't wake up after a week of Dude Diet dinners with Timberlake abs and a free pass to crush Domino's for the rest of the year. Sorry. However, if you embrace The Dude Diet's basic commandments and rely on the cleanish recipes in this book and its predecessor, you will undoubtedly feel better and look hotter long-term. That's a pretty sweet deal given that you're still able to enjoy epic meals without having to count calories or give up entire food groups/your life. Not to mention the fact that spending some quality time cooking for yourself and the people you love is guaranteed to up your culinary street cred and boost your confidence both inside the kitchen and out.

I'd also like to note that you may fall off the wagon from time to time, and that's okay. Just remember to pick yourself up, wipe the barbecue sauce from your various body parts, and climb right back on there. In reality, this shouldn't be too difficult. The Dude Diet bandwagon is awesome. It's packed with happy people (still plenty of breathing room, though, thanks to the lean nature of their wonderland bodies), and there's a bunch of nutritious and delicious food being served.

Go forth and conquer, dudes.

You Got This.

CHAPTER 2

BOMB BURGERS AND SANDWICHES

Turkey Reuben Patty Melts

FOR THE RUSSIAN DRESSING:

¼ cup mayonnaise

¼ cup nonfat plain Greek yogurt

2 tablespoons ketchup

2 teaspoons sriracha sauce

2½ tablespoons minced bread-and-butter pickles

½ teaspoon onion powder

1 teaspoon fresh lemon juice

FOR THE SANDWICH:

1 pound 93% lean ground turkey (not 99% lean!)

½ teaspoon dried dill weed

½ teaspoon kosher salt

¼ teaspoon freshly ground black pepper

2¼ cups sauerkraut, divided

Four 1-ounce slices Swiss cheese

5 teaspoons extra-virgin olive oil, divided

8 slices whole-grain rye bread

I always like to lead with the bad news, so here it is: The average overstuffed deli Reuben knows no nutritional bounds and tends to leave its wildly enthusiastic consumers bloated and in dire need of a rollaway cot. The good news? If you replace corned beef with a lean ground turkey patty and top it with digestion-friendly sauerkraut, a responsible amount of Swiss, and lightened-up Russian dressing, you can satisfy a raging Reuben craving *and* do a body good. It's Dude Diet sandwich sorcery at its finest.

1. Combine all the ingredients for the Russian dressing in a small bowl. Briefly set aside.
2. Place the ground turkey in a medium bowl. Add the dill, salt, pepper, and ¼ cup of the sauerkraut and mix until well combined. (I recommend using your hands for this.)
3. With damp hands, mold the turkey mixture into 4 oval or rectangular patties, about 6 inches long (roughly the length of your slices of bread) and ¼ inch thick, and place them on a piece of parchment or wax paper.
4. Heat 1 teaspoon of the oil in a large nonstick skillet over medium heat. When the oil is hot and shimmering, carefully add the patties to the pan. Cook for 2½ to 3 minutes per side, until cooked through. Transfer to a plate.
5. To assemble, spread one side of each slice of bread with 1 tablespoon Russian dressing. Add a turkey patty to each of 4 pieces of the bread and top each patty with ½ cup sauerkraut and a slice of cheese. Close the sandwiches with the remaining 4 slices of bread, dressing side down. Lightly brush the outside of each sandwich with 1 teaspoon oil.
6. Wipe out the pan used for the turkey patties and return it to the stovetop. Heat the pan over medium heat. When hot, add 2 of the sandwiches to the pan and place another heavy skillet (or a sandwich press) on top. Cook for about 3 minutes per side, until the outside is golden brown and the cheese has melted. Repeat with the remaining sandwiches.
7. Slice each sandwich in half and serve immediately.

Coconut Chicken Patties with **Mango** and **Cherry Tomato Salsa**

SERVES 4

Fruit salsa lovers will be all over this sweet-tangy mango and cherry tomato situation, which gets its unbeatable herbal freshness courtesy of mint *and* cilantro. You'll be tempted to mainline the stuff with a spoon—which I support given its stellar vitamin and mineral content—but do yourself a favor and save enough to top these crispy, coconut-infused chicken patties. Each bite of chicken and salsa is a little tropical vacation for your taste buds.

1. Start by whipping up the mango salsa. In a medium bowl, gently combine all the salsa ingredients and season with salt and pepper. Cover the bowl with plastic wrap and refrigerate until ready to use.

2. Place the chicken, lime zest, scallions, 3 tablespoons of the shredded coconut, 3 tablespoons of the almond meal, and the salt in a medium bowl and mix until well combined. (I like to use my hands for this, but a fork also works.) With damp hands, mold the chicken mixture into 4 roughly 1-inch-thick patties.

3. Combine the remaining 2 tablespoons shredded coconut and 1 tablespoon almond meal on a small plate. Lightly coat both sides of each patty with this mixture, pressing gently with your hands to help it adhere.

4. Heat ½ tablespoon of the oil in a large nonstick skillet over medium heat. When the oil is hot and shimmering, carefully add the chicken patties to the pan and cook for 6 minutes or until the underside is lightly browned. Add the remaining ½ tablespoon oil to the pan and flip the patties. Cook for another 5 to 6 minutes, until cooked through.

5. Serve the patties topped with plenty of salsa.

JUST THE TIP: You can find almond meal in almost every grocery store these days—check next to the flours in the baking aisle—but you can also make your own by pulverizing raw almonds in a food processor until they mimic the texture of flour. (Be careful not to overprocess, though, or you'll end up with almond butter.)

FOR THE SALSA:

1 ripe mango, peeled, pitted, and diced small

¼ cup minced red onion

1 cup cherry tomatoes, quartered

¼ cup loosely packed fresh mint leaves, finely chopped

¼ cup loosely packed fresh cilantro leaves, finely chopped

Juice of ½ lime

Kosher salt to taste

Freshly ground black pepper to taste

FOR THE CHICKEN:

1 pound ground chicken breast

Zest of 1 lime

¼ cup finely chopped scallions

5 tablespoons unsweetened finely shredded coconut, divided

4 tablespoons almond meal, divided

¾ teaspoon kosher salt

1 tablespoon extra-virgin coconut oil, divided

California Burgers with Guacamole and Quick Pickled Onion

FOR THE ONION:

½ medium red onion, very thinly sliced

¼ cup water

¼ cup distilled white vinegar

2 teaspoons pure cane sugar

¾ teaspoon kosher salt

FOR THE GUACAMOLE:

2 ripe avocados

1 tablespoon fresh lime juice

1 garlic clove, grated or finely minced

Pinch of kosher salt, plus extra as needed

2 tablespoons finely chopped fresh cilantro leaves

Freshly ground black pepper

FOR THE BURGERS:

1½ pounds 90% lean ground beef (preferably grass-fed)

Kosher salt to taste

Freshly ground black pepper to taste

1 tablespoon avocado oil, divided

A few years ago, Logan sat next to a certain rapper/actor/legend on a cross-country flight. The Dude was enamored for obvious reasons, but he felt a real connection to the mogul after witnessing him crush a giant burger and six White Russians in-flight. Logan arrived home craving his new soulmate's meal, but as it was not Sunday, I suggested a lettuce-wrapped burger and a couple of light beers. Given how well it went over, I recommend keeping this recipe in mind the next time you're on the brink of a burger binge. Chickity-check yo'self before you wreck yo'self.

1. Start by making the quick pickled onion. Place the onion in a small jar or bowl. In a small saucepan, combine the water, vinegar, sugar, and salt and bring to a simmer over medium heat. Pour this brine over the onion and let it cool to room temperature. This should take about 25 minutes, at which point the onion should be sufficiently pickled. (You can also pickle the onion in advance and refrigerate it in an airtight container for 3 to 5 days.)

2. Moving on to the guac! Cut each avocado in half lengthwise and remove the pit. Scoop the flesh into a small bowl. Immediately add the lime juice, garlic, and salt and mash with a fork until relatively smooth. Stir in the cilantro and season with extra salt and black pepper to taste. Press plastic wrap onto the surface of the guacamole and briefly set aside.

3. Form the meat into four ½-inch-thick patties. (These will seem rather large, but they're going to shrink as they cook.) Season the patties on both sides with salt and black pepper. Make a small indent with your thumb in the center of each burger to keep it from puffing up while it cooks—this is crucial, people.

4. Heat ½ tablespoon of the oil in a large skillet over medium-high heat. (If you have a two-burner griddle, use it; otherwise you're going to have to cook two burgers at a time.) When the oil is hot and shimmering, add 2 burgers to the pan, thumbprint-side down, and cook for about 4 minutes per side for a medium-rare burger. During the last minute of the cook time, add a slice of Gouda to each patty and cover the pan with the lid to melt the

cheese. Transfer the burgers to a plate and cover loosely with aluminum foil to keep warm. Add the remaining ½ tablespoon oil to the pan and repeat the cooking process with the remaining 2 burgers.

5. Fold each romaine leaf in half crosswise, to make sure you've got a double-lined "lettuce bun." To assemble the burgers, place each patty on a piece of folded romaine. Top with the guacamole, pickled onion, and sprouts. Drizzle with some hot sauce if that's your jam and top with another piece of folded romaine. Get after it.

Four 1-ounce slices
  smoked Gouda
  cheese

FOR SERVING:

8 romaine lettuce
  leaves

2 loosely packed cups
  alfalfa sprouts

Hot sauce of your
  choice (optional)

YOU DO YOU: These are messy, so a fork and knife are always an option. You can serve the burgers on real buns if you must, but please use a whole-grain option.

Sloppy Josés

FOR THE SLOPPY JOSÉS:

1 tablespoon extra-virgin olive oil

1 pound ground chicken breast (93% lean ground turkey is cool too)

1 small red bell pepper, seeded and cut into small dice

½ medium red onion, finely chopped

1 teaspoon dried oregano

¾ teaspoon ground cumin

½ teaspoon crushed red pepper flakes

½ teaspoon garlic powder

2 tablespoons tomato paste

One 15-ounce can tomato puree

½ teaspoon honey

One 15-ounce can pinto beans, drained and rinsed

Juice of ½ lime

Kosher salt to taste

4 whole-grain rolls or buns

FOR SERVING:

½ cup grated sharp cheddar cheese (optional)

1 romaine heart, finely chopped

1 ripe avocado, pitted, peeled, and sliced

Sloppy Joes may be a classic childhood food, but I've found that most adults still carry a torch for the messy sandwiches. In fact, unveiling a tray of them happens to be one of my favorite ways to elicit high-pitched squeals from grown men, and the recipe from *The Dude Diet* has become both a weeknight staple and a football party favorite for exactly that reason.

However, in recent years Joe's had some serious competition from his friend José. José brings all the same saucy ground meat goodness to the table (he's a lean chicken type of guy), just with a little more spice and some pinto beans thrown in for good measure. He's also slightly sloppier to consume than your average Joe, thanks to his fondness for toppings, but I'm guessing that's a good thing. I know how you kids like 'em extra sloppy!

1. Heat the oil in a large skillet over medium heat. When the oil is hot and shimmering, add the ground chicken and cook for about 5 minutes, stirring and breaking up the meat with a spatula, until no longer pink.

2. Add the bell pepper, onion, oregano, cumin, red pepper flakes, and garlic powder and cook for about 6 minutes, until the vegetables begin to soften. Stir in the tomato paste and cook for 1 minute (just to mellow the acidity), then stir in the tomato puree, honey, and pinto beans. Simmer gently for 10 minutes to allow the flavors to mingle and the sauce to thicken slightly. Turn off the heat and stir in the lime juice. Taste and season with a little salt if needed.

3. Pile the chicken mixture onto the rolls and top with cheese (if using), romaine, and avocado. Get sloppy.

JUST THE TIP: Since most recipes call for only 1 to 2 tablespoons of tomato paste, I recommend buying it in a tube with a screw cap to ensure you get your money's worth. Trying to save it in the can is just annoying.

Dude Diet Meatball Subs

FOR THE MEATBALLS:

1 pound 99% lean ground turkey

1½ cups grated zucchini (roughly 1 medium zucchini grated on the large holes of a box grater)

3 large garlic cloves, grated or finely minced

1 teaspoon kosher salt

½ teaspoon freshly ground black pepper

1½ teaspoons Worcestershire sauce

2 tablespoons chia seeds (I prefer white chia seeds for aesthetic purposes.)

⅓ cup freshly grated Parmesan cheese

¼ cup fresh basil leaves, finely chopped

¼ cup fresh flat-leaf parsley leaves, finely chopped

FOR THE MARINARA:

1½ tablespoons extra-virgin olive oil

½ small yellow onion, minced

2 garlic cloves, minced

¼ teaspoon kosher salt, plus extra as needed

Just to break it down for you, a traditional meatball sub packs upwards of 1,100 calories, 50 grams of fat, and 2,500 milligrams of sodium. In short? Said monstrosity is an enormous fat bomb that will blow you up like an Oompa Loompa faster than you can say, "Pass the Zantac!" I don't believe in deprivation, however, so if you're inclined to inhale such button-popping subs on the reg, I'm hoping you'll embrace this Dude Diet–friendly version instead.

I know turkey is often dismissed as the saddest of ball bases, but these babies are the super moist meatballs of food porn fantasies thanks to . . . wait for it . . . **grated zucchini**. The waterlogged vegetable keeps the balls from drying out while also providing a hefty serving of hidden nutrients.

1. Put all the ingredients for the meatballs in a medium bowl. Using your hands, gently mix until well combined. (If you're super squeamish, you can do this with a fork, but hands are best! Just be sure to wash your paws after mixing before you touch anything else.) Cover the meatball mixture and refrigerate for 30 minutes to allow the chia seeds to work their binding magic.

2. Preheat the oven to 375°F. Line a large baking sheet with parchment paper and set aside.

3. With damp hands, very gently roll the meat mixture into 12 balls (roughly 2¼ inches in diameter) and place them an inch or so apart on the prepared baking sheet. Bake for 25 minutes, or until cooked through.

4. Meanwhile, get going on the sauce. Heat the oil in a medium Dutch oven or sauté pan over medium heat. When the oil is hot and shimmering, add the onion, garlic, and salt and cook for 4 to 5 minutes, until the onion is very soft and the garlic is fragrant. Add the crushed tomatoes and red pepper flakes. Reduce the heat to low and simmer the sauce for 15 to 20 minutes, until slightly thickened, then stir in the basil. Taste and season with a little extra salt and crushed red pepper if needed.

5. Add the meatballs to the sauce and simmer for 5 minutes more.

6. Preheat the broiler to high.

7. Slice the sub rolls three-quarters of the way through and hollow out their insides, leaving a ½-inch shell. (You won't miss the extra bread, I promise.) Place the prepared rolls side by side on a baking sheet. Add

3 meatballs to each roll along with plenty of sauce and top with ¼ cup mozzarella cheese.

8. Place the subs underneath the broiler for 1 to 2 minutes, until the cheese is melted and bubbling. Serve warm, garnished with a little extra basil if you're feeling fancy.

YOU DO YOU: Not into subs or avoiding gluten? Try serving these meatballs over quinoa, brown rice, or zucchini noodles.

One 28-ounce can crushed tomatoes

¼ teaspoon crushed red pepper flakes, plus extra as needed

⅓ cup fresh basil leaves, finely chopped

FOR SERVING:

1 cup shredded part-skim mozzarella cheese

Four 6-inch whole-wheat sub rolls

Fresh basil leaves (optional)

Sheet Pan Sausage and Cauliflower Pitas

SERVES **2** GENEROUSLY

3 links fully cooked spicy Italian chicken sausage, sliced into ½-inch rounds

3 cups cauliflower florets (roughly ½ medium head of cauliflower)

1 small red bell pepper, seeded and cut into 1-inch pieces

2 tablespoons extra-virgin olive oil, divided

¾ teaspoon ground cumin

½ teaspoon garlic powder

¼ teaspoon kosher salt

1 small shallot, minced

Juice of ½ lemon

1 canned chipotle pepper in adobo sauce, minced (Seed the chipotle if you fear spice.)

¼ cup fresh cilantro leaves, chopped

2 tablespoons slivered almonds

2 ounces goat cheese, crumbled

2 whole-wheat pitas with pockets

This pita's hybrid Mexican-Mediterranean vibe will rock your world, but its impressive nutritional profile is equally thrilling. Each sandwich boasts two full servings of vegetables, and the lean chicken sausage and goat cheese add a solid amount of satiating protein to the mix. Did I mention that all the components of the filling cook together on a single sheet pan in twenty-five minutes? Pita pocket full of Dude Diet dreams!

1. Preheat the oven to 450°F. Line a sheet pan with parchment paper.

2. Place the sausage, cauliflower florets, and bell pepper in a large bowl. Drizzle with 1 tablespoon of the oil; sprinkle with the cumin, garlic powder, and salt; and toss to coat. Transfer the mixture to the prepared baking sheet and arrange in an even layer. Roast for 25 minutes, stirring once halfway through the cooking time, until the vegetables are tender and the sausage is lightly browned.

3. Meanwhile, whisk the remaining 1 tablespoon oil, the shallot, lemon juice, and chipotle in the same large bowl you used for the sausage mixture.

4. Add the cooked sausage mixture to the dressing in the bowl along with the cilantro and almonds. Fold everything together until well combined. Gently fold in the goat cheese.

5. Warm those pitas! I recommend placing them directly on your gas burner, but you can also use the microwave if you prefer.

6. Cut each pita in half. Stuff each half with one quarter of the sausage mixture and dig in.

JUST THE TIP: Chipotles canned in adobo sauce are dried and smoked jalapeños in a sweet and tangy red sauce, and you can find them in the Mexican section of most supermarkets. (If you can't locate them, ask!!) Since most recipes call for only a single chipotle, store what's left of the can in an airtight container in the fridge for up to two months.

Spinach-Artichoke Grilled Cheese

Is this a grilled cheese stuffed with spinach artichoke dip? Yes. Is that a crispy layer of cheese on the *outside* of the sandwich? Yes, yes it is. Is such an outrageous creation actually Dude Diet–friendly? Shockingly, the answer is still YES. This whole-grain, veggie-heavy sando scraps the traditional mayo and sour cream, getting its creaminess from Greek yogurt and a responsible amount of flavor-blasted Pecorino Romano and melty mozzarella.

If you haven't passed out from excitement, should you make this sandwich immediately? That was a rhetorical question . . .

1. Heat 1 teaspoon of the olive oil in a large nonstick skillet over medium heat. (A true nonstick pan is critical here.) When the oil is hot and shimmering, add the garlic and cook for 1 minute, just until fragrant. (Be very careful not to burn it!!) Add the spinach, red pepper flakes, and a pinch of salt, and cook just until wilted, about 90 seconds. Transfer the spinach to a bowl and stir in the artichoke hearts, scallions, yogurt, and Pecorino Romano. Taste and season with a little salt if needed.

2. Assemble your sandwiches! Divide the filling between two slices of bread and top each with ¼ cup mozzarella. Close the sandwiches with the remaining two slices of bread. Lightly brush the outside of the sandwiches with the remaining 2 teaspoons of olive oil.

3. Wipe out the skillet used for the filling and return it to the stovetop. Heat the pan over medium heat. When hot, add the sandwiches to the pan. Cover the pan with a lid, and cook for about 3 minutes or until the undersides are golden brown. Carefully flip the sandwiches, and sprinkle half of the remaining mozzarella on the top of each one (a little less than a tablespoon on each). Cover and cook for another 3 minutes until the opposite sides have browned. Flip the sandwiches so the cheesy side is in direct contact with the pan. (You're creating a crispy cheesy crust on your grilled cheese here, dudes.) Sprinkle with the remaining cheese, cover, and cook for a minute or so until the cheese is browned and crisp. Flip the sandwiches one more time and cook for 1 minute to brown the cheese on the opposite sides.

4. Slice the cheesy sandos in half and serve immediately.

Ingredients

- 1 tablespoon extra-virgin olive oil, divided
- 1 garlic clove, minced
- 4 packed cups baby spinach, chopped
- ¼ teaspoon crushed red pepper flakes (optional)
- Kosher salt to taste
- One 6-ounce jar marinated artichoke hearts, drained well and finely chopped
- 2 scallions, whites and light green parts only, finely chopped
- 2 tablespoons nonfat plain Greek yogurt
- 3 tablespoons grated Pecorino Romano cheese
- ⅔ cup shredded part-skim mozzarella cheese
- 4 slices whole-grain bread (I love whole-wheat sourdough for this.)

Marinated Flank Steak Wraps with Chipotle Romesco

FOR THE WRAPS:

2 tablespoons balsamic vinegar

1 tablespoon extra-virgin olive oil

2 garlic cloves, grated or finely minced

1 teaspoon Dijon mustard

1 pound flank steak

Kosher salt to taste

Freshly ground black pepper to taste

4 whole-grain lavash (or whole-grain wrap of your choice)

1 medium English cucumber (aka seedless cucumber), very thinly sliced at an angle

4 cups baby arugula

FOR THE ROMESCO:

One 12-ounce jar roasted red peppers, drained

2 tablespoons balsamic vinegar

1 tablespoon extra-virgin olive oil

1 garlic clove

½ cup slivered almonds

1 canned chipotle pepper in adobo sauce, seeded (Just scrape the seeds from the pepper with the side of a knife.)

1½ teaspoons adobo sauce from the chipotle can

Pinch of kosher salt, plus extra as needed

"Healthy" and "steak sandwich" aren't typically said in the same breath, but that's exactly what you're looking at here, folks. Lean marinated steak, lots of greens, and smoky red pepper sauce wrapped up in whole-grain flatbread make for a swoon-worthy steak sandwich that won't send your wonderland body into a tailspin. HAL-LELUJAH.

1. Start by marinating the steak. Whisk the vinegar, oil, garlic, and mustard in a small bowl. Place the flank steak in a large zip-top food storage bag and pour in the marinade. Seal the bag, removing as much air as humanly possible, and very gently squish the steak around to make sure it's well coated. Marinate for 20 minutes at room temperature.

2. Meanwhile, put all the ingredients for the romesco in the bowl of a food processor or high-speed blender. Process until nice and smooth. Taste and season with a little extra salt if needed. Briefly set aside.

3. Preheat a lightly oiled grill or grill pan (yes, a skillet is fine too) over medium-high heat.

4. Remove the steak from the marinade, shaking off any excess, and season generously on both sides with salt and pepper. Grill for 4 to 5 minutes per side for medium-rare. Transfer the steak to a cutting board and let it rest for a full 10 minutes. Using a sharp knife, thinly slice the steak across the grain.

5. Warm the lavash. I recommend placing them directly on the grill or grill pan just until grill marks appear, but you can also warm them for about 10 seconds in the microwave.

6. Load up each lavash with a quarter of the steak, cucumber, and arugula and smother with a generous amount of romesco. Roll up the lavash and go to town.

Asian-Style Turkey Burgers with Creamy Peanut Slaw

SERVES 4

FOR THE TURKEY BURGERS:

1 pound 93% lean ground turkey (do NOT use 99% lean)

2 whole scallions, very finely chopped

1½ tablespoons low-sodium soy sauce

2 large garlic cloves, grated or finely minced

2½ teaspoons peeled and grated fresh ginger

½ teaspoon freshly ground black pepper

1½ teaspoons light sesame oil

4 whole-grain buns or English muffins

FOR THE SLAW:

½ cup canned light coconut milk

¼ cup crunchy peanut butter

1 tablespoon unseasoned rice vinegar

1 tablespoon sriracha sauce

2 cups thinly sliced napa cabbage

1 cup shredded carrots

½ cup very thinly sliced red onion

⅓ cup fresh cilantro leaves, roughly chopped

Kosher salt to taste

Freshly ground black pepper to taste

While turkey burgers of yore may have been the driest of poultry pucks, we now live in the era of the trashed-up turkey burger, where flavor and moisture reign supreme. A few basic ingredients—soy sauce, garlic, ginger, and scallions, to be precise—set these patties apart, and a heaping serving of coconut-infused peanut slaw provides crazy flavor and crunch along with plenty of health benefits. If you're off bread (proud of you), double the slaw and serve it salad-style with a turkey patty on top.

1. Make the turkey burgers. Place the ground turkey, scallions, soy sauce, garlic, ginger, and black pepper in a medium bowl. Using your hands, gently mix until the ingredients are well combined.

2. With damp hands, mold the turkey mixture into 4 patties, about ¾ inch thick, and place them on a piece of parchment or wax paper. Make a small indent with your thumb in the center of each burger to keep it from puffing up as it cooks.

3. Heat the oil in a large nonstick skillet over medium heat. When the oil is hot and shimmering, carefully add the burgers, thumbprint-side down, to the pan. (I like to spray a thin metal spatula with cooking spray and use it to transfer the burgers to the pan.) Cook the patties for 6 to 7 minutes, undisturbed, until lightly browned on the undersides and beginning to firm, then flip with the spatula and cook for another 6 minutes on the opposite sides, or until cooked through.

4. Meanwhile, make the slaw. Whisk the coconut milk, peanut butter, rice vinegar, and sriracha in a medium bowl. Add the cabbage, carrots, red onion, and cilantro and toss to combine. Taste and season with a little salt and pepper if needed.

5. If you dig toasted buns, toast them now.

6. Serve the turkey burgers on buns, piled high with peanut slaw.

JUST THE TIP: Use the remaining coconut milk in a smoothie or Indian Spiced Chicken Stew (page 37) later in the week.

Curried Chicken Salad Sandwiches

When it comes to this chicken salad, the curry-spiked Greek yogurt dressing is a home run, but it's the mix-ins that really knock it out of the park. A particularly addictive combo of dried apricots, roasted cashews, scallions, and cilantro lends modern flair to a retro recipe that deserves a spot in your regular rotation.

The best part about this recipe is that it provides endless opportunities for you to do you. If you use Idiotproof Chicken Breasts (page 136), this chicken salad will run you about forty minutes from start to finish (including chicken cooling time), but you could just as easily dice or shred the breast meat from a store-bought rotisserie bird for a quicker fix. The apricots and cashews can be swapped for whatever dried fruit and nuts you like or have on hand, and the serving possibilities are endless.

1. Combine all the ingredients for the dressing in a large bowl. (If you like a sweeter dressing, feel free to add a tiny bit more honey.)

2. Add the salad ingredients to the bowl with the dressing and fold everything together until well combined. (Depending on the thickness of your Greek yogurt, you may want to add a couple of teaspoons or so of water to loosen it to your liking.) Taste and season with extra salt and pepper if needed.

3. Toast your bread to your preferred level of toastiness. Divide the chicken salad among 3 or 4 pieces of toast. Top with lettuce leaves and sandwich everything together with the remaining slices of toast.

4. Slice the sandwiches in half and serve.

> JUST THE TIP: Read your herb measurements carefully! This recipe calls for "⅓ cup fresh cilantro leaves, chopped," so measure the leaves *before* chopping them. However, if a recipe calls for "⅓ cup chopped fresh cilantro leaves," measure the herbs once chopped.

FOR THE DRESSING:

- 1 cup nonfat plain Greek yogurt
- 2 tablespoons curry powder
- 1 tablespoon fresh lemon juice
- 1 teaspoon honey
- ½ teaspoon kosher salt
- Pinch of cayenne pepper (optional)
- Freshly ground black pepper to taste

FOR THE SALAD:

- 1 pound cooked chicken breast, diced or shredded (about 2 heaping cups diced chicken)
- 3 whole scallions, finely chopped
- ⅓ cup fresh cilantro leaves, chopped
- ⅓ cup finely chopped dried apricots
- ⅓ cup chopped roasted cashews
- 1½ tablespoons hemp hearts (optional)

FOR SERVING:

- 6 to 8 slices whole-grain sandwich bread
- 1 head Bibb lettuce

Awesome Avocado Tuna Melts

Tuna melts are controversial. I get it—warm fish plus mayo and cheese seems all kinds of wrong. But I'm gonna go out on a limb here and say that this particular version of the divisive sandwich may just recruit you to team tuna melt. (I speak from personal experience.) The tuna salad itself ditches ~~the devil's condiment~~ mayo for heart-healthy mashed avocado, while turkey bacon ups the savory factor, shallots provide a gentle kick, and sweet and tangy bread-and-butter pickles add necessary crunch. This tuna salad is damn near perfect eaten straight from the bowl, but a toasted English muffin, tomato slices, and a little bit of bubbling cheddar elevate it to "blow your mind" status. I can't explain how or why it works, so I just need you to trust me and take a tiny tuna melt leap of faith.

1. Cook the turkey bacon in a skillet over medium heat until browned and crispy. (This will take 9 to 12 minutes total, depending on the bacon you use.) Transfer to a paper towel–lined plate to cool slightly, then finely chop.

2. Meanwhile, slice the avocado in half lengthwise and remove the pit. Scoop the flesh into a medium bowl and mash until very smooth. Add the shallot, pickles, pickle juice, lemon juice, and mustard and mix to combine. Add the tuna and chopped turkey bacon and mix again. Season with salt and pepper.

3. Preheat the broiler to high.

4. Toast your English muffins. Top each muffin half with a quarter of the tuna mixture, a slice of tomato (if using), and 1 tablespoon of cheese. Broil for 1 to 2 minutes, until the cheese is melted and bubbling.

5. Serve immediately. Don't be afraid to get some hot sauce involved if you're into spice.

2 slices turkey bacon

½ large ripe avocado

1 small shallot, minced

2 tablespoons minced bread-and-butter pickles

1 tablespoon pickle juice from the pickle jar

2 teaspoons fresh lemon juice

1 teaspoon Dijon mustard

One 5-ounce can albacore tuna in water, drained

Kosher salt to taste

Freshly ground black pepper to taste

2 whole-wheat English muffins, split in half (or 2 large slices whole-grain bread)

1 small tomato, sliced into 4 rounds (optional)

¼ cup grated mild cheddar cheese

Hot sauce (optional)

ONE-PAN WONDERS

Hurricane Turkey Chili

FOR THE CHILI:

- 1 tablespoon extra-virgin olive oil
- 1 pound 93% lean ground turkey
- 1 medium yellow onion, cut into small dice
- 1 red bell pepper, seeded and cut into small dice
- 1 yellow bell pepper, seeded and cut into small dice
- 4 garlic cloves, minced
- 2½ tablespoons chili powder
- 1½ teaspoons ground cumin
- 1½ teaspoons dried oregano
- ¾ teaspoon cayenne pepper, plus extra as needed
- One 15-ounce can kidney beans, drained and rinsed
- One 15-ounce can pinto beans, drained and rinsed
- 2 tablespoons low-sodium soy sauce
- One 15-ounce can diced fire-roasted tomatoes with their juices
- One 15-ounce can tomato puree
- ¾ cup low-sodium chicken broth
- 1 tablespoon plus 1 teaspoon balsamic vinegar
- Kosher salt to taste

FOR SERVING (OPTIONAL):

- ¾ cup grated pepper Jack cheese (or regular Jack cheese if you're heat-sensitive)
- ¼ cup chopped fresh cilantro leaves

This chili is the perfected iteration of a recipe that Logan and I ate for three days straight in the wake of Hurricane Sandy back in 2012. I whipped up a big batch before the power went out, which sustained us with all kinds of comfort while we rode out the storm. (It also provided a much-needed healthy foil to the box of Snickers ice cream bars the Dude ate as soon as the lights started flickering, in an effort to "reduce food waste.") It's a crowd-pleasing option for chilly weeknights (and a slam dunk for meal preppers), and the recipe is easily doubled for game day extravaganzas.

p.s. This chili is SPICY. If you're sensitive, make sure to cut back on the cayenne.

1. Heat the oil in a medium Dutch oven or heavy-bottomed soup pot over medium-high heat. When the oil is hot and shimmering (but not smoking!), add the ground turkey and cook for 5 to 6 minutes, stirring and breaking up the meat into small pieces with a spatula, until lightly browned. Add the onion, bell peppers, garlic, and spices and cook for about 5 minutes, until the peppers have softened and the onions are translucent.

2. Stir in the kidney and pinto beans, the soy sauce, diced tomatoes, tomato puree, and chicken broth. Bring the chili to a boil, then lower to a gentle simmer and cook for 30 minutes, uncovered, to allow all the awesome flavors to combine.

3. Turn off the heat and stir in the vinegar. Taste the chili and season with a little salt or extra cayenne if it needs it.

4. Ladle the chili into bowls and garnish with cheese and cilantro if you're feeling festive.

Indian Spiced Chicken Stew

I like to think of this one-pot wonder as cheater's chicken tikka masala. It serves up complex flavors reminiscent of the Indian favorite but has a much more impressive nutritional pedigree and can be on your table in about forty-five minutes flat. Talk about curry in a hurry.

This recipe calls for a couple of spices you may not have in your arsenal. Relax. You can find garam masala and coriander in the spice aisle at most supermarkets, and while they may set you back about six bucks each, I promise they're worth the investment. You can use each of these spices in an endless variety of dishes, from roasted vegetables to baked goods.

1. Heat the oil in a large Dutch oven or sauté pan over medium heat. When the oil is hot and shimmering, add the onion and garlic and cook for about 5 minutes, until the onion is soft and translucent.

2. Add the coriander, paprika, garam masala, cumin, salt, cayenne, ginger, and tomato paste and cook for 2 minutes to toast the spices and mellow the acidity of the tomato paste. Stir in the cauliflower, chickpeas, tomato puree, coconut milk, and chicken broth, scraping the bottom of the pan with a spatula to release any toasted spice remnants, and bring to a simmer. Slice the chicken breasts in half crosswise, then add them to the stew. Cover the pan with a lid and cook for 20 minutes, or until the cauliflower is tender and the chicken is cooked through.

3. Carefully transfer the chicken to a cutting board. Shred the meat with two forks, then return it to the pot. Turn off the heat and stir in the lemon juice. Taste and season with a little extra salt and/or lemon juice if needed.

4. Divide the brown rice (if using) among 4 bowls. Ladle the stew over the rice and top with plenty of cilantro.

FOR THE STEW:

1½ tablespoons extra-virgin coconut oil (Yes, you can use olive oil.)

1 small yellow onion, minced

4 large garlic cloves, minced

2 teaspoons ground coriander

2 teaspoons paprika

1½ teaspoons garam masala

1½ teaspoons ground cumin

½ teaspoon kosher salt, plus extra as needed

½ teaspoon cayenne pepper

1 tablespoon peeled and grated fresh ginger

1 tablespoon tomato paste

3 cups finely chopped cauliflower florets (aim for ½-inch pieces)

One 15-ounce can chickpeas, drained and rinsed

One 15-ounce can tomato puree

1 cup light coconut milk (from a can)

½ cup low-sodium chicken broth (water also is fine)

1 pound boneless, skinless chicken breasts

1 tablespoon fresh lemon juice, plus extra as needed

FOR SERVING:

2 cups cooked brown basmati rice (optional)

Chopped fresh cilantro leaves

Sweet Potato and Black Bean Enchilada Stew

FOR THE STEW:

1½ pounds tomatillos (about 12 tomatillos), rinsed well and halved crosswise

2 jalapeños, halved lengthwise, stems and seeds removed

½ packed cup fresh cilantro leaves

1 tablespoon extra-virgin olive oil

1 medium yellow onion, finely chopped

4 garlic cloves, minced

¾ teaspoon kosher salt, plus extra as needed

2 teaspoons ground cumin

1½ teaspoons dried oregano

1 quart low-sodium vegetable broth

1 large sweet potato, peeled and cut into ¾-inch cubes (about 3 cups diced sweet potatoes)

One 15-ounce can black beans, drained and rinsed

½ cup pearled or semi-pearled farro

Freshly ground black pepper to taste

FOR SERVING:

2 ounces crumbled goat cheese

Chopped fresh cilantro leaves

Enchiladas are bomb, but the prep time can be a little over the top sometimes. So can the heaviness that accompanies several tortillas and a layer of bubbling cheese. *Enter*: easy enchilada stew. This sweet and savory comfort food fiesta always hits the spot; is packed with fiber, potassium, and disease-fighting antioxidants; and requires zero tortilla stuffing or rolling. (You're welcome.) I beg you to try this vegetarian wonder as is, but if you or a loved one is prone to "where's the meat?!" meltdowns, go ahead and add some shredded chicken or browned chicken sausage to your pot.

1. Preheat the broiler to high. Line a large baking sheet with aluminum foil and spray with nonstick cooking spray.

2. Place the tomatillos and jalapeños cut side down on the prepared baking sheet. Broil for 8 minutes, turning the baking sheet 180 degrees halfway through the cooking time, until the tomatillos and jalapeños are softened and charred in spots. Transfer them to a food processor or high-speed blender and add the cilantro. Process until nice and smooth.

3. Meanwhile, heat the oil in a medium Dutch oven or heavy-bottomed soup pot over medium heat. When the oil is hot and shimmering, add the onion, garlic, and salt and cook for 5 minutes, or until the onion is very soft and translucent. (Be careful not to burn the garlic here! If it starts to brown, turn down the heat.) Add the cumin and oregano and cook for 1 minute just to toast the spices. Stir in the tomatillo puree, vegetable broth, sweet potato, and black beans and bring to a boil. Lower to a simmer and add the farro. Simmer, uncovered, for 30 minutes, or until the sweet potatoes and farro are tender. Taste and season with a little extra salt or some pepper if needed.

4. Ladle the stew into bowls, garnish with the goat cheese and cilantro, and serve piping hot.

JUST THE TIP: Tomatillos, aka Mexican husk tomatoes, are small green fruits with a distinctive tangy flavor. Look for tomatillos that are bright green and firm, and take a peek under the husk to make sure the fruit isn't shriveled or bruised. If you can't find fresh, you can use canned tomatillos.

Lasagna Soup with Sausage and Greens

FOR THE SOUP:

1½ tablespoons extra-virgin olive oil

12 ounces (3 to 4 links) uncooked sweet Italian turkey sausage, casings removed

½ medium yellow onion, finely chopped

4 ounces baby bella or cremini mushrooms, halved, then thinly sliced crosswise

3 large garlic cloves, minced

1 medium zucchini, diced

1½ tablespoons tomato paste

¼ cup dry red wine

One 28-ounce can crushed fire-roasted tomatoes

1 teaspoon dried oregano

½ teaspoon crushed red pepper flakes (optional)

3½ cups low-sodium chicken or vegetable broth

4 ounces whole-wheat or brown rice lasagna noodles, broken into 1½-inch pieces

3 packed cups baby kale or spinach

Kosher salt

FOR SERVING:

½ cup ricotta cheese

½ cup grated or shredded mozzarella cheese (I like to grate fresh mozzarella, but you do you.)

Thinly sliced fresh basil leaves

I'm thrilled to inform you that this soup delivers all the badass, comforting flavors of lasagna—noodles! meaty tomato sauce! melting cheese!—without the gut-busting consequences or crazy time commitment. And since the soup keeps deliciously for three to four days in the fridge and makes an awesome Dude Diet desk lunch, leftovers are something to be psyched about. You can also reheat a little soup in a small skillet and poach an egg or two in it for breakfast. (Definitely do that.)

1. Heat the oil in a medium Dutch oven or heavy-bottomed soup pot over medium heat. When the oil is hot and shimmering, add the sausage to the pan and cook, stirring the meat and breaking it up into small pieces with a spatula, for 7 to 8 minutes, until lightly browned.

2. Add the onion, mushrooms, and garlic to the pan and cook for 4 to 5 minutes, until the onion is translucent and the mushrooms have softened. Add the zucchini and tomato paste and cook for 1 minute (just to mellow the acidity of the tomato paste). Add the red wine and cook for a minute or so, making sure to scrape up any delicious browned bits from the bottom of the pan, until the liquid has evaporated. Stir in the crushed tomatoes, oregano, crushed red pepper (if using), and broth. Bring to a boil, then lower to a simmer and add the lasagna noodles. Cover and cook for 15 to 20 minutes, stirring occasionally, until the noodles are al dente.

3. Add the kale to the soup. (It will seem like a lot, but it's going to cook down, I promise.) Cook for 1 to 2 minutes, just until the greens have wilted. (If your soup is thicker than you'd like, feel free to thin it with an extra splash of broth.) Taste and season with salt if needed.

4. Ladle the soup into bowls and top each bowl with a little ricotta and shredded mozzarella cheese. Sprinkle with plenty of fresh basil and serve immediately.

Dude Diet Dirty "Rice" and Beans

While most food fads fall by the wayside after a few months, cauliflower "rice"—aka cauliflower florets that have been grated or pulsed in a food processor until they resemble said grain—has serious staying power. Not only is swapping cauliflower for regular rice one of the most painless ways to work more vegetables into a meal, but it also requires a fraction of the cooking time and is far less fickle than the actual grain. Win-win.

While you can and should season cauliflower rice six ways to Sunday as a sexy side, here it serves as a clean base for dirty "rice" and beans. The recipe may not call for the typical heap of refined carbs or chicken livers, but the Cajun flavor party is still raging.

1. Put half of the cauliflower florets in the bowl of a food processor. Pulse until the florets become coarse granules that resemble rice. (Be careful not to overprocess, or you'll end up with cauliflower mush.) Transfer the cauliflower rice to a large bowl. Repeat this process with the remaining cauliflower florets. Briefly set aside. (Note that you can also use the food processor to chop the celery, bell pepper, and onion.)

2. Heat the oil in a large skillet or sauté pan over medium heat. When the oil is hot and shimmering, add the sausage and cook for about 6 minutes, stirring and breaking up the meat with a spatula, until no longer pink. Add the celery, bell pepper, onion, garlic, spices, and salt to the pan and cook for about 7 minutes, until tender. Stir in the kidney beans and cauliflower rice. Cover the pan with a lid and cook for 3 minutes, or until the cauliflower is just tender. (The cauliflower cooks quickly and will continue cooking off the heat, so don't overdo it!)

3. Turn off the heat and stir in the lemon juice and parsley. Taste and season with extra salt if needed.

4. Divide the rice among 4 bowls. Garnish with scallions and hot sauce. Lemon wedges are also encouraged if you're a serious citrus fan.

FOR DIRTY "RICE" AND BEANS:

4 cups cauliflower florets (or 3 cups prepackaged cauliflower "rice")

1 tablespoon extra-virgin olive oil

12 ounces uncooked Italian turkey sausage (hot or sweet, your choice)

2 celery ribs, finely chopped

1 green bell pepper, seeded and cut into small dice

½ medium yellow onion, finely chopped

2 garlic cloves, minced

2 teaspoons smoked paprika

1 teaspoon chili powder

1 teaspoon dried thyme

½ teaspoon ground cumin

¼ teaspoon freshly ground black pepper

¼ teaspoon cayenne pepper

¼ teaspoon kosher salt, plus extra as needed

One 15-ounce can red kidney beans, drained and rinsed

1 tablespoon fresh lemon juice

¼ cup fresh flat-leaf parsley leaves, chopped

FOR SERVING:

3 whole scallions, thinly sliced

Hot sauce

Lemon wedges (optional)

Buffalo Chicken and White Bean Chili

FOR THE CHILI:

Two 15-ounce cans great northern beans, drained and rinsed

2 tablespoons extra-virgin olive oil

2 medium carrots, minced

1 celery rib, minced

1 medium yellow onion, minced

5 garlic cloves, minced

2 teaspoons smoked paprika

½ teaspoon ground cumin

¼ teaspoon freshly ground black pepper

¼ cup plus 3 tablespoons Frank's Red Hot Buffalo Wing Sauce, plus extra as needed

2 cups low-sodium chicken broth

Two 8-ounce boneless, skinless chicken breasts

½ teaspoon dried dill weed

Kosher salt to taste

FOR SERVING:

½ cup crumbled blue cheese or grated sharp cheddar cheese

2 whole scallions, thinly sliced

1 celery rib, thinly sliced crosswise into half-moons

In the market for a new game day go-to? Thank God you're here. Kicked up with Frank's finest, this fiery chili will crush your Buffalo chicken cravings while keeping your football season physique in check. It's also been known to induce extreme excitement freak-outs among adult males, which you know is my perpetual culinary goal. Think "Gronk making his sixty-ninth touchdown" levels of joy . . .

1. Place half of the beans in a large bowl and roughly mash them with a fork. Set aside.

2. Heat the oil in a medium Dutch oven or heavy-bottomed soup pot. When the oil is hot and shimmering, add the carrots, celery, onion, and garlic and cook for about 5 minutes, until the vegetables have softened and the onion is translucent. Add the paprika, cumin, and black pepper and cook for 1 minute just to toast the spices. Add the wing sauce, mashed beans, whole beans, and chicken broth and bring to a simmer.

3. Slice the chicken breasts in half crosswise (to help them cook more quickly) and add them to the pot. Cover the pot with a lid and simmer for 15 minutes, or until the chicken is cooked through.

4. Carefully transfer the chicken to a cutting board. Shred the meat with two forks, then return it to the pot. Stir in the dill and simmer, uncovered, for 10 minutes more, or until the chili has thickened slightly.

5. Taste and season with a little salt or extra wing sauce if necessary.

6. Ladle the chili into bowls. Garnish with the cheese, scallions, and celery, and get after it.

JUST THE TIP: Save prep time by using your food processor to finely chop the carrots, celery, onion, and garlic.

Manly Minestrone

SERVES 4 to 6

FOR THE MINESTRONE:

1 tablespoon extra-virgin olive oil

4 ounces diced pancetta (Thick-cut bacon will also work.)

1 medium yellow onion, finely chopped

2 large garlic cloves, minced

2 medium carrots, peeled and cut into small dice

2 ribs celery, cut into small dice

1 medium zucchini, cut into small dice

One 28-ounce can fire-roasted tomatoes with their juices

1 quart low-sodium vegetable broth

1 teaspoon dried oregano

½ teaspoon kosher salt, plus extra as needed

¼ teaspoon crushed red pepper flakes (optional)

One 15-ounce can butter beans, drained and rinsed (Cannellini beans are also great.)

8 fresh basil leaves, chopped, plus extra for serving

FOR SERVING (OPTIONAL):

½ cup shaved Parmesan or Pecorino cheese

Should you go a little too HAM on No-Calorie Sunday or fall off the healthy eating wagon altogether, this rustic Italian soup is the perfect "reset" meal to help get your Dude Diet mojo back. It's chock-full of vegetable goodness, and a very modest amount of crisped pancetta goes a long way in the flavor department. Most minestrone recipes call for some sort of pasta, but I KO'd the unnecessary carbs here in the name of your wonderland body. Trust me, you won't miss them.

This soup is the ultimate light dinner (you'll want to get a side salad and/or some whole-grain bread involved), but it also slays as a smart snack. Based on field research, eating a small bowl before hitting a party or going out to a restaurant will fill you up enough to avoid ~~attacking finger food servers~~ making poor hunger-induced choices.

1. Heat the oil in a Dutch oven or heavy-bottomed soup pot over medium-high heat. When the oil is hot and shimmering (but not smoking!), add the pancetta and cook for about 5 minutes, until lightly browned.

2. Reduce the heat to medium and add the onion, garlic, carrots, and celery. Cook for 5 minutes, or until the vegetables have softened slightly and the onion is translucent. Add the zucchini, tomatoes, vegetable broth, oregano, salt, and crushed red pepper to the pot and bring to a boil. Lower to a simmer, stir in the beans, and cook for 20 to 25 minutes, until all the vegetables are very tender. Turn off the heat and stir in the basil. Taste and season with a little extra salt if needed.

3. Ladle the soup into bowls and garnish with the cheese and a little extra basil if you're feeling fancy.

Super Green Stir-Fry

This stir-fry epitomizes a Dude Diet meal. It's hearty and huge on flavor but made with real, whole foods that pack a serious nutritional punch. On top of its healthy deliciousness, this recipe—which comes together in under half an hour despite the seemingly long ingredient list, I promise—gets major props for versatility. It's equally great with shrimp, thinly sliced beef, or dry-fried tofu, and the topping possibilities are endless. I love basil for sweetness and raw cashews for healthy fat and crunch, but any combo of fresh herbs, scallions, nuts, sesame or hemp seeds, and even furikake would be killer. I support your creativity.

1. In a small bowl, combine the soy sauce, ginger, rice vinegar, sriracha sauce or chili paste (if using), and honey. Place this sassy stir-fry sauce by the stove.

2. Season the chicken cubes with salt and pepper.

3. Heat ½ tablespoon of the coconut oil in a wok or large non-stick skillet over medium-high heat. When the oil is hot and shimmering, add the chicken to the pan in an even layer. Let the chicken cook for 3 minutes, undisturbed (you want to get some light browning action going), then continue cooking, stirring occasionally for about 2 minutes or until cooked through. Transfer the chicken to a bowl and place it by the stove.

4. Return the pan to the heat and add the remaining tablespoon of coconut oil. When the oil is hot and shimmering, add the broccoli, zucchini, onion, and garlic to the pan. Cook until the vegetables are tender (but not mushy!), about 4–6 minutes. (I like to brown my vegetables a little, but if you're not into that, simply turn the heat down to medium.)

5. Add the edamame and baby kale to the pan and cook for about 1 minute just until the greens are wilted.

6. Strain any excess liquid from the cooked chicken, and return it to the pan along with the stir-fry sauce. Cook for a minute or so until heated through.

7. Serve your stir-fry warm topped with basil and cashews if you have them.

3 tablespoons low-sodium soy sauce

1 tablespoon peeled and grated fresh ginger

2 teaspoons unseasoned rice vinegar

1-2 teaspoons sriracha sauce or sambal oelek chili paste (optional)

1 teaspoon honey

1 pound boneless, skinless chicken breasts, cut into ¾-inch cubes

½ teaspoon kosher salt

Freshly ground black pepper to taste

1½ tablespoons extra-virgin coconut oil, divided

2 cups broccoli florets, chopped into roughly ½-inch pieces

1 large zucchini, diced

½ medium yellow onion, finely chopped

3 garlic cloves, minced

1 cup shelled edamame (If using frozen edamame, defrost according to the package directions.)

3 packed cups baby kale (or leafy green of your choice)

FOR SERVING: (OPTIONAL)

⅓ cup fresh basil leaves, chopped

¼ cup roasted cashews, chopped

Butternut Squash Cheesy Rice with Sausage

SERVES 4 to 6

2 tablespoons extra-virgin olive oil

1 small yellow onion, minced

5 garlic cloves, minced

¼ teaspoon kosher salt

¾ pound (3 to 4 links) uncooked sweet Italian turkey sausage, casings removed

¼ teaspoon ground cinnamon

1½ cups short-grain brown rice

4 cups cubed butternut squash (cut into ½-inch cubes)

4 cups low-sodium vegetable broth

3 sprigs fresh thyme plus 1 tablespoon fresh thyme leaves, divided

6-8 fresh sage leaves

⅓ cup freshly grated Parmesan cheese

1 cup grated Fontina cheese

Freshly ground black pepper to taste (optional)

I originally created this dish as a sexy side but quickly recognized it as an epic one-pot meal in and of itself. The brown rice takes on a dreamy risotto-like texture, and the combo of savory turkey sausage, slightly sweet butternut squash, creamy Fontina, and fresh thyme is a big fat seasonal bear hug for the soul. The recipe is super simple, but it's definitely fancy enough to serve to guests should you choose to cook for compliments. Just throw a fresh thyme sprig on top of each bowl for presentation purposes. People love that shit.

1. Heat the olive oil in a Dutch oven or large sauté pan over medium heat. When the oil is hot and shimmering, add the onion, garlic, and salt, and cook for about 5 minutes or until the onions are very soft and translucent. Add the sausage and cinnamon and cook, stirring and breaking up the meat into small pieces with a spatula, for about 5 minutes or until no longer pink. Add the brown rice and cook for 2 minutes, stirring constantly, to toast the grains.

2. Stir in the butternut squash cubes, and then add the vegetable broth, thyme sprigs, and sage leaves. Bring to a boil, then immediately lower to a simmer. Cover with a lid and cook for 35 minutes until the rice is just tender, the butternut squash is soft, and most of the liquid has been absorbed. (You still want a little liquid in the pan to help create the creamy texture of the finished rice.)

3. Remove the thyme sprigs and sage leaves with a fork and discard. (Careful, they're hot!) Give the rice a really good stir, breaking down some of the butternut squash cubes. (Your rice will have a risotto-like consistency.)

4. Turn off the heat and stir in the Parmesan and Fontina cheeses, then stir in the thyme leaves. Taste and season with a little extra salt if needed and freshly ground black pepper (if using). Serve warm.

JUST THE TIP: Cut prep time in half by buying pre-cubed fresh or frozen butternut squash.

Quickie Chicken Pozole

SERVES 4

FOR THE POSOLE:

Two 4-ounce cans diced green chiles (preferably fire-roasted)

1 quart low-sodium chicken broth, divided

1 tablespoon extra-virgin olive oil

1 small yellow onion, finely chopped

2 garlic cloves, minced

1½ teaspoons ground cumin

1 teaspoon chili powder

1 teaspoon dried oregano

Kosher salt to taste

One 15-ounce can white hominy, drained and rinsed

1 pound boneless, skinless chicken breasts

Juice of ½ lime

FOR SERVING:

Lime wedges

2 cups finely chopped romaine hearts

1 cup fresh cilantro leaves, chopped

2 to 3 radishes, thinly sliced

1 ripe avocado, pitted, peeled, and diced

½ red onion, minced

If you've never had pozole, you're in for a serious treat. Pozole (or posole) is a Mexican soup traditionally made with pork shoulder and hominy, but this quickie version uses shredded chicken breast for a couple of reasons: (1) pork shoulder is fatty and chicken is not, and (2) chicken cooks in a fraction of the time.

The soup itself is hearty and comforting—it's also spicy enough to do some mild sinus clearing—but it's the toppings that make the meal. You're going to want to get very, *very* weird with the toppings, amigos. Don't be alarmed if your bowl ends up resembling a taco salad. It's cool.

1. Place the green chiles and ½ cup of the chicken broth in a blender and blend until relatively smooth. Briefly set aside.

2. Heat the oil in a medium Dutch oven or heavy-bottomed soup pot over medium heat. When the oil is hot and shimmering, add the onion and garlic and cook for about 4 minutes, until the onion is soft and translucent and the garlic is fragrant. (Be very careful not to burn them, people!) Stir in the cumin, chili powder, oregano, and a generous pinch of salt and cook for 1 minute to toast the spices. Add the chile puree, hominy, and remaining 3½ cups chicken broth and bring to a simmer. Slice the chicken breasts in half crosswise and add them to the pot. Cover the pot with a lid and simmer for 15 minutes, or until the chicken is cooked through.

3. Carefully transfer the chicken to a cutting board. Shred the meat with two forks (or your hands), then return it to the pot. Turn off the heat and stir in the lime juice. Season the pozole with more salt to taste. (FYI, you'll likely need a decent amount of salt here.)

4. Ladle the pozole into bowls and really go to town with the toppings.

> JUST THE TIP: Hominy is made from whole corn kernels that have been soaked in a lye or lime solution to remove the bran and germ. This process causes the grain to puff up to about twice its normal size, leaving you with giant corn kernels that taste almost potato-like. It's sold in most major grocery stores near the canned corn and beans, but you can always sub corn or your favorite bean in a pinch.

One-Pot Cheeseburger Fusilli

Given the dude community's rabid enthusiasm for both cheeseburgers and pasta, it only made sense to combine the two into a single culinary masterpiece. You'd think the mash-up of such notoriously unhealthy items would be a nutritional disaster, but thanks to portion-controlled lean ground beef and fiber-rich brown rice pasta, this one-pot meal actually aligns with your healthy eating efforts. Think of it as Hamburger Helper with a little more pizzazz and zero chemical additives.

1. Heat the oil in a large sauté pan or Dutch oven over medium heat. When the oil is hot and shimmering, add the onion and garlic and cook for 4 to 5 minutes, until the onion is soft and translucent and the garlic is fragrant.

2. Add the ground beef, salt, paprika, and black pepper to the skillet. Cook for about 7 minutes, stirring the meat and breaking it up into small pieces with a spatula, until no longer pink.

3. Stir in the tomato paste, mustard, and Worcestershire sauce and cook for 2 more minutes, then stir in the diced tomatoes and tomato puree. Bring to a gentle simmer and cook for 10 minutes to allow the flavors to mingle, then stir in the beef broth and pasta. Simmer for 12 to 15 minutes, stirring occasionally, until the pasta is al dente.

4. Stir in the spinach and cook just until wilted, about 1 minute, then stir in the cheese.

5. Ladle the pasta into bowls and top with avocado, red onion, and a sprinkling of sesame seeds if you're feeling the garnishes.

FOR THE CHEESEBURGER FUSILLI:

1 tablespoon extra-virgin olive oil

1 medium yellow onion, finely chopped

3 garlic cloves, minced

1 pound 90% lean ground beef (preferably grass-fed)

1¼ teaspoons kosher salt

1 teaspoon paprika

½ teaspoon freshly ground black pepper

2 tablespoons tomato paste

2 tablespoons Dijon mustard

2 tablespoons Worcestershire sauce

One 14.5-ounce can diced fire-roasted tomatoes with their juices

One 8-ounce can tomato puree

2 cups low-sodium beef broth

8 ounces brown rice or whole-wheat fusilli pasta

3 packed cups baby spinach, chopped

1 cup grated extra-sharp cheddar cheese

FOR SERVING (OPTIONAL):

1 ripe avocado, pitted, peeled, and diced

½ small red onion, minced

2 teaspoons sesame seeds

Suped-Up Sweet Potato Soup

In addition to their blood sugar–regulating and anti-inflammatory nutrients, sweet potatoes are jam-packed with every Dude Dieter's favorite antioxidant, beta-carotene. Not only does beta-carotene boost immunity, improve vision, and lower the risk of heart disease and cancer, but it also does wonders for your skin. So please try not to let all the compliments go to your head when you put this recipe into regular rotation and start resembling a young Brad Pitt.

Thanks to the satiating power of crispy bacon and sharp cheddar, this smoky-sweet soup is 100 percent hearty enough to be eaten for dinner, but I also recommend it as an easy appetizer for fancy dinner parties. It truly amuses the bouche.

1. Heat a medium Dutch oven or heavy-bottomed soup pot over medium heat. When hot, add the sliced bacon and cook for about 8 minutes, until browned and crisp. Using a slotted spoon, transfer the bacon to a paper towel–lined plate. (Careful, the oil may spit a little!)

2. Pour off all but 2 tablespoons of the bacon grease from the pot and return it to the stovetop. Reduce the heat to medium and add the onion, garlic, and salt to the pan. Cook for 5 minutes, or until the onion is soft and translucent. Add the paprika and cayenne pepper (if using) and cook for 1 more minute to toast the spices. Add the sweet potatoes, cauliflower, and chicken broth and bring to a boil over high heat. Lower to a simmer, cover the pot with a lid, and cook for 25 minutes, or until the vegetables are very tender.

3. Transfer the soup to a blender—depending on the size of your blender, you'll likely need to do this in two batches—and puree until smooth. Make sure you remove the cap from the center of your blender lid and hold a dish towel over the gap while blending to let steam escape and prevent a soup explosion. (If you happen to have an immersion blender, definitely use it.)

4. Return the soup to the pot and stir in half of the cooked bacon, half of the cheese, and half of the chives. Taste and season with a little extra salt and pepper if needed.

5. Ladle the soup into bowls and serve garnished with the remaining bacon, cheese, and chives. Drizzle with hot sauce if that's your style.

10 slices bacon (preferably with no added nitrates), sliced crosswise into ½-inch pieces

1 small yellow onion, finely chopped

3 garlic cloves, minced

½ teaspoon kosher salt

1½ teaspoons smoked paprika

Pinch of cayenne pepper (optional)

2 medium sweet potatoes, peeled and cut into ½-inch pieces (about 5 cups)

2 cups chopped cauliflower florets

1 quart low-sodium chicken broth

¾ cup sharp cheddar cheese

⅓ cup finely chopped fresh chives

Hot sauce for serving (optional)

Summer Jambalaya with Chicken and Sausage

1 pound boneless, skinless chicken thighs, cut into 1½-inch pieces

½ teaspoon kosher salt, divided, plus extra as needed

Freshly ground black pepper to taste

2 tablespoons extra-virgin olive oil, divided

3 links fully cooked andouille chicken sausage, sliced into rounds

1 medium yellow onion, diced

1 red bell pepper, seeded and diced

1 cup fresh or frozen sweet corn kernels

3 garlic cloves, minced

1 tablespoon smoked paprika

1 teaspoon dried oregano

½ teaspoon ground cumin

¾ cup green lentils, rinsed well

One 14.5-ounce can diced fire-roasted tomatoes with their juices

3 cups low-sodium chicken broth

1 tablespoon hot sauce of your choice, plus more for serving (I like Cholula for this.)

1 teaspoon Worcestershire sauce

1 medium zucchini, diced

2 whole scallions, thinly sliced (optional)

Loaded with tender chicken thighs, sausage, and summer's finest produce, this smoky, rice-free interpretation of the Creole classic will fill you up without weighing you down. If you're worried that this jambalaya won't have the same staying power without a grain . . . think again. A surprise lentil cameo adds heft to this dish along with some impressive health benefits—the legume's high fiber and mineral content promotes digestive and heart health, stabilizes blood sugar, and boosts energy in a big way. If you're not a lentil lover, I beg you to give them a shot in this recipe. Truth be told, you may not even notice them in your bowl. Logan didn't . . .

1. Season the chicken with ¼ teaspoon of the salt and a few cranks of pepper.

2. Heat a large Dutch oven or sauté pan over medium-high heat. When hot, add 1 tablespoon of the oil, swirling to coat the bottom of the pan. Immediately add the chicken and chicken sausage to the pan (careful, the oil may pop and spit!) and cook for 8 to 10 minutes, until both are lightly browned all over. Transfer to a large plate or bowl using a slotted spoon.

3. Add the remaining 1 tablespoon oil to the pan and add the onion, bell pepper, corn, garlic, and remaining ¼ teaspoon salt and cook for about 6 minutes, until the vegetables are just tender. Add the smoked paprika, oregano, and cumin and cook for 1 minute to toast the spices. Return the chicken and sausage to the pan. Stir in the lentils, tomatoes, chicken broth, hot sauce, and Worcestershire sauce and bring the mixture to a simmer. Simmer for about 30 minutes, until the lentils are tender. Stir in the zucchini and cook for 5 to 7 minutes, until just tender. Taste the jambalaya and season with a little extra salt if needed.

4. Ladle the jambalaya into bowls and garnish with scallions (if using). Serve with extra hot sauce.

Greek Steak Skillet with Tzatziki

As far as quick and dirty weeknight meals go, a low-maintenance meat and vegetable stir-fry is a no-brainer. Most stir-fry recipes tend to be Asian-inspired, but I urge you to think outside the box and experiment with other flavor combinations like this Mediterranean-themed steak skillet. Topped with a cooling, protein-packed tzatziki sauce, each veggie-heavy serving will have you feeling like a Greek god in thirty minutes flat.

1. Place the steak in the freezer for 15 minutes. (This will make it so much easier to slice.)

2. Make the tzatziki: Wrap the grated cucumber in a clean dish towel. Twist the towel tightly (over the sink, obviously) to wring out the excess moisture from the cucumber. Add the cucumber to a small bowl along with the rest of the ingredients for the tzatziki and stir to combine. Cover the bowl tightly with plastic wrap and refrigerate until ready to use.

3. Remove the steak from the freezer and slice it across the grain as thinly as humanly possible. Season the steak with ¼ teaspoon of the salt and the black pepper.

4. Heat 1½ teaspoons of the oil in a large skillet over medium-high heat. When the oil is hot and shimmering, add the steak to the pan and cook for 3 to 4 minutes, until no longer pink. Transfer the steak to a bowl or plate and briefly set aside.

5. Wipe out the skillet and return it to the stove over medium-high heat. Add the remaining 1½ teaspoons oil, then add the red pepper, zucchini, onion, garlic, oregano, and remaining ¼ teaspoon salt. Cook for about 7 minutes, until tender (but not mushy) and lightly browned.

6. Drain any excess liquid from the steak and return it to the skillet. Stir in the lemon juice.

7. Divide the contents of the skillet between 2 bowls or plates. Serve topped with the tzatziki and parsley (if using). If necessary, some whole-wheat pita or naan is allowed.

FOR THE STEAK:

12 ounces top round steak

½ teaspoon kosher salt, divided

½ teaspoon freshly ground black pepper

1 tablespoon avocado oil, divided (Olive oil is also fine.)

1 red bell pepper, seeded and thinly sliced

1 large zucchini, quartered lengthwise and sliced into ½-inch pieces

½ small red onion, thinly sliced

2 large garlic cloves, minced

2 teaspoons dried oregano

1 tablespoon fresh lemon juice

Chopped fresh flat-leaf parsley for serving (optional)

FOR THE TZATZIKI:

½ cup grated or finely chopped English cucumber (aka seedless cucumber)

½ cup nonfat plain Greek yogurt (I like Fage for this.)

1 garlic clove, grated or finely minced

1½ teaspoons fresh lemon juice

2 teaspoons fresh dill weed or 1 teaspoon dried dill weed

Pinch of kosher salt

Turkey Teriyaki Noodles with Bok Choy and Brussels Sprouts

SERVES 3 to 4

FOR THE NOODLES:

4 ounces brown rice pad Thai noodles (such as Annie Chun's brand)

2 cups thinly sliced Brussels sprouts (roughly 8 medium sprouts)

1 pound turkey cutlets, sliced into ¼-inch-thick pieces

6 ounces baby bok choy (about 3 small heads)

2 tablespoons light sesame oil, divided (Coconut oil is also great.)

Freshly ground black pepper to taste

FOR THE TERIYAKI SAUCE:

¼ cup low-sodium soy sauce

¼ cup water

2 tablespoons honey

1½ tablespoons rice vinegar

1½ teaspoons peeled and grated fresh ginger

1 large garlic clove, grated or finely minced

1 tablespoon cornstarch

½ teaspoon Thai fish sauce (optional)

Early in the process of writing this book, I asked the Dude Diet Instagram community for their most burning recipe requests, and countless individuals slid into my DMs with some iteration of the same demand: SEND NOODS. Ask and ye shall receive, my wordplaying friends. I did my very best to fulfill all your sweet and savory fantasies.

p.s. I look forward to seeing these fresh noods #BreakTheInternet.

1. Fill a medium saucepan or baking dish with hot water. Soak the noodles according to the package directions (usually about 10 minutes). Drain the noodles, rinse them with cold water, and set aside.

2. Meanwhile, whisk all the ingredients for the teriyaki sauce in a medium bowl. Set the sauce by the stove.

3. I'm assuming you can thinly slice the Brussels sprouts and turkey, but the bok choy needs some special attention. Cut each bok choy crosswise into ½-inch slices, **keeping the sliced leaves separate from the sliced stalks.** (They have different cooking times!)

4. Place the Brussels sprouts, turkey, and bok choy stalks and leaves by the stove, along with an empty mixing bowl. Things are going to happen fast once you start cooking, and you want to have all the goods handy.

5. Heat 1 tablespoon of the oil in your largest nonstick sauté pan or wok over medium-high heat. When the oil is hot and shimmering, add the bok choy stems and Brussels sprouts. Cook for 3 to 4 minutes, until crisp-tender. Add the bok choy leaves and cook just until wilted, about 1 minute. Transfer the veggies to the empty bowl.

6. Return the pan to the heat and add ½ tablespoon of the remaining oil. Add half of the turkey to the pan in an even layer and season with a little black pepper. Cook for 1 minute, undisturbed, until lightly browned on the underside. Then cook for another 1 to 2 minutes, stirring regularly, until the turkey is just cooked through (turkey cooks quickly and has a tendency to dry out, so be careful not to overdo it!). Transfer the turkey to the bowl with the vegetables. Add the remaining ½ tablespoon oil to the skillet and repeat the cooking process with the remaining turkey.

7. Give the teriyaki sauce a whisk to smooth out any clumps and pour it

into the pan with the second batch of turkey. Cook for about 30 seconds, until it thickens slightly. Add the rest of the turkey, vegetables, and noodles to the pan and cook for about 1 minute, tossing with tongs, just until everything is heated through.

8. Divide the teriyaki noodles among 3 or 4 bowls. Serve immediately, garnished (if you like) with the peanuts and scallions and some sriracha.

FOR SERVING (OPTIONAL):

¼ cup chopped roasted peanuts or cashews

¼ cup thinly sliced scallions

Sriracha sauce

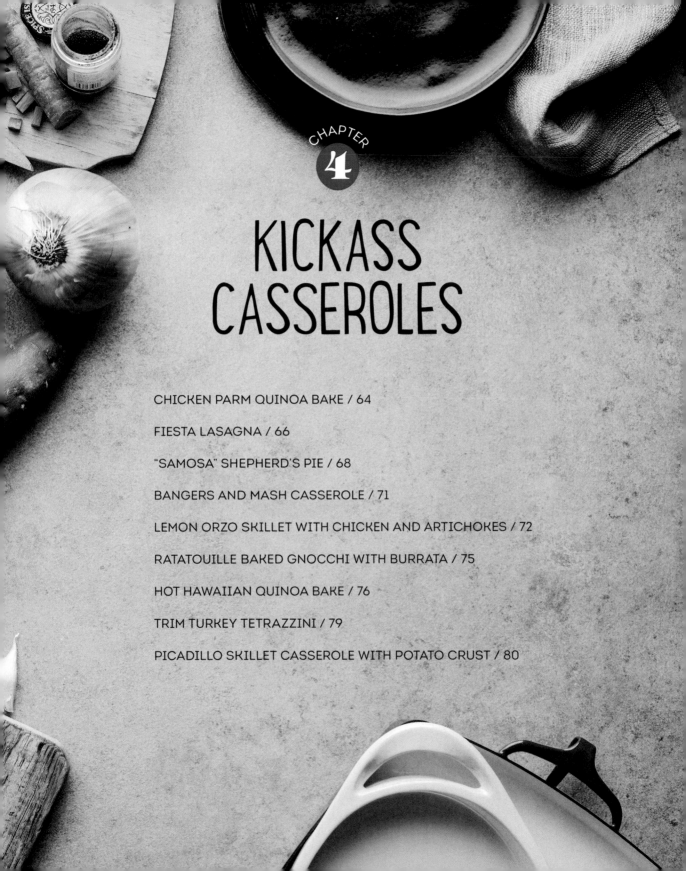

KICKASS CASSEROLES

Chicken Parm Quinoa Bake

¾ cup quinoa, rinsed and drained

1¼ cups low-sodium chicken broth

4 cups broccoli florets

2 tablespoons extra-virgin olive oil

Kosher salt to taste

Freshly ground black pepper to taste

3 garlic cloves, minced

⅓ cup whole-wheat panko bread crumbs

¼ teaspoon crushed red pepper flakes (optional)

One 8-ounce ball fresh mozzarella, divided

1 recipe Idiotproof Chicken Breasts (page 136), diced (Or use 2 cups diced or shredded chicken breast—no judgment if you want to use a store-bought rotisserie bird.)

2½ cups marinara sauce, divided (I like Rao's brand for this.)

¼ cup freshly grated Parmesan cheese

Chopped fresh basil for serving (optional)

If The Dude Diet had a singular food mascot, it would be the humble quinoa bake. No contest. Various iterations of this whole-grain casserole have introduced many a dude to the wonders of quinoa and helped hordes of quinoa haters change their tune, which is pretty thrilling given quinoa's laundry list of health perks. The grain (which is technically a seed, but whatever) is packed with fiber, iron, and magnesium among other essential vitamins and minerals, and it happens to be a complete protein, meaning that it provides your body with all nine essential amino acids required to build and repair protein tissues in the body. In short, quinoa is a nutritional all-star, and the versatile fluffy grain makes quite the kickass casserole base.

The formula for a quinoa bake is simple: **quinoa + lean protein + vegetables + something saucy + a responsible amount of cheese + crispy topping.** This formula can be adapted in infinite awesome ways, but I highly recommend the recipe below, which rocks all the flavors of chicken Parmesan in Dude Diet–friendly form. Whether you're a quinoa bake virgin or devotee, you're going to want to get on this one ASAFP.

1. Preheat the oven to 425°F.
2. Combine the quinoa and chicken broth in a small saucepan and bring to a boil. Lower to a simmer, cover the saucepan with a lid, and cook for 14 minutes, or until all of the liquid has been absorbed. Let the quinoa rest, covered, for 5 minutes, then fluff with a fork.
3. Place the broccoli in a large (12-inch) ovenproof skillet. Drizzle with 1 tablespoon of the oil and sprinkle with a pinch of salt and a few cranks of black pepper. Toss to coat. Arrange the broccoli in a single layer in the skillet. Transfer to the oven and roast for 13 to 15 minutes, until tender and lightly browned in spots. When you take the broccoli out of the oven, reduce the temperature to 375°F.
4. While the broccoli is roasting, heat the remaining 1 tablespoon oil in a small skillet over medium heat. When the oil is hot and shimmering, add the garlic and cook for about 2 minutes, until golden brown. (Be very careful not to burn the garlic!! If it looks like it's browning too quickly, turn down the heat.) Stir in the bread crumbs and red pepper flakes (if using) and cook for 2 to 3 minutes, until the crumbs are nicely toasted and have darkened a shade in color. Transfer the garlicky bread crumbs to a small bowl.

5. Grate half of the mozzarella ball on the large holes of a box grater. Slice the remaining half into very thin rounds. (The rounds don't need to be perfect—they're going to melt!)

6. Add the chicken, cooked quinoa, 2 cups of the marinara sauce, and the grated mozzarella to the skillet with the broccoli. (Be careful, the skillet is HOT!!) Fold everything together with a spatula until well combined. Taste and season with a little salt and pepper if necessary. Smooth the top of the filling with a spatula. Spread the remaining ½ cup marinara sauce on top, then add the sliced mozzarella cheese and sprinkle with the Parmesan cheese and the garlicky bread crumbs. Bake for 20 to 25 minutes, until the cheese has melted and the topping is lightly browned.

7. Let your badass bake rest for 10 minutes. (Trust me, you will burn your tongue!) Serve warm, topped with fresh basil, if you like.

JUST THE TIP: To make grating and slicing fresh mozzarella a breeze, pop the ball into the freezer for 15 minutes beforehand to firm up the cheese.

Fiesta Lasagna

FOR THE LASAGNA:

1 tablespoon extra-virgin olive oil

1 pound 90% lean ground beef

2 portobello mushroom caps (stems and gills removed), finely chopped

1 red bell pepper, seeded and cut into small dice

¾ cup fresh or frozen sweet corn kernels

½ medium yellow onion, finely chopped

1 jalapeño, finely chopped

1 tablespoon chili powder

1½ teaspoons smoked paprika

1 teaspoon kosher salt, plus extra as needed

¾ teaspoon ground cumin

½ teaspoon dried oregano

½ teaspoon garlic powder

One 28-ounce can tomato puree

1 cup low-sodium beef broth

3 packed cups baby spinach, chopped

Six 8-inch whole-wheat tortillas

1½ cups grated sharp cheddar cheese

The first time I whipped up this Mexican masterpiece was Super Bowl Sunday 2018. As you may recall, the Eagles were up against the Patriots, and it was an angsty game. Especially for die-hard Philly fans like Logan. There was a lot of screaming, creative expletives, and stress eating of this layered casserole that evening, and then something miraculous happened . . . *the Eagles won.*

Since the Dude is extremely superstitious, this casserole has since become his lucky meal. It's now mandatory on all important game days, which I feel great about given that it's made with lean beef, plenty of vegetables, and whole-grain tortillas. Imagine if we had ordered Domino's that day . . .

1. Heat the oil in your largest sauté pan or a Dutch oven over medium heat. When the oil is hot and shimmering, add the beef and cook, stirring and breaking up the meat with a spatula, for 5 to 6 minutes, until lightly browned. Add the mushrooms, bell pepper, corn, onion, jalapeño, and the spices and cook for about 6 minutes, just until the vegetables are tender. Stir in the tomato puree and beef broth and simmer for 5 minutes to allow the flavors to marry. Add the spinach and cook just until wilted, about 1 minute. Remove that fiery fiesta sauce from the heat. Taste and season with a little extra salt if necessary.

2. Preheat the oven to 375°F.

3. Spread the bottom of a 9 × 13-inch baking dish with 1 cup of the sauce. Layer two tortillas over the sauce. (They will overlap in the middle—it's cool.) Top the tortillas with 2 cups of the sauce. Sprinkle with ⅓ cup of the cheese. Repeat these layers—tortillas, sauce, cheese—a second time, then top with a third and final layer of tortillas. Spread the remaining sauce on top of the tortillas and sprinkle evenly with the remaining cheese.

4. Bake for 25 minutes, or until the cheese has melted and the sauce is bubbling.

5. Let the casserole cool for 5 to 10 minutes (it will be scary hot!) before cutting and serving. Feel free to garnish with avocado, cilantro, and plenty of hot sauce or your favorite toppings.

66 THE DUDE DIET DINNERTIME

YOU DO YOU: I like to garnish this lasagna with avocado, cilantro and hot sauce, but don't be afraid to get creative with your toppings.

"Samosa" Shepherd's Pie

SERVES 4

FOR THE SHEPHERD'S PIE:

3 medium
  sweet potatoes
  (approximately 6 to 8
  ounces each), sliced
  in half lengthwise

1 tablespoon plus 2
  teaspoons extra-
  virgin olive oil,
  divided

½ teaspoon ground
  cinnamon, divided

1¼ teaspoons kosher
  salt, divided

2 cups finely chopped
  cauliflower florets
  (about ½ small head
  of cauliflower)

1 cup finely chopped
  carrots

1 small yellow onion,
  minced

3 large garlic cloves,
  minced

1 tablespoon plus
  2 teaspoons curry
  powder

2 teaspoons chili
  powder, plus extra
  (optional) for topping

½ teaspoon ground
  cumin

¼ teaspoon ground
  ginger

(continued)

Inspired by the warmly spiced filling of the beloved samosa, this stick-to-your-ribs meat and (sweet) potato casserole serves up big flavor and even bigger health benefits. Each serving boasts an impressive amount of fiber, essential minerals, and antioxidants such as beta-carotene. Grass-fed lamb—which contains levels of anti-inflammatory omega-3 fatty acids similar to those of some fish—adds richness and depth to this recipe, but if you're not down with its distinctive flavor, swap in your favorite lean ground meat. (But, for the love of God, do not use 99% lean ground turkey or your casserole will be sad and dry.)

1. Preheat the oven to 425°F. Line a baking sheet with parchment paper or aluminum foil.

2. Brush the cut sides of the sweet potatoes with 1 teaspoon of the oil and place them cut-side down on the prepared baking sheet. Roast for 25 minutes, or until very tender when pierced with the tip of a sharp knife. Let cool slightly. When the sweet potatoes are cool enough to handle, remove their skins. (They should peel right off.) Transfer the flesh to a medium bowl and add 1 teaspoon of the remaining oil, ¼ teaspoon of the cinnamon, and ¼ teaspoon of the salt and mash with a fork until very smooth. Set aside.

3. Reduce the oven temperature to 375°F.

4. Meanwhile, heat the remaining 1 tablespoon oil in a large skillet over medium heat. When the oil is hot and shimmering, add the cauliflower, carrots, and onion and cook for 5 to 6 minutes, until the cauliflower and carrots have softened slightly and the onion is translucent. Add the garlic, curry powder, chili powder; the remaining ¼ teaspoon cinnamon; the cumin, ginger, cayenne; and the remaining 1 teaspoon salt. Cook for 1 minute more to toast the spices. Add the lamb and cook for about 4 minutes, breaking up the meat with a spatula, until no longer pink. Stir in the chicken broth and simmer for 5 minutes, or until most of the liquid has been absorbed. Turn off the heat and stir in the peas and lemon juice.

5. Transfer the filling to a medium baking dish (a 9 × 9-inch or a 7 × 11-inch dish is ideal) and top with the sweet potato mash, spreading it out in an even layer. Add a couple of dashes of chili powder if you like.

⅛ teaspoon cayenne
 pepper

12 ounces ground
 lamb (preferably
 grass-fed)

¾ cup low-sodium
 chicken broth

1 cup frozen sweet
 peas

Juice of ½ lemon

FOR SERVING (OPTIONAL):

¼ cup fresh cilantro
 leaves, finely
 chopped

6. Bake the casserole for 20 minutes, or until piping hot and bubbling around the sides. Remove from the oven and let cool for 5 to 10 minutes. Serve garnished with cilantro if you appreciate a little fresh greenery.

JUST THE TIP: In a rush? Bypass baking and serve the lamb filling in bowls over the sweet potato mash. It will be more stew-like (and less pretty), but it will still taste delicious.

Bangers and Mash Casserole

This casserole channels the British comfort food favorite with a few minor tweaks to keep your meat sweats and carb comas at bay. Don't panic, the essentials—sausage, mash, gravy—are all present and accounted for here. The sausage just happens to be chicken, the cheesy mash cauliflower, and the gravy made sans flour and butter. Not that you'll be able to tell . . .

1. Put the cauliflower florets and 3 cups of the chicken broth in a Dutch oven or large saucepan and bring to a boil over high heat. Lower to a simmer, cover with a lid, and cook for about 20 minutes, until the cauliflower is very tender when pierced with the tip of a sharp knife. Using a slotted spoon, transfer the florets to a blender or food processor and puree until smooth. Transfer the puree to a bowl, stir in ½ cup of the cheese, and season generously with salt.

2. Meanwhile, whisk the remaining 1 cup chicken broth, the cornstarch, mustard, and vinegar in a small bowl. Set this sauce by the stove.

3. Heat the oil in your largest ovenproof skillet or sauté pan over medium-high heat. When the oil is hot and shimmering (but not smoking!), add the sausage and cook for 5 minutes, or until well browned. Add the onion, bell pepper, and cabbage and cook for about 6 minutes, just until the vegetables are tender (but not mushy!). Give the sauce another whisk to smooth out any cornstarch clumps, then add it to the pan. Reduce the heat to medium and cook for 5 minutes, or until the vegetables are very soft and the sauce has thickened slightly.

4. Preheat the broiler to high.

5. Top the contents of the skillet with the cheesy cauliflower puree, spreading it out in an even layer. Sprinkle with the remaining ½ cup cheese. (If you don't have an ovenproof skillet, transfer the contents of the skillet to a medium baking dish before topping with the cauliflower puree and broiling.)

6. Place the casserole under the broiler for about 5 minutes, until the cheese is bubbling and lightly browned. Let cool for 5 to 10 minutes before serving. Serve garnished with the parsley, if you have it.

FOR THE CASSEROLE:

1 large head cauliflower, cored and broken into florets

4 cups low-sodium chicken broth, divided

1 cup grated Dubliner cheddar cheese, divided (Gruyère or Fontina is also great.)

Kosher salt to taste

1 tablespoon cornstarch

1 tablespoon plus 2 teaspoons whole-grain mustard

1 tablespoon plus 2 teaspoons balsamic vinegar

1 tablespoon extra-virgin olive oil

12 ounces fully cooked chicken sausage (any kind will do, but I'm partial to andouille or sweet Italian), sliced into ¼-inch rounds

1 large yellow onion, thinly sliced

1 red bell pepper, seeded and thinly sliced

4 cups thinly sliced green cabbage

FOR SERVING (OPTIONAL):

2 tablespoons chopped fresh flat-leaf parsley

Lemon Orzo Skillet with Chicken and Artichokes

1½ pounds boneless, skinless chicken thighs

Kosher salt to taste

Freshly ground black pepper to taste

1½ tablespoons extra-virgin olive oil

3 garlic cloves, minced

1 cup whole-wheat orzo pasta (uncooked)

One 12-ounce jar marinated artichoke hearts, drained and roughly chopped

1 tablespoon herbes de Provence

2½ cups low-sodium chicken broth

1¼ cups grated Fontina cheese, divided (Gouda or Gruyère is also great.)

1 teaspoon freshly grated lemon zest

1 tablespoon fresh lemon juice

¼ cup grated Parmesan cheese

¼ cup flat-leaf parsley leaves, finely chopped

While this cheesy chicken, artichoke, and whole-wheat orzo casserole is the perfect thing to eat on your couch in polar vortex situations, it's equally awesome for entertaining given the sophisticated flavor profile (artichokes and "notes of citrus" = instant fancy) and alluring, herb-sprinkled blanket of bubbling cheese. The best part? Everything cooks together in a single skillet, so you can spend less time cleaning and more time basking in your casserole compliments.

1. Pat the chicken thighs dry and season all over with salt and pepper.

2. Heat 1 tablespoon of the oil in a large (12-inch) ovenproof skillet over medium-high heat. When the oil is hot and shimmering, add the chicken to the pan and sear for 3 minutes per side, or until it's a nice golden brown. (The oil may pop and spit a little, so please be careful not to burn yourself!) Transfer the seared chicken to a plate.

3. Reduce the heat to medium and add the remaining ½ tablespoon oil to the skillet. Add the garlic and orzo and cook for 2 minutes, just to lightly toast the orzo. Add the artichoke hearts, herbes de Provence, and chicken broth to the pan and bring to a boil over high heat. Lower the heat to a simmer and return the chicken thighs to the skillet. Cover the pan with a lid and cook for 20 minutes, or until the chicken is cooked through and the orzo is tender. There should still be some liquid in the pan—you need it to keep things saucy.

4. Preheat the broiler to high.

5. Transfer the chicken thighs to a cutting board and shred the meat with two forks. Return the chicken to the skillet along with half of the Fontina cheese, folding everything together with a spatula. Turn off the heat and stir in the lemon zest and lemon juice. Taste and season with more salt and pepper if needed. Sprinkle the remaining Fontina cheese and the Parmesan cheese over the skillet and top with a few extra cranks of black pepper (if you like).

6. Place the skillet under the broiler. Broil until the cheese is bubbling and lightly browned. This should take about 4 minutes, but broilers are fickle, so keep an eye on it!

7. Garnish with the parsley and serve warm.

JUST THE TIP: This dish makes a killer main dish or sexy side for parties! The casserole can be fully prepped through step 4 up to a day in advance, then all you have to do is add the cheeses and bake.

Ratatouille Baked Gnocchi with Burrata

Traditional ratatouille (rat-uh-too-ee) is a medley of vegetables sautéed with plenty of olive oil, garlic, an herb or two, and cooked down until the veggies are melt-in-your-mouth tender. The resulting dish is somehow much more than the sum of its simple parts, and it's both delicious and surprisingly nutritious. This recipe combines the aforementioned goodness with pillowy whole-wheat gnocchi and burrata—aka the creamiest, most delicious fresh mozzarella on the planet—to create an obscenely flavorful vegetarian casserole that will satisfy cheesy carb cravings without derailing your Dude Diet efforts.

Yes, you can add some browned chicken or turkey sausage if you must. (I knew you'd ask.)

1. Preheat the oven to 375°F. Bring a large pot of salted water to a boil.

2. Heat the oil in your largest ovenproof skillet, sauté pan, or braiser. (If you don't have something ovenproof, no worries. You can transfer everything to a casserole dish before baking.) When the oil is hot and shimmering, add the bell pepper, onion, garlic, salt, and crushed red pepper. Cook for about 5 minutes, until the onions are translucent and the peppers are lightly softened. Add the zucchini and squash and cook for about 6 minutes, until just tender, then stir in the tomatoes. Simmer gently for 10 minutes.

3. Meanwhile, cook the gnocchi according to the package directions.

4. Add the gnocchi and basil to the ratatouille sauce and fold everything together.

5. Tear the burrata cheese into 6 to 8 pieces on top of everything (cream will run out of the cheese, and that's a beautiful thing), then sprinkle with the Pecorino Romano cheese.

6. Transfer the gnocchi madness to the oven and bake for 20 minutes, or until the cheese is melted and the sauce is bubbling slightly. Remove from the oven and let cool for 5 to 10 minutes. Serve garnished with extra basil if you're feeling fresh.

¾ teaspoon kosher salt, plus more for cooking the gnocchi

2 tablespoons extra-virgin olive oil

1 small red bell pepper, seeded and diced

½ medium yellow onion, finely chopped

5 garlic cloves, minced

½ teaspoon crushed red pepper flakes

1 medium zucchini, diced

1 small summer squash, diced

One 28-ounce can diced fire-roasted tomatoes with their juices

1 pound whole-wheat gnocchi

¼ cup fresh basil leaves, chopped, plus extra (optional) for serving

One 8-ounce ball burrata cheese

¼ cup Pecorino Romano cheese

Hot Hawaiian Quinoa Bake

1 cup quinoa, rinsed and drained

1½ cups low-sodium chicken broth

1 tablespoon plus 1 teaspoon extra-virgin olive oil, divided

8 ounces Canadian bacon, diced

1 large red bell pepper, seeded and diced

1 small red onion, diced

1 large garlic clove, minced

1¼ teaspoons dried oregano, divided

1½ tablespoons tomato paste

One 14.5-ounce can diced fire-roasted tomatoes with their juices

1 cup diced fresh pineapple

1 tablespoon finely chopped pickled jalapeño rounds, plus more (optional) for serving

¼ cup whole-wheat panko bread crumbs

Tiny pinch of kosher salt

¾ cup shredded part-skim mozzarella cheese

¾ cup grated sharp cheddar cheese

I don't want to get ahead of myself here, but this one seems to have "cult classic" written all over it. If you're a fan of Hawaiian pizza, this quinoa bake featuring the sweet-savory-spicy trifecta of Canadian bacon, pineapple, and plenty of pickled jalapeños is going to blow your damn mind. And since the casserole reheats amazingly well, leftovers are something to get hot and bothered about.

1. Combine the quinoa and chicken broth in a small saucepan and bring to a boil. Lower to a simmer, cover the saucepan with a lid, and cook for 14 minutes, or until all of the liquid has been absorbed. Let the quinoa rest, covered, for 5 minutes, then fluff with a fork.

2. Preheat the oven to 375°F.

3. Meanwhile, heat 1 tablespoon of the oil in a large (12-inch) ovenproof skillet over medium heat. When the oil is hot and shimmering, add the bacon and cook until lightly browned and crispy, about 4 minutes. (Careful, the bacon may pop and spit a little!) Add the bell pepper, onion, garlic, and 1 teaspoon of the oregano and cook for about 5 minutes, just until the vegetables are tender. Add the tomato paste and cook for 1 minute just to mellow the acidity, then add the diced tomatoes and simmer for 5 minutes. Stir in the pineapple and half of the jalapeños.

4. Meanwhile, toast the bread crumbs! Heat the remaining 1 teaspoon oil in a small skillet over medium heat. When hot, add the bread crumbs, the remaining ¼ teaspoon oregano, and a tiny pinch of salt and cook for about 2 minutes, until the bread crumbs are nicely toasted and have darkened a shade in color. Transfer to a small bowl.

5. Turn off the heat and fold in the quinoa and half of the mozzarella and cheddar cheeses. Smooth the top of the filling with a spatula. Add the remaining cheeses in an even layer and sprinkle with the panko topping. Bake for 25 minutes, or until the cheese has melted and the top is very lightly browned.

6. Let your delicious quinoa bake rest for 10 minutes. (It will remove your taste buds if you cheat. Trust.) Serve with extra jalapeños if you're wild like that.

Trim Turkey Tetrazzini

This comfort food classic is usually a vehicle for leftover turkey or chicken, and most recipes call for canned "cream of something" soup and/or heavy cream plus a boatload of white pasta. Not only does the resulting dish have little nutritional value, it will also send your blood sugar levels into outer space. Swapping in whole-wheat spaghetti and zucchini noodles significantly boosts the fiber and nutrients in this casserole, and a responsible amount of full-fat sour cream and Italian cheeses adds indulgently creamy flavor to the sauce without a crazy amount of chemical additives (or calories).

1. Preheat the oven to 425°F. Grease a 9 × 13-inch baking dish with a little oil.

2. Heat the oil in a Dutch oven or large sauté pan over medium-high heat. When the oil is hot and shimmering, add the mushrooms (if using) and salt and cook for about 2 minutes, until just beginning to soften. Add the onion, garlic, oregano, thyme, and black pepper and cook for about 5 minutes, until the onion is translucent and the garlic is fragrant. Add the turkey and cook for about 5 minutes, breaking up the meat into small pieces with a spatula, until no longer pink. Sprinkle the flour over everything and cook for 2 minutes, stirring constantly, then add the wine and cook for 1 minute more, or until most of the liquid has been absorbed. Stir in the chicken broth and bring to a gentle simmer.

3. Break the spaghetti in half and add to the pot. Simmer for about 8 minutes, stirring occasionally—be careful not to let the spaghetti stick to the bottom of the pan!—until the pasta is just shy of al dente. Turn off the heat and stir in the zucchini noodles, peas, sour cream, and ⅓ cup of the cheese. Taste and season with a little extra salt and pepper if needed.

4. Transfer the mixture to the prepared casserole dish and smooth the top. Sprinkle with the remaining ⅓ cup cheese, the bread crumbs, and extra black pepper if you like. Bake for 20 minutes, or until the casserole is bubbling and the top is lightly browned.

5. Let cool for at least 5 minutes to allow the sauce to thicken before serving. Garnish with fresh herbs, if you like.

1 tablespoon extra-virgin olive oil, plus extra for greasing the baking dish

8 ounces baby bella mushrooms, stemmed and thinly sliced (optional)

1 teaspoon kosher salt, plus extra as needed

½ medium yellow onion, finely chopped

3 garlic cloves, minced

1¼ teaspoons dried oregano

1 teaspoon dried thyme

½ teaspoon freshly ground black pepper, plus extra as needed

1 pound 93% lean ground turkey

¼ cup whole-wheat flour

½ cup dry white wine, such as Sauvignon Blanc

3 cups low-sodium chicken broth

8 ounces whole-wheat spaghetti

3 cups zucchini noodles

1 cup fresh or frozen green peas

¾ cup sour cream

⅔ cup Italian cheese blend, divided

⅓ cup whole-wheat panko bread crumbs

Chopped fresh parsley or chives for serving (optional)

Picadillo Skillet Casserole with Potato Crust

SERVES 4

1 pound 90% lean ground beef (preferably grass-fed)

2 tablespoons extra-virgin olive oil, divided

1 medium carrot, finely chopped

1 small bell pepper (I like red), seeded and finely chopped

1 small sweet onion, finely chopped

3 garlic cloves, minced

½ teaspoon kosher salt, plus extra as needed

2 teaspoons ground cumin

2 teaspoons dried oregano

¼ teaspoon cayenne pepper (optional)

¼ teaspoon ground cinnamon

One 14.5-ounce can tomato puree

½ cup beef bone broth (regular beef or chicken broth also will do)

⅓ cup pitted green olives, sliced into thin rounds

¼ cup golden raisins (optional)

2 tablespoons finely chopped fresh cilantro

2 teaspoons apple cider vinegar

Featuring a parade of awesome and unexpected flavors, including warming spices, briny olives, and sweet golden raisins, picadillo is an outrageously tasty ground beef dish favored in several Latin American countries and the Philippines. While many traditional recipes call for simmering potatoes in the picadillo, I like to thinly slice some spuds and layer them on top of the meat to create a satisfying skillet casserole with a golden potato crust. Talk about a crowd-pleaser.

1. Preheat the oven to 425°F.

2. Heat a 12-inch cast iron or other ovenproof skillet over medium-high heat. When hot, add the beef and cook for about 5 minutes, stirring and breaking up the meat into small pieces with a spatula, until lightly browned. Drain the beef in a mesh colander to get rid of excess grease and briefly set aside.

3. Wipe out the skillet and return it to the stove over medium heat. Add 1 tablespoon of the oil to the pan. When the oil is hot and shimmering, add the carrot, bell pepper, onion, garlic, and salt and cook for 5 minutes, or until the onion is translucent and the vegetables are beginning to soften. Add the cumin, oregano, cayenne (if using), and cinnamon and cook for 1 minute to toast the spices.

4. Return the beef to the pan and stir in the tomato puree, broth, olives, raisins (if using), cilantro, and vinegar. Season with black pepper and a little extra salt if needed. Turn off the heat and smooth the top of the picadillo with a spatula.

5. Top the filling with an even layer of sliced, slightly overlapping potatoes. (I like to make concentric circles starting at the border of the skillet and working my way in.) Brush the top of the potatoes with the remaining 1 tablespoon oil and season with a little salt and pepper.

6. Cover the skillet with aluminum foil or a lid and transfer it to the oven. Bake for 20 minutes. Remove the foil (some of the sauce will have bubbled up around the potatoes, which is fine) and bake for 20 more minutes, or until the potatoes are lightly browned and crisp around the

edges. If the potatoes haven't browned, pop the casserole under the broiler for a couple of minutes to give them some color.

7. Let cool for 5 minutes before serving. Garnish with extra cilantro if you like.

Freshly ground black pepper to taste

1 pound Yukon gold potatoes (about 3 potatoes), scrubbed and sliced into ⅛-inch-thick disks

YOU DO YOU: In a hurry or simply not a potato fan? Skip the spuds and simmer the picadillo for 10 to 15 minutes after step 4 to allow the flavors to get friendly and the sauce to thicken. Serve it over brown rice or with a side of tortillas.

CHAPTER
5

FINGERS, WINGS, AND OTHER THINGS

Honey-Chipotle BBQ Wings

FOR THE WINGS:

3 pounds chicken wings ("Wingettes and drumettes" or "cut chicken wings" are ideal, but whole chicken wings are also fine!)

1 tablespoon paprika

1 teaspoon kosher salt

¾ teaspoon garlic powder

¼ teaspoon freshly ground black pepper

Chopped fresh cilantro leaves for serving (optional)

FOR THE SAUCE:

¼ cup plus 1 tablespoon tomato paste

1 canned chipotle pepper in adobo sauce, finely minced (For tips on chipotles in adobo, see the sidebar on page 22.)

2 tablespoons adobo sauce from the chipotle can

3 tablespoons honey

2 tablespoons apple cider vinegar

1 tablespoon low-sodium soy sauce

¼ teaspoon garlic powder

½ cup water

Not gonna lie, watching the Dude eat these sweet and spicy chicken wings makes me nervous. Somehow whole wings go into his mouth and only bones come out. This is impressively efficient, yes, but it also happens at warp speed, and the choking risk feels very real. With that said, I'm selfish, so I regularly sideline my fears of becoming a young widow in favor of treating myself to one of Logan's baked wing–induced excitement freak-outs. At least I'm not clogging his arteries at the same time, right?

1. Preheat the oven to 400°F. Line two large baking sheets with aluminum foil and spray them with cooking spray. (The spray is KEY.)

2. If you're working with whole chicken wings, you'll need to do a little prep work. Remove and discard the wing tips (just cut them off at the joint), then separate the wings into wingettes (or flats) and drumettes. This sounds scary, but it's pretty easy, I swear. Just bend each wing backward at the joint until the bones separate, and then use your sharpest knife to cut between them.

3. Pat the wings dry with paper towels and place them in a large bowl. Sprinkle with the paprika, salt, garlic powder, and pepper and toss to coat. Arrange the wings on the prepared baking sheets, leaving a little space between each one. Bake for about 45 minutes, turning the wings once halfway through the cooking time, until crispy and nicely browned.

4. Meanwhile, get going on your bomb barbecue sauce! Put all the ingredients for the sauce into a large skillet or sauté pan (you need something large because you'll be adding the wings to it later) and whisk until well combined. Bring to a boil, then lower to a very gentle simmer and cook for 10 minutes, stirring periodically. Turn off the heat.

5. When the wings are done, add them to the pan with the sauce (no need to reheat the sauce) and toss to lightly coat each wing. Depending on the size of your pan, you may need to do this in two batches. (Tongs are very helpful here.) Return the wings to the baking sheet, drizzle with any sauce left in the pan, and place them back in the oven for another 5 minutes to get them nice and sticky.

6. Pile the wings on a large plate or platter. Sprinkle with cilantro if you like, and serve warm with a pile of napkins.

JUST THE TIP: If you decide to double or triple this recipe for a crew, separate the flats and drumettes and make the sauce up to a day in advance. Then all you'll have to do come party time is bake the wings. Boom done.

Lavash Pizzas with Prosciutto, Roasted Red Peppers, and Honey

MAKES 2 PERSONAL PIZZAS

I hate to fearmonger here, but many well-known pizza delivery players put some seriously questionable things in their pies (cheese shouldn't have several unpronounceable ingredients!), while others refuse to disclose their ingredient lists altogether. It's safe to say that your average order isn't doing your health or hot body any favors, so please slow your pizza delivery roll and consider partying with this semi-homemade personal pie.

The real waist-saving aspect of this recipe lies in the "crust." Whole-grain lavash is an Armenian flatbread that crisps up beautifully in the oven and makes an ideal base for thin-crust 'za. It's also higher in fiber and protein and much lower in calories than your average pizza dough. You should be able to pick up lavash next to the pitas and tortillas in most large markets, but if you can't find it, any type of flatbread will do.

1. Preheat the oven to 450°F. (If you have a pizza stone and want to use it, by all means, go ahead.)

2. Place both flatbreads on a large baking sheet and brush very lightly with the olive oil. Bake for about 3 minutes or until very lightly crisped but not browned.

3. Remove the flatbreads from the oven and spread each with an even layer of marinara sauce. Sprinkle with crushed red pepper flakes and top with cheese, roasted red peppers, and prosciutto.

4. Bake the pizzas for 6 to 8 minutes or until the cheese is melted and bubbling and the edges of the lavash are dark brown. (Pay attention! Things go from brown to burned shockingly fast.)

5. Top the pizzas with basil and drizzle with honey. Slice each pizza into four pieces and dig in.

2 whole-grain lavash (Trader Joe's makes a great one) or flatbread of your choice

1 teaspoon extra-virgin olive oil

2/3 cup marinara sauce (I recommend Rao's brand.)

1/2 teaspoon crushed red pepper flakes

One 4-ounce ball fresh mozzarella, sliced into thin rounds or grated

2/3 cup roasted red peppers bottled in water, drained and chopped

2 ounces thinly sliced prosciutto (4 slices), torn into large pieces

8 fresh basil leaves, torn into small pieces

1 teaspoon honey

Cuban Chicken Tacos

SERVES 4 to 6

FOR THE TACOS:

1 tablespoon extra-virgin olive oil

½ medium white onion, minced

3 garlic cloves, minced

½ teaspoon kosher salt

2 teaspoons dried oregano

1½ teaspoons ground cumin

½ teaspoon crushed red pepper flakes

¼ teaspoon freshly ground black pepper

2 teaspoons coarse-grain mustard

Juice of 1 lime

Juice of 1 orange

One 12-ounce bottle light beer

1½ pounds boneless, skinless chicken breasts (approximately 3 breasts)

FOR SERVING:

12 corn tortillas (Flour tortillas are also fine.)

1 romaine heart, finely chopped

2 medium tomatoes, diced

½ cup fresh cilantro leaves, chopped

½ cup sour cream or plain Greek yogurt (optional)

1 lime, cut into wedges

Given that tacos are one of the dude community's staple food groups, you can never have enough healthy recipes for the handheld flavor bombs. Here, the pulled chicken filling is simmered in a mojo-inspired combo of spices and citrus along with a bottle of (light) beer, and it serves up killer Cuban flavor with a solid kick. Meal prep enthusiasts, take note—these tacos are the ultimate make-ahead dinner for busy weeknights. And if you're lucky enough to have leftovers, the chicken is an epic addition to nachos, bowls, salads, quesadillas, and sandwiches.

1. Heat the oil in a Dutch oven or large sauté pan over medium heat. When the oil is hot and shimmering, add the onion, garlic, and salt and cook for about 3 minutes, until the onion becomes translucent and the garlic is fragrant. Stir in the oregano, cumin, crushed red pepper, and black pepper and cook for 1 minute more.

2. Stir in the mustard, lime juice, orange juice, and beer and bring to a boil. Lower to a simmer. Slice each chicken breast in half crosswise (this will help them cook more quickly) and add halves to the pan. Cover the pan with a lid and cook for 20 minutes, or until the chicken is cooked through.

3. Transfer the chicken to a cutting board and shred the meat with two forks. Return the shredded chicken to the sauce and simmer, uncovered, for another 10 to 15 minutes, until about half of the liquid has been absorbed.

4. Warm the tortillas! You can either wrap 4 tortillas at a time in a damp paper towel and microwave in 30-second increments or heat each tortilla right on your stovetop burner for 5 to 10 seconds per side.

5. Spoon the meat onto the tortillas and garnish with the romaine heart, tomatoes, cilantro, and sour cream (if using). Serve with the lime wedges.

88 THE DUDE DIET DINNERTIME

YOU DO YOU: If you're looking to turn up on the taco front, get a fresh salsa like Mango and Cherry Tomato Salsa (page 15), Peach-Jalapeño Salsa (page 183), Grilled Pineapple Relish (page 148), or your favorite pico de gallo involved.

Chicago Dog Baked Potatoes

When it comes to dressing up a dog, the fine folks of Chicago go a Dude Diet–friendly route by pure happenstance. Garnished with tomatoes, sport peppers, pickles, yellow mustard, and celery salt, the famous Chicago dog is "dragged through the garden," and the result is undeniably funky fresh.

I'm sure many Chicagoans won't take kindly to my deconstructing their city's famous hot dog and stuffing it inside a baked potato, but here's my pitch: Have you ever eaten your dog with a side of fries??? Crushing this loaded spud is like getting a mouthful of fluffy french fry interior with each bite. Try it. It's weirdly awesome.

Ingredients:

- 4 medium russet potatoes
- 3½ tablespoons extra-virgin olive oil, divided
- Kosher salt to taste
- Freshly ground black pepper to taste
- 1 teaspoon celery salt, plus extra as needed
- 3 cups finely chopped romaine hearts
- 1 medium tomato, diced
- ½ cup chopped dill or bread-and-butter pickles (dealer's choice)
- ½ cup sport peppers or pepperoncini, sliced into rounds
- ⅓ cup finely chopped white onion
- 3 tablespoons yellow mustard, plus extra for serving
- 1 tablespoon apple cider vinegar
- 1 teaspoon honey
- Six 100% beef hot dogs, preferably with no added nitrates

1. Position the oven racks in the top and bottom thirds of the oven. Preheat the oven to 425°F.

2. Scrub the potatoes and dry them well. Using a fork, poke deep holes all over the potatoes (4 good stabs will do it) so that steam can escape during cooking. Rub the potatoes with 2 teaspoons of the oil and sprinkle with a little salt and pepper. Place the potatoes directly on the top oven rack (no baking sheet necessary). Bake for 50 minutes to 1 hour, until very tender when pierced with the tip of a sharp knife. Let the potatoes cool slightly. Create a dotted line from end to end on each potato, then push the ends toward each other to crack it open. Drizzle the inside of each potato with 1 teaspoon oil, sprinkle with ¼ teaspoon celery salt, and mash the insides with a fork.

3. Meanwhile, toss the romaine hearts, tomato, pickles, sport peppers, and onion in a medium bowl. In a small bowl, combine 1 tablespoon of the remaining oil, the mustard, vinegar, and honey. Briefly set both bowls aside.

4. Slice the hot dogs in half lengthwise. Then slice them crosswise at an angle into roughly ½-inch pieces. Heat the remaining 1½ teaspoons oil in a large skillet over medium-high heat. When the oil is hot and shimmering (but not smoking!), add the sliced hot dogs and cook for about 5 minutes, until browned and crispy.

5. Toss the salad with the dressing just before serving.

6. Top each potato with hot dog slices and a heap of salad. Drizzle with extra yellow mustard if you like.

Veggie Moo Shu Wraps

SERVES **3 to 4**

4 garlic cloves, minced

1 tablespoon peeled and grated fresh ginger

3 tablespoons hoisin sauce, plus extra for serving

2 tablespoons low-sodium soy sauce

2 tablespoons unseasoned rice vinegar

¼ teaspoon freshly ground black pepper

One 8-ounce block tempeh

2½ tablespoons light sesame oil, divided

8 ounces shiitake mushrooms, stems discarded and caps thinly sliced (about 4 cups sliced mushrooms)

¼ teaspoon kosher salt

One 12-ounce bag coleslaw mix (containing shredded cabbage and carrots)

1 bunch whole scallions, roughly chopped, divided

1 teaspoon dark (aka toasted) sesame oil

8 medium (5- to 7-inch) whole-grain or grain-free tortillas (I love Siete foods cassava and coconut tortillas for this.)

*B*ack in the day, I used to order the occasional delivery meal from a little vegan joint in the West Village. For Logan, I always got the moo shu—a hearty blend of stir-fried tempeh, portobellos, and cabbage that he would roll up in thin pancakes with fragrant hoisin sauce. And despite what he will say after reading this and discovering its meatless nature, *he loved it*. I've re-created that winning recipe here in the hope that you might just love it too.

1. In a small bowl, combine the garlic, ginger, hoisin sauce, soy sauce, rice vinegar, and black pepper. Set that magic moo shu sauce by the stove.

2. Prep the tempeh. Using a sharp knife, slice the block of tempeh in half horizontally into 2 very thin slabs. Slice these slabs crosswise into roughly ⅛-inch-thick pieces. (Think tempeh matchsticks.)

3. Heat 1 tablespoon of the light sesame oil in your largest nonstick skillet or sauté pan over medium-high heat. When the oil is hot and shimmering, add the tempeh and cook for 4 to 5 minutes, until lightly browned in spots. (It won't brown evenly—you just want to get a little color and crisp going.) Transfer the tempeh to a bowl and briefly set aside.

4. Add the remaining 1½ tablespoons light sesame oil to the pan. When the oil is hot and shimmering, add the mushrooms and salt and cook for about 2 minutes, until the mushrooms soften slightly and release some of their water. Add the coleslaw mix (it will seem like too much, but it will cook down!) and half of the scallions to the pan and cook for about 3 minutes, until the vegetables are lightly softened. Return the tempeh to the pan along with the moo shu sauce and cook for 1 minute more. Turn off the heat and stir in the remaining scallions and toasted sesame oil.

5. Warm the tortillas! Wrap 4 tortillas at a time in damp paper towels and microwave them in 30-second increments or heat each tortilla in a skillet over medium heat for about 10 seconds per side.

6. To serve, top each tortilla with plenty of moo shu and drizzle with a tiny bit of extra hoisin. Roll everything up and go to town.

> YOU DO YOU: Thanks to its hearty texture and mild, nutty flavor, tempeh is arguably the least scary "meat alternative" out there, but you can always sub in thinly sliced chicken, turkey cutlets, or a heaping cup of shredded rotisserie chicken if you must.

Buffalo Chicken Taquitos with Yogurt Ranch

FOR THE YOGURT RANCH:

1½ cups nonfat plain Greek yogurt

1 teaspoon dried parsley, crushed (Just use your fingers to crush the flakes.)

½ teaspoon dried dill weed

½ teaspoon kosher salt

¼ teaspoon garlic powder

¼ teaspoon freshly ground black pepper

FOR THE TAQUITOS:

2 tablespoons extra-virgin olive oil, divided

2 medium carrots, minced

1 celery rib, minced

½ medium yellow onion, minced

½ red bell pepper, seeded and minced

2 cups shredded chicken breast (I recommend using the breast meat from a store-bought rotisserie bird.)

¼ cup plus 2 tablespoons Frank's Red Hot Cayenne Pepper Sauce, plus extra for serving

¾ cup shredded part-skim mozzarella cheese

Fourteen 6-inch flour tortillas

Early in our courtship, Logan professed his love for "dirt sticks," which I later learned were the taquitos served at a very fine establishment called 7-Eleven. His passion for these crispy stuffed treats has inspired many a cleaner dirt stick over the years, but these fiery Buffalo chicken bad boys have been the most celebrated by far.

I suppose taquitos are typically considered an app or a snack rather than dinner, but . . . whatever. You're an adult (or at least a very advanced child if you're reading this book), and you can eat whatever the hell you want for dinner. I would appreciate it if you ate a vegetable on the side, though.

1. In a medium bowl, mix together all the ingredients for the yogurt ranch until well combined. Briefly set aside.

2. Heat 1 tablespoon of the oil in a large skillet or a sauté pan over medium heat. When the oil is hot and shimmering, add the carrots, celery, onion, and bell pepper and cook for 8 to 10 minutes, until the vegetables are nice and soft. Add the chicken and Frank's to the pan and stir to combine. Turn off the heat and stir in the cheese and ½ cup of the yogurt ranch. Cover the remaining ranch with plastic wrap and refrigerate until ready to use.

3. Preheat the oven to 425°F. Line a large baking sheet with aluminum foil and spray it with cooking spray. Set aside.

4. Lightly brush one side of each tortilla with the remaining 1 tablespoon oil. Spoon about 2 tablespoons of the filling onto the bottom third of the un-oiled side of each tortilla. Roll up the taquitos tightly like cigars and place them, seam side down, on the prepared baking sheet about 1 inch apart. Bake for 15 to 17 minutes, until the edges are nicely browned and crispy.

5. Pile the taquitos on a large serving plate or platter. Drizzle with extra Frank's if you're freaky like that and serve with the reserved yogurt ranch for dipping.

JUST THE TIP: Pulsing all the vegetables in a food processor until finely chopped will save you a good fifteen minutes of prep time.

Pulled Pork Tostadas

SERVES 4

FOR THE PORK:

1 tablespoon extra-virgin olive oil

1 small yellow onion, minced

3 garlic cloves, minced

1¼ teaspoons ground cumin

1 canned chipotle pepper in adobo sauce, minced

One 8-ounce can tomato sauce

1¼ cups low-sodium chicken broth

2 teaspoons honey

1 pound pork tenderloin, trimmed of excess fat and cut crosswise into 4 pieces

¼ teaspoon kosher salt

FOR THE TOSTADA SHELLS:

1 tablespoon extra-virgin olive oil

¾ teaspoon chili powder

¼ teaspoon kosher salt

8 corn tortillas

FOR THE BEANS:

One 15-ounce can fat-free refried beans

1 tablespoon fresh lime juice

¼ packed cup fresh cilantro leaves, finely chopped

If there were ever a time for sexy-sounding Spanish expletives, it would be now. But I don't know any, so I'm just gonna go with HOT DAMN, these pulled pork tenderloin tostadas are en fuego!! And while the recipe seems to have a lot going on, you'll have plenty of time to tackle the crispy shells, beans, and garnishes while the pork simmers. For those looking to feast with friends, double the recipe and set out a DIY tostada bar so people can build their own. Just make sure you have plenty of napkins on hand. These are messy in the best possible way.

1. Preheat the oven to 400°F. Line 2 large baking sheets with parchment.

2. Make the pork. Heat the oil in a medium Dutch oven or sauté pan over medium heat. When the oil is hot and shimmering, add the onion and garlic and cook for 5 minutes, or until the onion is soft and translucent and the garlic is fragrant. (Be very careful not to burn the garlic! If it starts to brown, reduce the heat.) Add the cumin and cook for 1 minute to toast the spice, then stir in the chipotle pepper, tomato sauce, chicken broth, and honey. Bring to a boil, then lower to a simmer. Season the pork pieces with the salt and add them to the pan. Cover and simmer for 30 minutes, or until the meat is cooked through. Transfer the pork to a cutting board and shred the meat with two forks. Return the shredded pork to the sauce and simmer, uncovered, for 10 minutes more.

3. Meanwhile, make the tostada shells. In a small bowl, combine the oil, chili powder, and salt. Lightly brush both sides of each tortilla with the seasoned oil and place them on the prepared baking sheets. Bake for 10 to 12 minutes, until lightly browned and crisp, turning once halfway through the cooking time. (Keep a close eye on them during the last few minutes—they can burn quickly!) Briefly set aside.

4. Next up, beans. Combine the refried beans and lime juice in a medium skillet or saucepan and cook over medium-low heat just until warmed through, about 5 minutes. Turn off the heat and stir in the cilantro.

5. Assembly time! Spread each tortilla with a layer of refried beans.

Top with a little cabbage and a scoop of pulled pork and garnish with the radishes and a sprinkling of queso fresco. Serve immediately, with the lime wedges.

YOU DO YOU: You can easily skip the tortilla crisping and make soft tacos instead, or ditch the tortillas altogether and serve the pork and beans bowl-style over a base of brown rice, quinoa, or extra cabbage.

FOR SERVING:

2 cups finely shredded cabbage

2 baby radishes, thinly sliced

¼ cup crumbled queso fresco (Feta is also great.)

1 lime, cut into wedges

Supreme Pizzadillas

If you love pizza, quesadillas, and looking extremely sexy, I sincerely hope you're crying tears of joy right now. (Or at the very least doing some heavy breathing.) Stuffed with melty mozzarella and slimmed-down supreme toppings, this crispy 'dilla is a Dude Diet dream come true. And since it can be prepped, cooked, and ready for shameless marinara dunking all in less time than it would take to get a pizza or quesadilla delivered, I'm hoping it will help keep you on the straight and narrow when either craving strikes.

1. Heat a large nonstick skillet over medium-high heat. When hot, add the sausage and cook for 6 to 7 minutes, stirring and breaking up the meat with a spatula, until lightly browned. Transfer to a small bowl and briefly set aside.

2. Reduce the heat to medium and add the oil to the pan. When the oil is hot and shimmering, add the bell peppers, onion, mushrooms, garlic, oregano, salt, and crushed red pepper and cook until the vegetables are very tender (but not mushy), about 8 minutes. Transfer to a bowl.

3. Assembly time! To assemble each 'dilla: Sprinkle ¼ cup of the cheese on one half of the tortilla. Top with one quarter of the browned sausage and one quarter of the vegetable mixture. Sprinkle with the olives (if using) and basil and top with another ¼ cup cheese. Fold the empty half of the tortilla over the filling to close the quesadilla.

4. Wipe out the pan and return it to the stovetop over medium heat. When hot, add two pizzadillas to the pan and cook for 3 to 4 minutes, until the underside of each tortilla is lightly browned and crispy. Flip them carefully and cook for another 2 minutes or so on the opposite side. Transfer the quesadillas to a cutting board. Repeat this process with the remaining quesadillas.

5. Slice each pizzadilla into 4 triangles and serve with the warm marinara for dipping.

3 links (10 to 12 ounces) uncooked sweet Italian turkey sausage, casings removed

1 tablespoon extra-virgin olive oil

1 red bell pepper, seeded and thinly sliced

1 green bell pepper, seeded and thinly sliced

1 small yellow onion, thinly sliced

4 ounces baby bella mushrooms, sliced (about 1½ cups)

2 garlic cloves, minced

1½ teaspoons dried oregano

¼ teaspoon kosher salt

¼ teaspoon crushed red pepper flakes

2 cups shredded part-skim mozzarella cheese

4 large (10- to 12-inch) whole-grain tortillas

¼ cup black olives (optional)

8 to 10 fresh basil leaves, torn

1 cup warm marinara sauce for serving

JUST THE TIP: If you don't have/can't find buttermilk, mix 1 cup regular milk with 1 tablespoon lemon juice or distilled white vinegar. Let it stand for 10 minutes to thicken, then give it a stir.

Buttermilk Chicken Tenders with **Secret Sauce**

To all the fingie fans out there looking to keep it tight, I see you! These "oven-fried" tenders bypass the traditional coating of flour, eggs, and white bread crumbs, taking a lighter dip in fat-free buttermilk and toasted whole-wheat panko instead. Not only are they shockingly tender and truly crispy, but they also clock in at roughly half the fat and calories of their deep-fried counterparts. Don't even get me started on the secret sauce, people.

1. Preheat the oven to 425°F. Line a large baking sheet with aluminum foil.
2. Make the tenders. In a shallow baking dish, whisk the buttermilk, garlic, paprika, oregano, cayenne pepper, and ½ teaspoon of the salt. Add the chicken tenders to the baking dish and make sure they're fully coated in the marinade. Cover the baking dish with plastic wrap and refrigerate for 30 minutes (or up to overnight).
3. Spread the panko in an even layer on the prepared baking sheet. Mist with cooking spray and transfer to the oven. Bake for about 3 minutes, until the crumbs become a deep golden brown. (Keep a close eye on them—they will darken quickly!) Transfer the toasted panko to a shallow bowl and toss with the remaining ¼ teaspoon salt and the black pepper.
4. Spray a wire rack with cooking spray and place it on top of the baking sheet you used for the panko. (If you don't have a wire rack, you can cook your tenders directly on the aluminum foil–lined baking sheet.)
5. Place the bowl of panko next to the prepared baking sheet and get your marinated chicken from the fridge. One at a time, remove the chicken tenders from the marinade, shaking off any excess, and dredge them in the bowl of panko. Use your fingers to gently press the panko onto the chicken tenders, making sure they're well coated. Transfer the breaded tenders to the prepared wire rack.
6. Bake for 15 minutes, or until the tenders are cooked through. (If your tenders are superthick, you may need to cook them for an extra 5 minutes.)
7. Meanwhile, combine all the ingredients for the secret sauce in a small bowl.
8. Transfer the fingies to a plate and serve with secret sauce for shameless dipping.

FOR THE TENDERS:

1 cup nonfat buttermilk

2 large garlic cloves, grated or finely minced

1 teaspoon paprika

1 teaspoon dried oregano

¼ teaspoon cayenne pepper

¾ teaspoon kosher salt, divided

1 pound boneless, skinless chicken tenders (sometimes labeled "tenderloins")

1 cup whole-wheat panko bread crumbs

¼ teaspoon freshly ground black pepper

FOR THE SECRET SAUCE:

⅓ cup nonfat plain Greek yogurt

3 tablespoons ketchup

½ teaspoon freshly ground black pepper

½ teaspoon Dijon mustard

¼ teaspoon garlic powder

¼ teaspoon Worcestershire sauce

JUST THE TIP: The salad atop this pizza can also make an extremely versatile sexy side. Try it alongside your favorite soups, sandwiches, meat, or fish.

The Great Salad Pizza

MAKES **1** LARGE PIZZA/SERVES **3 to 4**

While I like to think you always consume pizza with a side of greens, I'm also a realist, which is why I put a salad ON this pizza. I know many will be skeptical about a pile of greens atop their pie, but once you try this particular combo, you may just come around to the "salad pizza" concept. Lightly dressed greens add freshness and crunch while ensuring that you get some necessary nutrients with each slimmed-down slice.

1. Make the pizza. Take your dough out of the refrigerator and let it come to room temperature for about 30 minutes (this will make it so much easier to roll out!).

2. Place a pizza stone (if you have one) or an overturned baking sheet in the bottom third of your oven and preheat the oven to 450°F. You want your stone/baking sheet to be ridiculously hot before you put your pizza in.

3. Place a large piece of parchment paper (at least 18 × 15 inches) over your biggest cutting board and sprinkle it generously with flour. Place the dough in the center of the paper and sprinkle with more flour. Roll the dough out until it has a uniform thickness of ⅛ inch. (If you don't have a rolling pin, a wine bottle works.) You can make any shape pizza you like—rectangle, circle, oval—just make sure it's very thinly and evenly rolled out.

4. In a small bowl, combine the oil, garlic, and oregano. Brush the dough with the oil mixture. Sprinkle half the cheese all over the dough. Top with the salami and jalapeños and sprinkle with the remaining cheese.

5. Carefully slide the pizza (still on the parchment paper) onto the hot pizza stone or baking sheet.

6. Bake for 12 to 15 minutes, until the crust is lightly browned and cooked through. Keep a close eye on it—it can burn quickly. Let cool for about 5 minutes. (If the crust is superhot, the salad will wilt immediately when you add it.)

7. Meanwhile, make the salad. Place the spring mix in a large bowl, add the salt, and toss to combine. Add the cucumber, onion, vinegar, and oil and toss again. Season with black pepper.

8. Top the pizza with the salad. Slice into 8 pieces and serve immediately.

FOR THE PIZZA:

1 pound whole-wheat pizza dough (Whole Foods and Trader Joe's both make a good whole-wheat dough.)

All-purpose flour, for rolling out the dough

1½ tablespoons extra-virgin olive oil

2 large garlic cloves, grated or finely minced

1 teaspoon dried oregano

¾ cup grated Italian cheese blend

3 ounces thinly sliced salami

½ cup pickled jalapeño slices

FOR THE SALAD:

5 ounces (roughly 5 cups) spring mix (Arugula and mesclun are also great.)

Pinch of kosher salt

1 cup very thinly sliced English cucumber

½ cup very thinly sliced red onion

3 tablespoons red wine vinegar

1 tablespoon extra-virgin olive oil

Freshly ground black pepper to taste

Chicken Cheesesteak Lettuce Wraps

1½ pounds boneless, skinless chicken breasts, very thinly sliced crosswise (I'm talking ⅛-inch slices if possible.)

Kosher salt

Freshly ground black pepper

2 tablespoons avocado oil, divided (Olive oil also is fine.)

1 large red bell pepper, seeded and thinly sliced

1 large yellow bell pepper, seeded and thinly sliced

1 medium yellow onion, thinly sliced

¾ teaspoon dried oregano

½ teaspoon garlic powder

½ teaspoon onion powder

2 tablespoons Worcestershire sauce

2 tablespoons low-sodium soy sauce

Four 1-ounce slices smoked provolone cheese (Regular provolone is obviously fine.)

Roughly 1 head large lettuce leaves (I like Bibb, Boston, or romaine hearts.)

Finely chopped pickled jalapeños or cherry peppers (optional)

A few months after we started dating, Logan suggested that we get cheesesteaks from his favorite spot. I happily agreed, admitting that I had never actually had one before. Horrified, the Dude ordered three different cheesesteaks to cover all our bases—one traditional with extra Whiz, one pizza steak, and one Buffalo chicken. To be perfectly honest, I wasn't that impressed. When I told Logan as much, he was both upset and confused, and I'm pretty sure he questioned our compatibility as a couple.

Much to Logan's delight, I've come around to the taste over the years, but I'll never be on board with the cheesesteak brick that sits uncomfortably in my stomach for hours after consumption. That's why I appreciate these hearty but not too heavy chicken lettuce wraps starring the flavors of Philly's famous sando. Luckily, Logan loves them too.

1. Sprinkle the chicken with a little salt and pepper.

2. Heat ½ tablespoon of the oil in a large nonstick skillet over medium-high heat. When the oil is hot and shimmering, add half of the chicken to the pan in an even layer. Cook for 2 to 3 minutes, undisturbed, until the chicken is lightly browned. Cook for another minute or so, stirring regularly and breaking up the chicken into smaller pieces with a spatula, until opaque throughout. Transfer the chicken to a bowl. Return the skillet to the stove and add another ½ tablespoon of the oil. Repeat the cooking process with the remaining chicken and add it to the bowl.

3. Add the remaining 1 tablespoon oil to the skillet. When hot, add the bell peppers, onion, oregano, garlic powder, and onion powder to the pan and cook for about 8 minutes, until tender (but not mushy) and lightly browned.

4. Return the chicken to the skillet and stir in the Worcestershire sauce and soy sauce.

5. Reduce the heat to medium, place the slices of provolone on top of the chicken and vegetables, and cover the skillet with a lid. Cook for about 1 minute, until the cheese has melted.

6. Spoon the filling onto lettuce leaves—I like to stack 2 leaves per wrap for stability—and serve garnished with the pickled jalapeños (if using).

JUST THE TIP: Avocado oil is loaded with heart-healthy oleic acid and plenty of antioxidants. Its mellow flavor makes it a great addition to marinades, salad dressings, and dips, and its high smoke point also makes it a much better, healthier option for high-heat cooking than canola, grapeseed, or other highly processed oils. To reap its full health benefits, look for a cold-pressed version.

Loaded Bean and Cheese Burritos

1 tablespoon extra-virgin olive oil

1½ cups sweet corn kernels (from 2 ears of corn)

1 medium zucchini, diced small

1 red bell pepper, seeded and diced small

½ small red onion, finely chopped

1½ teaspoons chili powder

1½ teaspoons smoked paprika

¾ teaspoon ground cumin

½ teaspoon garlic powder

¼ teaspoon kosher salt

Juice of 1 lime

1 tablespoon hot sauce, plus extra for serving (I like Cholula for this.)

One 15-ounce can fat-free refried beans

¼ cup salsa of your choice, plus extra for serving

¼ packed cup fresh cilantro leaves, chopped

2 tablespoons finely chopped pickled jalapeños (optional)

Logan is a big fan of a little jam band called Widespread Panic. Since becoming a "Spreadhead" back in high school, the Dude has been to over a hundred of their shows, many of which I attended with him in the spirit of togetherness. I was never one for the music, but I did appreciate the good vibes and excellent burritos sold in the parking lot at outdoor shows (usually by a friendly, tie-dye-clad individual manning a portable griddle). Filled with spiced beans, veggies, rice, and cheese, these taste treats always hit the spot for both me and the Dude post-show, which was somewhat of a surprise, given their meatless nature.

Much to Logan's dismay, I retired from Widespread concerts a few years ago, but he takes comfort in sharing a lot-inspired burrito with me from time to time. I make mine with doctored fat-free refried beans and ditch the rice in favor of an extra serving of fresh vegetables, peace, and love . . .

1. Heat the oil in a large skillet over medium-high heat. When the oil is hot and shimmering (but not smoking!), add the corn, zucchini, bell pepper, and onion and cook for about 10 minutes, until softened and lightly browned. Add the chili powder, paprika, cumin, garlic powder, and salt and cook for 1 minute to toast the spices. Stir in the lime juice and hot sauce and remove from the heat. Transfer the veggies to a bowl and cover with aluminum foil to keep warm. Wipe out the skillet.

2. Meanwhile, drain any excess liquid from the beans and place them in a medium bowl. Stir in the salsa, cilantro, and pickled jalapeños (if using).

3. Warm the tortillas so that they're pliable and easy to roll. You can pop them in the microwave for 20 to 30 seconds or warm them in a skillet on the stove for about 20 seconds per side.

4. Assembly time! Spread about ⅓ cup of the bean mixture down the center of each tortilla (you don't need to measure it, but keep in mind you want to have enough for all 6 burritos), then top with ¼ cup cheese, and about ½ cup of the veggie mixture. Fold the top and bottom of each tortilla over the filling and roll up tightly.

5. Return the skillet you used for the veggies to the stove over medium heat. When the pan is nice and hot, add 3 burritos seam side down. Cook for about 3 minutes, until the undersides are golden brown. Flip the burritos and cook for another 3 minutes, or until golden brown on the opposite sides. (If you want to brown the sides of your burritos as well, go for it!) Repeat this process with the remaining burritos.

6. Serve your burritos warm with extra salsa and/or hot sauce. Guacamole also is allowed.

6 burrito-size (10-inch) whole-wheat tortillas

1½ cups grated sharp cheddar cheese

JUST THE TIP: These burritos can be fully prepped through step 4 and refrigerated for up to 3 days or frozen for a couple months. To reheat, microwave the burritos for 3 to 4 minutes or wrap them in aluminum foil and bake at 350°F for about 15 minutes before browning them in a skillet.

Choose Your Own Adventure Sheet Pan Fajita Bowls

Broiling spiced veggies and your choice of protein on a single baking sheet pan is the fajita hack you've been waiting for. The minimal prep and cleanup should be enough to sell you on this quick and dirty Mexican feast, but the recipe gets extra credit for using a fraction of the oil found in most fajita skillets. If you're throwing down for a crowd, double or triple the recipe, set out a toppings bar, and let people assemble their fantasy fajita bowl. Needless to say, tortillas are also an option for the traditionalists, but please remember your lessons on portion control.

1. Cook the rice according to the package directions. Cover and keep warm until ready to serve.

2. Preheat the broiler to high. Position an oven rack about 6 inches beneath the heat source. Line a large baking sheet with aluminum foil.

3. Combine the chili powder, salt, black pepper, oregano, garlic powder, onion powder, and cayenne pepper in a small bowl.

4. Add the bell peppers and onion to the prepared baking sheet. Drizzle with 1½ tablespoons of the oil, sprinkle with half of the spice mixture, and toss to coat. Broil for roughly 8 to 10 minutes, stirring once halfway through the cooking time, until the veggies are softened. (The veggies are going to continue cooking once you add the protein, so don't overdo it here.)

5. If using chicken or steak, thinly slice it into roughly ¼-inch pieces. Drizzle your meat or shrimp with the remaining ½ tablespoon oil, sprinkle with the remaining spice mixture, and toss to coat. Add the meat or shrimp in an even layer on top of the veggies. Broil the chicken for about 5 minutes, until cooked through; steak for 3 to 4 minutes, until the desired degree of doneness; and shrimp for 3 to 4 minutes, until just opaque. Add the lime juice and stir to combine the meat/shrimp and veggies.

6. Divide the rice and romaine among 4 bowls, then add the fajita mixture. Garnish each bowl with the avocado or guacamole, salsa, and lime wedges. Serve immediately.

FOR THE BOWLS:

¾ cup brown rice (Quinoa is also great.)

1 tablespoon chili powder

1 teaspoon kosher salt

½ teaspoon freshly ground black pepper

½ teaspoon dried oregano

½ teaspoon garlic powder

½ teaspoon onion powder

¼ teaspoon cayenne pepper

3 bell peppers (I like a combo of colors), seeded and thinly sliced

1 medium red onion, thinly sliced

2 tablespoons extra-virgin olive oil, divided

1 pound boneless, skinless chicken breast; flank or skirt steak; or large shrimp, peeled and deveined

Juice of 1 large lime

FOR SERVING:

2 cups finely chopped romaine hearts

1 ripe avocado, pitted, peeled, and sliced (or sub 1 cup guacamole)

Salsa of your choice

1 lime, cut into wedges

Stovetop Broccoli Mac

3 cups cauliflower florets, chopped into roughly ½-inch pieces (about ½ medium head cauliflower)

2 cups 2% milk

¾ teaspoon kosher salt, plus more for cooking the pasta

8 ounces whole-grain or grain-free macaroni or shells

2½ cups finely chopped broccoli florets

1 cup grated smoked Gouda cheese (You can also use four 1-ounce slices if necessary.)

¾ cup extra-sharp cheddar cheese (Pepper Jack is also great if you like heat.)

¼ cup finely chopped whole scallions, plus extra for serving

1 tablespoon hot sauce of your choice, plus extra for serving

1 teaspoon Dijon mustard

¼ teaspoon garlic powder

¼ cup crushed whole-grain crackers or whole-wheat panko (optional)

I have outlined the perils of refined carbohydrates before, but just to reiterate, white pasta is a Dude Dieter's kryptonite. Coating it with more white flour, butter, cream, and cheese? HOT MESS. Please relegate standard mac and cheese to the special occasion/No-Calorie Sunday category and indulge your weekday cravings with a significantly more slimming stovetop mac.

This boss recipe ditches the white pasta, works in a serving of green vegetables, and relies on the healthy magic of cauliflower puree to thicken the luscious cheese sauce. It's a great thirty-minute meatless meal, but don't hesitate to add a little lean protein (shredded chicken, ground meat, and chicken sausage are all excellent), or serve it as a family-friendly side dish.

1. Combine the cauliflower and milk in a medium sauté pan or Dutch oven. Bring to a simmer, then cover partially with a lid (just offset the lid slightly so there's about an inch of space for steam to escape) and simmer for 20 minutes, or until the cauliflower is very tender.

2. Meanwhile, bring a separate large pot of salted water to a boil for the pasta and broccoli. Once boiling, add the pasta and cook until a couple of minutes shy of al dente. Add the broccoli to the pot and cook for 2 minutes, or until bright green and tender. Drain. If using gluten-free pasta (brown rice, chickpea etc.), rinse the pasta and broccoli with tepid water. Briefly set aside.

3. Transfer the cauliflower and milk to a blender and blend until it's silky smooth (this can take up to a full minute). Return the cauliflower to the pan over medium-low heat and stir in the Gouda and cheddar cheeses, the scallions, hot sauce, mustard, salt, and garlic powder. Continue stirring until the cheese has completely melted and the sauce is nice and smooth.

4. Add the pasta and broccoli to the cheese sauce and stir to combine. Cook for a minute or two, until piping hot.

5. Serve your mac and cheese topped with crushed crackers or panko, extra scallions, and hot sauce if that tickles your fancy.

BBQ Turkey Stuffed Sweet Potatoes

SERVES 4

4 medium sweet potatoes

1 tablespoon extra-virgin olive oil

1 red bell pepper, seeded and cut into small dice

½ small red onion, minced

2 large garlic cloves, minced

¼ teaspoon kosher salt, plus extra as needed

¼ teaspoon freshly ground black pepper, plus extra as needed

2 teaspoons smoked paprika

2 teaspoons chili powder

1 pound 93% lean ground turkey

⅔ cup barbecue sauce of your choice

1 cup cherry tomatoes, quartered

½ cup fresh cilantro leaves, chopped

¼ cup chopped pickled jalapeños (or more if you like heat)

2 ounces goat cheese, crumbled

Stuffed with BBQ-sauced ground turkey and a killer medley of fresh and spicy toppings, each sweet spud is a perfectly portioned Dude Diet meal with nutrition benefits that just won't quit. The potatoes need roughly fifty minutes in the oven to get soft and stuffable, but the filling comes together in about fifteen minutes with minimal mess, leaving you plenty of time for a pre-dinner activity (jumping jacks! call your mom! walk a dog!). You could even prep a second recipe for later in the week if you're feeling like a real go-getter. Virtual butt slap.

1. Preheat the oven to 400°F. Line a baking sheet with aluminum foil.

2. Scrub the sweet potatoes and dry them well. Pierce the skin of each sweet potato all over with a fork (4 good stabs should do it) so that steam can escape during cooking and place them on the prepared baking sheet. Bake for 45 minutes to 1 hour (cooking time will vary depending on the size of the sweet potatoes), until very tender when pierced with the tip of a sharp knife. Let the sweet potatoes cool slightly.

3. Meanwhile, heat the oil in a large skillet over medium heat. When the oil is hot and shimmering, add the bell pepper, onion, garlic, salt, and black pepper to the pan and cook for about 6 minutes, until the onion is translucent and the bell pepper has softened. Add the smoked paprika and chili powder and cook for 1 minute to toast the spices. Add the turkey to the pan and cook for about 6 minutes, stirring the meat and breaking it up into small pieces with a spatula, until no longer pink. Stir in the barbecue sauce. Taste and season with extra salt and pepper if needed.

4. Cut a slit lengthwise from end to end on each sweet potato and gently push the ends toward each other to "crack" it open. Season with a tiny bit of salt and pepper and roughly mash the insides of each spud with a fork.

5. Stuff your sweet potatoes! Add one quarter of the turkey mixture to each sweet potato. Top with the cherry tomatoes, cilantro, pickled jalapeños, and goat cheese. Serve warm.

CHAPTER 6

SERIOUS SALADS

Turkey Taco Salad with Avocado Ranch

FOR THE AVOCADO RANCH:

1 ripe Haas avocado

3 tablespoons nonfat plain Greek yogurt

¼ packed cup fresh cilantro leaves

½ teaspoon onion powder

¼ teaspoon dried dill weed

¼ teaspoon garlic powder

Juice of ½ large lime

3 to 4 tablespoons water

Kosher salt to taste

Freshly ground black pepper to taste

FOR THE SALAD:

1 teaspoon extra-virgin olive oil

1 pound 93% lean ground turkey

1 tablespoon tomato paste

2½ teaspoons chili powder

¾ teaspoon kosher salt

½ teaspoon ground cumin

¼ teaspoon freshly ground black pepper

Consider this highly textured flavor fiesta a gateway recipe to the salad lovers' club. It tastes every bit as awesome as its namesake finger food but packs a far more substantial nutrient punch thanks to a leafy green base, plenty of crunchy veggies, and a creamy, avocado-based ranch dressing. I like ground turkey for the Mexican-spiced meat component, as I tend to have it on hand, but any lean ground meat will do.

1. Start by making the avocado ranch. Slice the avocado in half lengthwise and remove the pit. Scoop the flesh into the bowl of a food processor and add the yogurt, cilantro, onion powder, dill weed, garlic powder, and lime juice. Process until smooth, scraping down the sides of the bowl a few times if necessary. With the motor running, add the water, 1 tablespoon at a time, until the dressing is thinned slightly. (It should be thick but dressing thick, not guacamole thick.) Season with salt and pepper and briefly set aside.

2. Make the salad. Heat the oil in a large skillet over medium heat. When the oil is hot and shimmering, add the turkey and cook for 5 to 6 minutes, breaking up the meat into small pieces with a spatula, until no longer pink. Add the tomato paste, chili powder, salt, cumin, and black pepper and cook for 2 minutes to mellow the acidity of the tomato paste and toast the spices. Add the chicken broth and lime juice and cook for 1 minute more, or until most of the liquid has been absorbed.

3. In a large bowl, combine the romaine, tomatoes, bell pepper, and baby radishes. Transfer to a serving bowl/platter or individual bowls and top with the cooked turkey, cheese, red onion, and tortilla chips.

4. Serve the salad topped with dollops of avocado ranch or allow people to dress their own salads.

¼ cup low-sodium chicken broth or water

Juice of ½ large lime

2 romaine hearts, finely chopped (about 6 cups)

1 dry pint cherry tomatoes, sliced into quarters

1 yellow bell pepper, seeded and diced

½ cup thinly sliced baby radishes

½ cup grated sharp cheddar cheese

½ cup minced red onion (about ½ small red onion)

½ cup crumbled whole-grain tortilla chips

Rubirosa Salad

Every No-Calorie Sunday at 5:30 p.m., Logan and I cozy up to the bar at Rubirosa Ristorante in SoHo for our much-anticipated weekly feast. There is a very large, non-negotiable pizza involved—half supreme, half vodka sauce with fresh mozzarella and pesto—but the meal always gets off on the right foot with the famous Rubirosa Salad. Since it's one of the few salads the Dude gets truly amped about, it felt necessary to spread the balsamic-glazed gospel. The recipe makes two light vegetarian meals (a meatless meal won't kill you, I swear) but is easily bulked up with Idiotproof Chicken Breasts (page 136), sliced steak, or pan-seared salmon.

1. Preheat the oven to 375°F.
2. Make the croutons. Place the bread cubes in a large bowl, drizzle with the oil, and add a pinch of salt and pepper. Toss to coat. Transfer to a small baking sheet and bake for 12 to 15 minutes, until lightly browned, turning them once halfway through the cooking time. (Keep a close eye on them!) Let cool slightly.
3. Meanwhile, whisk together the ingredients for the dressing in the same bowl you used for the croutons. Add the red onion, toss to coat with the dressing, and set aside for 10 minutes to allow the onion to marinate and lose a little of its bite.
4. Pour the vinegar into a small nonstick skillet or saucepan and heat over medium heat. Simmer for about 2 minutes, swirling the pan regularly, until the vinegar has thickened slightly. (You're going for the consistency of maple syrup here, folks.) Remove from the heat and let cool slightly.
5. Add the arugula, cucumber, celery, tomatoes, and mozzarella to the bowl with the dressing and onion. Toss to combine.
6. Divide the salad between 2 plates (or transfer it to a serving dish if you're planning to serve it as an appetizer/side) and top with the croutons. Drizzle with the balsamic reduction and serve immediately. Feel free to add a few extra cranks of black pepper if you like.

> **JUST THE TIP:** Skip reducing your own balsamic and drizzle the salad with 1½ tablespoons balsamic glaze.

FOR THE SALAD:

1 slice Ezekiel bread (or whole-grain bread of your choice), cut into ½-inch cubes

1 teaspoon extra-virgin olive oil

Pinch of kosher salt

Freshly ground black pepper to taste

¼ medium red onion, thinly sliced

3 tablespoons balsamic vinegar

5 cups baby arugula

½ English cucumber (aka seedless cucumber), thinly sliced into half-moons

2 ribs celery, thinly sliced into half-moons

1 cup cherry tomatoes, halved crosswise

3 ounces baby ciliegine fresh mozzarella (aka mozzarella cheese balls; you also can use ¾ cup diced fresh mozzarella)

FOR THE DRESSING:

3½ tablespoons red wine vinegar

1½ tablespoons extra-virgin olive oil

1 garlic clove, grated or finely minced

¾ teaspoon honey

Pinch of kosher salt

Freshly ground black pepper to taste

Chicken, Apple, Cheddar Salad

FOR THE DRESSING:

3 tablespoons red wine vinegar

2 tablespoons extra-virgin olive oil

1 tablespoon Dijon mustard

1 tablespoon minced shallot

½ teaspoon pure maple syrup

Tiny pinch of kosher salt

Freshly ground black pepper to taste

FOR THE SALAD:

5 cups torn butter or Boston lettuce

2 cups shredded chicken breast

1 small apple, thinly sliced (I recommend a Pink Lady apple, but you do you.)

¼ cup coarsely chopped raw walnuts

2 ounces (½ cup) shaved sharp cheddar cheese (Just use a vegetable peeler on a block of cheddar.)

2 tablespoons chopped fresh chives

A handful of fresh ingredients come together here to create a shockingly satisfying dinner salad, and its ease and familiar flavors make it the perfect back pocket recipe on the days when you lack dinner motivation/inspiration. I'm a fan of whipping up this quick recipe on Monday nights as a realistic recovery meal after a big weekend. Far from "rabbit food," it feels nourishing, not punishing, and adheres to my roommate's strict salad requirements: **more good shit, less lettuce.**

You can obviously roast your own chicken for this salad if you'd like (such a go-getter!!) or shred some Idiotproof Chicken Breasts (page 136), but there's no shame in picking up a store-bought rotisserie bird when you're short on time.

1. Whisk together all the ingredients for the dressing in a large bowl.
2. Add the lettuce, chicken, apple, walnuts, half of the cheese, and half of the chives and toss again.
3. Divide the salad between 2 plates. Top each with the remaining cheese and chives and serve.

Sweet and Spicy Steak Salad with Grapefruit and Avocado

SERVES 2

FOR THE SALAD:

One 8-ounce filet mignon

1 pink grapefruit

Kosher salt to taste

Freshly ground black pepper to taste

2 teaspoons extra-virgin olive oil

1 tablespoon unsalted butter

5 packed cups baby arugula

1 small avocado, pitted, peeled, and thinly sliced

1 small jalapeño, very thinly sliced into rounds

2 tablespoons slivered almonds

FOR THE DRESSING:

3 tablespoons fresh grapefruit juice (from the grapefruit above)

2 tablespoons finely chopped whole scallions

1 tablespoon extra-virgin olive oil

2 teaspoons fresh lemon juice

½ teaspoon pure maple syrup

Kosher salt to taste

Freshly ground black pepper to taste

Based on a number of field experiments, fanning a medium-rare filet on top of greens tends to entice even the most stubborn salad haters. And once the bait is set, it's impossible to fight the awesomeness of the sweet and spicy produce party happening beneath the beef. One bite is all it takes to get hooked . . .

1. Take your steak out of the fridge and let it hang out on the counter. Before you cook it, you want the meat to come up to room temperature, which will take about 20 minutes. (This is optional, but it will yield a much more tender steak, so . . .)

2. Meanwhile, prep the salad ingredients and dressing. First, segment the grapefruit. Using a sharp knife, carefully slice the top and bottom from the grapefruit. Slice the peel and white pith from all around the sides. (It doesn't have to be perfect!) Working over a medium bowl, cut between the membranes to release the grapefruit segments into the bowl.

3. Measure 3 tablespoons of grapefruit juice from the bowl of segmented grapefruit and put it in a large bowl. (If you don't have enough juice, squeeze some from the leftover grapefruit "carcass.") Add the remaining ingredients for the dressing to the bowl and whisk to combine. Set aside.

4. Preheat a medium skillet over medium-high heat. Pat the steak dry and season both sides generously with salt and black pepper. When the skillet is piping hot, add the oil and swirl to coat the pan. Add the steak and cook for 5 minutes. Turn the steak over, add the butter to the pan, and cook for about 5 minutes for medium-rare. During the last 2 minutes of the cook time, spoon the fat in the pan over the steak a few times to add flavor and keep things juicy. (Cook a few minutes longer for medium or medium-well.) Transfer the steak to a cutting board. Let the meat rest for 10 minutes, then slice it very thinly against the grain.

5. Add the grapefruit segments, arugula, avocado, jalapeño (if you're sensitive to spice, use half or seed the pepper first), and almonds to the bowl with the dressing and toss to coat.

6. Divide the salad between 2 plates or bowls. Fan half of the sliced steak over each salad and serve immediately.

Grilled Shrimp Cobb

FOR THE SALAD:

6 metal or bamboo skewers

1 pound large shrimp (about 24 shrimp), peeled and deveined with the tail shells still on

4 slices turkey bacon

2 ears sweet corn, shucked

2 medium zucchini, sliced lengthwise into ½-inch planks

1 tablespoon extra-virgin olive oil

Pinch of kosher salt

Freshly ground black pepper to taste

5 cups torn Bibb lettuce

1½ cups cherry tomatoes, sliced into quarters

1 ripe avocado, pitted, peeled, and sliced or diced

½ cup crumbled goat cheese

FOR THE DRESSING:

Juice of 2 lemons

¼ cup extra-virgin olive oil

3 garlic cloves, grated or finely minced

This salad is slightly more involved than most, but its extreme delicious-ness and nutritional benefits make it well worth your extra while. The steps are pretty painless, I swear, and if you're systematic about it (please read the recipe all the way through before you start, people!!), you can have dinner on the table in forty-five minutes.

Just to state the obvious, this Cobb is dressed to impress, so definitely add it to your summer entertaining shortlist.

1. If you're using bamboo skewers, make sure to soak them in a shallow baking dish filled with water for at least 30 minutes to prevent them from catching fire on the grill. Do NOT skip this step.

2. In a small bowl, whisk together the lemon juice, oil, garlic, mustard, salt, and pepper for the dressing.

3. Place the shrimp in a large zip-top bag and add ¼ cup plus 1 table-spoon of the dressing. Seal the bag, removing as much air as humanly possible, and gently squish the shrimp around to make sure they all get coated. Refrigerate for 30 minutes.

4. Add the yogurt, honey, and tarragon to the remaining dressing and whisk to combine. Cover with plastic wrap and refrigerate until ready to use.

5. Meanwhile, heat a large skillet over medium heat. When hot, add the turkey bacon and cook for 4 to 5 minutes per side, until browned and crisp. Transfer the bacon to a paper towel–lined plate and let cool to room tem-perature. Chop into small pieces.

6. Preheat a grill (or grill pan) over medium-high heat.

7. Remove the shrimp from the marinade and thread 4 or 5 shrimp onto each skewer. (You want the skewer to pierce each shrimp twice: once just above the tail shell and once near the head, to form a tight C-shape.) Brush the corn and zucchini all over with the oil and season with a little salt and pepper.

8. Get grilling! Grill the corn for 8 to 10 minutes, rotating every few min-utes, until tender and lightly charred in spots. Grill the zucchini for 4 to 5 minutes per side, until tender. Grill the shrimp skewers for about 2 min-

utes per side, until the shrimp are pink and opaque throughout. (Do not overcook them!!)

9. Roughly chop the grilled zucchini. Slice the corn kernels from the cob with a sharp knife. Remove the shrimp from the skewers.

10. Assembly time! Add the lettuce to a large salad bowl or platter. Drizzle with half of the dressing and toss to coat. Arrange the shrimp, corn, zucchini, tomato, avocado, turkey bacon, and goat cheese in lines on top of the greens. Drizzle with the remaining dressing and serve immediately. (You can also just toss everything together and serve, but sometimes a fancy aesthetic is cool.)

1 tablespoon Dijon mustard

¼ teaspoon kosher salt

¼ teaspoon freshly ground black pepper

¼ cup nonfat plain Greek yogurt

½ teaspoon honey

1½ tablespoons finely chopped fresh tarragon

Italian Stallion Chopped Salad with Basil Vinaigrette

SERVES **2 to 3** AS AN ENTRÉE / **4 to 6** AS A SIDE

Basically a deconstructed Italian sub, this irresistible recipe is the king of all studly salads. The usual suspects are present and accounted for—salami as the requisite cured meat component, pepperoncini for briny kick, and a little bit of Pecorino Romano for sharp cheese flavor—along with a few unexpected additions in the form of buttery cannellini beans and sun-dried tomatoes. Tied together with a bright and tangy basil vinaigrette, this powerhouse salad is molto bene for both your taste buds and your waistline.

Speaking of dressing, remember this one when you're looking to punch up everything from basic grilled meat and fish to sandwiches and pasta. For the smoothest consistency, I like to throw all the ingredients into a small food processor or personal cup blender attachment, but you can always mince the basil, shallot, and garlic and whisk a more "rustic" dressing by hand if you don't have the proper electronics. No biggie.

1. Put all the ingredients for the dressing in a food processor or blender. (Given the small amount, it's best to use a small blender like a NutriBullet, a personal cup blender attachment, or a mini food processor.) Process until smooth. Briefly set aside.

2. Place all of the ingredients for the salad in a large bowl and toss to combine. Add the dressing and toss to coat. Divide the salad between 2 or 3 plates or bowls. Serve topped with a little more black pepper if you're feeling it.

FOR THE BASIL VINAIGRETTE:

¾ packed cup fresh basil leaves

2 tablespoons minced shallot

1 small garlic clove, peeled and smashed

2 tablespoons red wine vinegar

3 tablespoons extra-virgin olive oil from the sun-dried tomato jar

Pinch of kosher salt

Freshly ground black pepper to taste

FOR THE SALAD:

One 15-ounce can cannellini beans, drained and rinsed (Chickpeas and great northern beans are also great.)

2 ounces salami, sliced into ribbons

½ cup sun-dried tomatoes packed in extra-virgin olive oil, patted dry with paper towels and sliced into ribbons

½ cup chopped pepperoncini (If using whole pepperoncini, remove the stems before chopping.)

½ English cucumber (aka seedless cucumber), diced

3 cups finely chopped romaine hearts

¼ cup shaved Pecorino Romano cheese

Freshly ground black pepper to taste

Spicy Tuna Poké Salad with Mango

3 tablespoons low-sodium soy sauce

1 tablespoon fresh lime juice

½–1 tablespoon sriracha sauce (depending on your heat preference)

½ teaspoon toasted sesame oil

1 garlic clove, grated or finely minced

12 ounces sushi-grade ahi tuna, sliced into ½-inch cubes

2 tablespoons minced sweet onion (such as Vidalia or Walla Walla)

2 teaspoons sesame seeds

½ teaspoon honey

½ cup shelled edamame

4 cups mixed baby lettuces

½ mango, peeled and diced

¼ cup slivered almonds

8 brown rice crackers, crumbled (feel free to use any flavor you like)

Tuna poké has exploded over the past few years for good reason. Made with cubed raw fish marinated in an umami-flavored sauce, the Hawaiian specialty is a knockout on both the flavor and nutrition fronts. Not only is ahi high in protein and low in calories, but it's also a great source of omega-3 fatty acids and essential minerals like magnesium, both of which promote brain health. And God knows I support foods that make you simultaneously hotter *and* smarter.

Poké is typically served over white rice, but since we've established that refined carbohydrates aren't your friends, this sriracha-spiked version is piled atop a giant salad featuring mango, edamame, and a chronic combo of crunchy almonds and brown rice crackers. In short, this salad tastes like I want you to feel at all times: light, fresh, and spicy as fuck.

1. In a medium mixing bowl, whisk the soy sauce, lime juice, sriracha sauce, sesame oil and garlic.
2. Transfer 2½ tablespoons of the soy sauce mixture to a second mixing bowl. Add the tuna, onion, and sesame seeds and toss gently to coat. Cover with plastic wrap and refrigerate for 10 minutes (or up to 2 hours).
3. Add the honey to the bowl with the remaining soy sauce mixture and whisk to combine. Roughly chop the edamame (just run your knife back and forth over the beans a few times to help them disperse better throughout the salad), and add it to the bowl along with the baby lettuces, mango, and almonds. Toss to combine.
4. Divide the salad between two plates. Top each bowl with half of the tuna poké. Sprinkle each bowl with rice crackers and serve immediately.

YOU DO YOU: Sushi-grade tuna is readily available in most major markets, but if you can't find it, wild salmon is a great sub. Don't do raw? Sear your fish first, or try tossing steamed shrimp or firm tofu with the dressing.

Falafel Salad with BBQ Tahini

FOR THE FALAFEL:

⅓ cup old-fashioned rolled oats

¼ medium yellow onion, roughly chopped

½ packed cup fresh flat-leaf parsley leaves

3 garlic cloves, peeled and smashed

1 teaspoon ground cumin

½ teaspoon kosher salt

One 15-ounce can chickpeas, drained, rinsed, and patted dry with paper towels

2 tablespoons extra-virgin olive oil

FOR THE BBQ TAHINI:

2 tablespoons tahini

2 tablespoons barbecue sauce of your choice

1 tablespoon fresh lemon juice

3 tablespoons lukewarm water

FOR SERVING:

2 cups finely chopped romaine hearts

1 medium tomato, diced (or 1 cup cherry tomatoes, quartered)

Logan and I first met in Paris, and the day after we got engaged, he whisked me off to the City of Light for a romantic long weekend. We had lunch one day at the famous L'As du Fallafel in the Marais neighborhood, and halfway through the most epic of pitas, the Dude looked at me lovingly and said through a mouthful of deep-fried chickpeas, "Next book, you make falafel!!" When the muse speaks, I listen.

This high-fiber, protein-packed falafel is bound with heart-healthy rolled oats and seared rather than deep-fried until crispy. Served over a "salad" of traditional toppings and drizzled with a distinctly nontraditional BBQ-laced tahini sauce, this recipe is the most delicious way to get a cleanish falafel fix.

1. Make the falafel. Put the oats in the bowl of a food processor (or high-speed blender) and pulse until they become a coarse flour. Add the onion, parsley, garlic, cumin, and salt to the processor. Pulse a few times, until everything is minced, then add the chickpeas. Pulse again until the mixture resembles a coarse mash, scraping down the sides of the bowl a few times if necessary. (Be *very* careful not to overprocess this mixture, dudes, or you'll end up with hummus instead of falafel!) Cover the falafel mixture and refrigerate while you prep the dressing and bowl fixings. (If you've got the time, let the mixture chill for an hour or two in the fridge to firm up.)

2. Make the BBQ tahini. In a medium bowl, whisk the tahini, barbecue sauce, and lemon juice until smooth. It will seize up a little, and that's okay. Add the lukewarm water and whisk until the sauce is completely smooth and pourable. If it's too thick, add a little more water. Cover with plastic wrap and refrigerate until ready to use.

3. Scoop out roughly 2-tablespoon measures of the falafel mixture onto a wax paper– or parchment-lined cutting board and roll them into balls. (You should have 10 balls.) Gently flatten the balls into roughly ¾-inch-thick patties.

4. Heat the oil in your largest nonstick skillet over medium-high heat. When the oil is hot and shimmering (but not smoking!), add the falafel, leaving a little space around each one. (Depending on the size of your pan, you may have to cook your falafel in two batches.) Cook for 4 to 5 minutes, undisturbed, until they are a deep golden brown on the underside. Carefully flip the falafel over and cook for another 4 to 5 minutes on the opposite side, until browned and crispy.

5. Assembly time! Divide the romaine, tomato, cucumber, red onion, and banana peppers between 2 bowls. Add the falafel patties to each bowl and drizzle with plenty of BBQ tahini. Go to town.

½ cup thinly sliced English cucumber

⅓ cup very thinly sliced red onion

¼ cup sliced banana peppers or dill pickles (or both!)

Chinese Chicken Salad

FOR THE DRESSING:

¼ cup unseasoned rice vinegar

2½ tablespoons low-sodium soy sauce

1½ tablespoons light sesame oil (Avocado oil also is great.)

1 tablespoon toasted (aka dark) sesame oil

2½ teaspoons honey

1½ teaspoons peeled and grated fresh ginger

1 teaspoon Dijon mustard

1 large garlic clove, grated or finely minced

½ teaspoon crushed red pepper flakes

FOR THE SALAD:

2 cups shredded chicken (from Idiotproof Chicken Breasts, page 136, or a store-bought rotisserie chicken)

2 cups thinly sliced purple cabbage

2 cups thinly sliced napa cabbage

2 cups shredded carrots

1 large ripe avocado, pitted, peeled, and diced

½ cup thinly sliced whole scallions

½ cup fresh cilantro leaves

¼ cup slivered almonds

Thanks to its big, bright flavors and signature crunch, Chinese chicken has become one of the dude community's few salad staples. While I applaud the attempt at making healthier choices, most restaurant versions are drenched in sugary, MSG-laced dressing and showered with deep-fried wonton strips, landing them firmly in the "you'd be better off ordering the burger" category of salads.

The good news is that you can easily whip up a cleaner version of the Asian-inspired favorite in your own kitchen with good-for-you ingredients, including lean shredded chicken breast, detoxifying cabbage and carrots, heart-healthy avocado and almonds, and plenty of fresh herbs. The zingy dressing ditches refined sugar altogether, getting its heat-balancing sweetness from a drizzle of honey instead. If you're looking to give your salad a little more staying power and/or eat with your hands, try wrapping it burrito-style in a whole-grain tortilla.

1. Whisk all the ingredients for the dressing in a large bowl.
2. Add the chicken, cabbage, carrots, avocado, scallions, cilantro, and almonds to the bowl and toss to combine.
3. Divide the salad among 3 or 4 plates or bowls and serve.

JUST THE TIP: If you have a food processor with a shredding attachment, use it to save on veggie prep time! You can also use 6 cups pre-shredded coleslaw mix.

MEATY MAINS

Idiotproof Chicken Breasts

Two 8-ounce boneless, skinless chicken breasts

Kosher salt to taste

Coarsely ground black pepper to taste

1 tablespoon extra-virgin olive oil

OG Dude Dieters, I'm hoping you're extremely familiar with this "recipe," but I'm rehashing it here for those who have yet to be introduced to the life-changing magic of Idiotproof Chicken Breasts. **To the newbies:** This is unequivocally the most reliable and anxiety-free method for cooking boneless, skinless chicken breasts. In just twenty minutes, you will be the proud producer of epically tender and juicy chicken that you can serve with your favorite sexy sides or add to everything from serious salads to kickass casseroles. By following the instructions below, you will never again deal with the undercooked squishiness/overcooked stringiness of improperly cooked BS breasts. This is the first day of the rest of your culinary life.

Please note that you can season these chicken breasts in infinite ways and/or serve them with your favorite sauces. I'm partial to rubbing them with a little of the jerk spice rub on page 148, the Cajun spice rub on page 189, or a little Chinese five-spice powder. When it comes to sauces, Arugula and Goat Cheese Pistou (page 206), Awesome Almond Sauce (page 140), Chipotle Romesco (page 26), Carrot-Ginger Dressing (page 154), and Creamy-Spicy Sauce (page 232) are great places to start.

1. Pat the chicken breasts dry with paper towels and season both sides generously with salt and pepper.
2. Heat a large skillet or sauté pan over medium-high heat. When hot, add the oil and swirl to coat the bottom of the pan. Lower the heat to medium and add the chicken breasts. Cook for 1 minute, then flip the breasts over. Reduce the heat to low, cover the pan with a tight-fitting lid, and cook for 10 minutes. DO NOT LIFT THE LID.
3. After 10 minutes, turn off the heat and let the chicken sit, covered, for an additional 10 minutes. Again, DO NOT LIFT THE LID. Resist the urge.
4. After the full 20 minutes, remove the lid. Boom, done. (Your chicken will be cooked, but if you're still nervous, you can check it with an instant-read thermometer to make sure it has an internal temperature of at least 165°F.)

Bolognese Stuffed Peppers

Stuffed with lean Bolognese filling and topped with a bubbling layer of melted cheese, these brightly colored bad boys are feel-good comfort food at its finest. I sneaked in an extra serving of vegetables in the form of finely chopped (and virtually undetectable) cauliflower, but feel free to throw in a couple of handfuls of baby spinach if you're feeling particularly ambitious on the health front.

The Bolognese filling can also be served over whole-grain pasta, zucchini noodles, or your go-to whole grain, or used as the base for a lightened-up lasagna. Got leftovers? #putaneggonit

1. Preheat the oven to 375°F.
2. Heat a large skillet over medium-high heat. When hot, add the ground beef to the pan and cook for about 6 minutes, stirring the meat and breaking it up into small pieces with a spatula, until completely browned. Drain the meat in a mesh colander (just like pasta!) to get rid of excess grease. Briefly set aside.
3. Wipe out the skillet and return it to the stove over medium heat. Add the oil to the pan and swirl to coat. Add the cauliflower, carrots, celery, onion, and garlic and cook for about 8 minutes, until the vegetables have softened. Add the tomato paste and cook for 1 minute just to mellow its acidity. Return the beef to the pan, then stir in the crushed tomatoes, 2 teaspoons of the oregano, the salt, and crushed red pepper. Simmer for 10 minutes to allow the flavors to combine. Turn off the heat and stir in the basil.
4. Meanwhile, slice the bell peppers in half lengthwise and remove the seeds and any white membrane. Arrange the pepper halves in an extra-large baking dish. (If you don't have a baking dish large enough, go ahead and use two baking dishes.) Season the inside of each pepper half with a tiny bit of salt and black pepper.
5. In a small bowl, combine the mozzarella cheese, Parmesan cheese, and the remaining ½ teaspoon oregano.
6. Spoon the filling into each of the pepper halves and top with the cheese mixture. Pour the broth into the bottom of the baking dish(es) and cover the dish(es) tightly with aluminum foil. Bake for 35 minutes, or until

1 pound 90% lean ground beef (preferably grass-fed)

1 tablespoon extra-virgin olive oil

1 cup very finely chopped cauliflower florets (You can use store-bought cauliflower rice if you like!)

2 medium carrots, minced (about ½ cup minced carrot)

1 celery rib, minced (about ¼ cup minced celery)

½ medium yellow onion, minced

3 large garlic cloves, minced

1 tablespoon tomato paste

One 28-ounce can crushed tomatoes (I like San Marzano.)

2½ teaspoons dried oregano, divided

1 teaspoon kosher salt, plus more for the bell peppers

¼ to ½ teaspoon crushed red pepper (depending on your heat preference)

(continued)

½ cup fresh basil leaves, finely chopped, plus extra for serving

5 large bell peppers (Any color will do!)

Freshly ground black pepper to taste

¾ cup shredded part-skim mozzarella cheese

¼ cup grated Parmesan cheese

½ cup low-sodium beef or chicken broth (Water will also do.)

the peppers are just tender. (I prefer a tiny bit of bite to my peppers for texture, but if you dig softer peppers, bake them for an extra 10 minutes or so.) If you'd like to brown the tops of your peppers, pop them under the broiler for a few minutes before serving.

7. Serve the stuffed peppers warm with a sprinkling of basil.

JUST THE TIP: Pulsing all the veggies in a food processor until very finely chopped will save you some serious prep time.

Five-Spice Pork Tenderloin with Charred Broccoli and Awesome Almond Sauce

SERVES 2 to 3

FOR THE PORK:

1 pork tenderloin (1 to 1¼ pounds), trimmed of excess fat

2 tablespoons extra-virgin olive oil, divided

2 teaspoons Chinese five-spice powder

1¼ teaspoons kosher salt, divided

6 cups broccoli florets

Freshly ground black pepper

FOR THE SAUCE:

¼ cup smooth almond butter

1 large garlic clove, grated or finely minced

Zest of 1 small lime

1½ tablespoons unseasoned rice vinegar

1 tablespoon sriracha sauce

1½ teaspoons low-sodium soy sauce

1 teaspoon honey

2 tablespoons water

Pork tenderloin is wildly underrated, probably because people tend to cook the hell out of the lean cut of meat until it resembles a sad, gray log. Never again! The simple roasting technique described below does for pork tenderloin what the Idiotproof Method does for boneless, skinless chicken breasts: *It yields perfectly tender, juicy meat* **every. single. time.** For your first foray into this method, I urge you to follow my lead and rub your tenderloin with warming Chinese five-spice powder, cook it alongside some crispy broccoli, and then douse everything in awesome almond sauce. Sweet baby Jesus, the sauce . . .

1. Place a large rimmed baking sheet in the oven. Preheat the oven to 450°F.

2. Pat the pork tenderloin dry with paper towels. Rub the tenderloin with 1 teaspoon of the oil, then season all over with the five-spice powder and 1 teaspoon of the salt.

3. Place the broccoli in a large bowl. Drizzle with the remaining 1 tablespoon plus 2 teaspoons oil and season with the remaining ¼ teaspoon salt and a few cranks of black pepper. Toss to coat.

4. Carefully remove the baking sheet from the oven. Add the pork tenderloin to the sheet and surround it with the broccoli in an even layer. (Try to leave a little space between the florets if you can, to help them crisp versus steam.) Roast for 10 minutes. Turn the tenderloin over and immediately return it to the oven. Reduce the oven temperature to 400°F and roast for another 10 minutes (20 minutes total!). Transfer the broccoli to a serving bowl and cover with aluminum foil to keep it nice and warm. Transfer the tenderloin to a cutting board and cover it loosely with aluminum foil. Let it rest for 10 minutes. (Do not cheat here!)

5. Meanwhile, combine all the ingredients for the sauce in a medium bowl and whisk until smooth. (The sauce should be thick but still pourable. If necessary, add another tablespoon of water to thin it out.)

6. Slice the tenderloin crosswise into ¼-inch-thick rounds. Serve with the charred broccoli and drizzle generously with that awesome almond sauce.

JUST THE TIP: Chinese five-spice powder is a blend of cinnamon, fennel, cloves, star anise, and white pepper that's warming, earthy, and delicious. You can find it in the spice aisle at most major markets.

Mediterranean Sheet Pan Chicken and Vegetables

SERVES 4

2 teaspoons dried oregano

2 teaspoons paprika

1 teaspoon kosher salt

½ teaspoon freshly ground black pepper, plus extra as needed

Florets removed from 1 medium head cauliflower (about 6 cups florets)

1 medium red onion, cut into 8 wedges

3 tablespoons extra-virgin olive oil, divided

2 pounds bone-in chicken thighs with skin on (4 to 6 thighs)

½ English cucumber (aka seedless cucumber), cut into medium dice

1 cup cherry or grape tomatoes, sliced crosswise into rounds

½ cup sliced black olives (optional)

¾ cup fresh flat-leaf parsley leaves, chopped

2 ounces feta cheese, crumbled (½ cup)

Juice of 1 large lemon

I obviously love it when you make Dude Diet recipes as written, but I love it even more when you make them your own. This sheet pan chicken dinner is the perfect example of a "road map recipe" that can be tweaked in endless delicious ways. The flavors and textures in this particular Mediterranean-themed meal are primo, but the concept of roasting crispy-skinned chicken thighs with a medley of vegetables and showering them with fresh, colorful toppings is the true takeaway. Dream big and do you, dudes.

1. Put a large rimmed baking sheet (or 2 smaller baking sheets) in the oven. Preheat the oven to 400°F.

2. Meanwhile, combine the oregano, paprika, salt, and black pepper in a small bowl.

3. Place the cauliflower florets and onion wedges in a large bowl. Drizzle with 2 tablespoons of the oil and sprinkle with half of the spice mixture. Toss to combine.

4. Pat the chicken thighs dry with paper towels. Rub the thighs all over with the remaining 1 tablespoon oil and season with the remaining spice mixture.

5. Carefully remove the hot baking sheet(s) from the oven. Place the thighs skin side down on the baking sheet(s) and arrange the cauliflower and onion around the chicken (not on top of it!) in an even layer, leaving a little space between the vegetables if possible.

6. Roast the chicken and vegetables for 15 minutes. Remove the baking sheet(s) from the oven, turn the chicken thighs over, and give the vegetables a quick stir. Roast for 15 minutes more (30 minutes total), or until the chicken is cooked through and the vegetables are tender and lightly browned. If you like particularly crispy skin on your chicken and a little char on your veggies, place the baking sheet under the broiler for 1 to 2 minutes, until the chicken skin is browned, bubbling, and crisp.

7. If you used two baking sheets to cook the chicken and veggies, transfer everything to one of the sheets or a serving platter. Top with the cucumber, tomatoes, olives (if using), parsley, and cheese. Squeeze the lemon juice over everything, season with a little extra black pepper if you like, and serve warm.

Tex-Mex Turkey Meatloaf

FOR THE TURKEY:

1 tablespoon extra-virgin olive oil

½ medium red onion, minced

½ red bell pepper, seeded and cut into small dice

2 large garlic cloves, minced

1 tablespoon chili powder

1 tablespoon smoked paprika

1 teaspoon ground cumin

2 tablespoons water

1 tablespoon tomato paste

2 pounds 93% lean ground turkey

1 ripe avocado, pitted, peeled, and mashed

1½ tablespoons Worcestershire sauce

½ cup fresh cilantro leaves, chopped

¼ cup chia seeds (I like to use white seeds for aesthetic purposes, but you do you.)

Turkey meatloaf is typically a semi-sad sub for the real thing, but this über-moist, fiesta-flavored recipe delivers, especially given that there are zero bread crumbs or grains involved. How, then, do we bind this miracle loaf? *Chia seeds.* If you're floored by this info, you must be a new Dude Dieter (welcome to the fold!) because I've (a) done this many times before, and (b) promoted the hell out of the tiny superfood seeds as a Dude Diet staple. Don't worry, you can't taste the chia, and the seeds don't have the same alien egg texture here as they do in a pudding or jam; they simply hold the meatloaf together while providing extra fiber, protein, and omega-3s. Magic!!

This meatloaf will run you close to two hours from start to finish (only about a quarter of which is active prep), but please don't let that put you off. Tackle it when you have a little extra time on your hands and save leftovers for busier days—it reheats perfectly.

1. Heat the oil in a medium skillet over medium heat. When the oil is hot and shimmering, add the onion, bell pepper, and garlic and cook for 5 to 6 minutes, until very soft but not browned. (Please be careful not to burn the garlic!) Stir in the chili powder, paprika, and cumin and cook for 1 minute to toast the spices. Add the water, stirring to loosen any spices from the pan, then stir in the tomato paste and cook for 1 minute (just to mellow the acidity), then transfer the veggie mixture to a large bowl. Let cool for at least 5 minutes.

2. Meanwhile, gather the remaining ingredients for the meatloaf. Add everything to the bowl with the cooled veggie mixture and gently mix with your hands (or a spatula) until well combined. Cover the mixture and refrigerate for 20 minutes to allow the chia seeds to work their gelling magic.

3. Meanwhile, preheat the oven to 350°F. Line a rimmed baking sheet with aluminum foil.

4. Whisk together all the ingredients for the glaze and set aside.

5. Dump the meat mixture onto the prepared baking sheet. Gently mold the meat with your hands into a roughly 9 × 5-inch rectangular loaf. Spread two-thirds of the glaze evenly on the top and sides of the loaf.

6. Bake for 45 minutes, add the remaining glaze, and bake for 15 minutes more (1 hour total), or until the meatloaf is cooked through. Let the loaf rest for a full 10 minutes.

7. Slice your Tex-Mex masterpiece into thick pieces (it will look slightly pink—don't panic, it's tinted from the spices) and serve garnished with cilantro and hot sauce if you like.

JUST THE TIP: Eliminate unnecessary bread crumbs by using chia seeds as a binder in meatloaf, meatballs, and burgers. Simply add 2 tablespoons of chia per pound of meat.

1½ teaspoons kosher salt

¼ teaspoon cayenne pepper

FOR THE GLAZE:

¼ cup plus 2 tablespoons tomato paste

1½ tablespoons hot sauce of your choice

1½ tablespoons fresh lime juice

1½ teaspoons honey

3 tablespoons warm water

FOR SERVING (OPTIONAL):

Chopped fresh cilantro

Hot sauce

Bulgogi Beef Bowls

FOR THE BEEF AND MARINADE:

1¼ pounds top round steak

¼ cup plus 1 tablespoon low-sodium soy sauce

3 garlic cloves, grated or finely minced

2 tablespoons brown sugar

1 tablespoon plus 1 teaspoon toasted (aka dark) sesame oil

1½ teaspoons peeled and grated fresh ginger

½ teaspoon crushed red pepper flakes

3 scallions, white and light green parts only, thinly sliced

1 tablespoon toasted sesame seeds

FOR THE SLAW:

¼ cup nonfat plain yogurt

Juice of ½ lime

2 cups very thinly sliced purple cabbage

2 cups shredded carrots

1 yellow bell pepper, seeded and very thinly sliced

1 ripe avocado, pitted, peeled, and thinly sliced

The literal translation of *bulgogi* is "fire meat," which is a pretty apt description of the Korean barbecue favorite. In this lightened-up version, lean beef gets marinated in a killer blend of soy sauce, sesame oil, fresh ginger, and spices and is panfried until beautifully browned and caramelized. The meat—which is, in fact, straight fire—is then piled atop a creamy, crunchy, vitamin-packed rainbow slaw and finished with cooling avocado. The resulting bowls serve up a special kind of magic.

1. Put your steak in the freezer for 10 to 20 minutes while you whip up the marinade and prep the slaw ingredients. (This is optional, but it will make the beef much easier to slice. Just do it.)

2. In a large bowl, whisk all the ingredients for the marinade. Transfer 3 tablespoons of the marinade to a separate large bowl (you're going to use it for the slaw). Briefly set both bowls aside.

3. Slice the steak against the grain as thinly as humanly possible. (I'm talking ⅛-inch slices if you can manage it.) Add the steak to the original marinade bowl. Using your hands, massage the marinade into the sliced beef, making sure each piece is well coated. Cover the beef with plastic wrap and refrigerate for 30 minutes.

4. Meanwhile, make the slaw. Add the yogurt and lime juice to the bowl with the reserved marinade and whisk to combine. Add the cabbage, carrots, and bell pepper and toss to coat. Cover with plastic wrap and refrigerate until ready to serve.

5. Heat a large nonstick skillet or wok over high heat. Place a medium bowl by the stove. When the pan is screaming hot, add half of the meat in an even layer. Cook undisturbed for 2 minutes, or until the meat is well browned on the underside, then give it a stir and cook for about 1 minute more, shaking the pan a few times, until browned all over. Transfer the meat to the waiting bowl. Repeat this process with the remaining meat.

6. Divide the slaw among 4 dinner bowls and top with the beef and sliced avocado. Serve immediately.

Jerk Turkey Cutlets with Grilled Pineapple Relish

2 pounds turkey
  breast cutlets
  (Chicken cutlets are
  also great.)

FOR THE RELISH:

1 medium pineapple

1½ teaspoons extra-
  virgin olive oil

¼ teaspoon kosher
  salt, plus extra as
  needed

¼ teaspoon freshly
  ground black pepper,
  plus extra as needed

Juice of 1 lime

½ cup thinly sliced
  whole scallions

¼ teaspoon ground
  cinnamon

FOR THE JERK SEASONING:

2 teaspoons light
  brown sugar

1½ teaspoons onion
  powder

1¼ teaspoons ground
  allspice

1 teaspoon cayenne
  pepper

1 teaspoon garlic
  powder

1 teaspoon kosher salt

1 teaspoon paprika

¼ teaspoon freshly
  ground black pepper

Logan is rarely happier than when he's rocking an apron (shirtless), sipping a heady IPA, and lovingly tending meats on a grill. Said grill master activities make his nutritional spirit guide very happy, as I happen to be a big proponent of cooking over an open flame. (Although I do recommend switching to a light brew for extended sessions.) Not only does grilling require minimal added fats like oil and butter to cook exceptionally flavorful proteins, vegetables, and fruits, but grill grates also allow for some of the existing fat in meat to drip away as it cooks. God bless the barbecue!

Heavier staples like steak, burgers, and sausages are fine in moderation, but grilling season is long, and you'll need plenty of lighter options in the rotation. Like these grilled turkey cutlets rubbed with a fiery jerk seasoning blend and topped with sweet and smoky pineapple relish. They'll tickle your taste buds while keeping belly bloat and meat sweats at bay, so bump this recipe to the top of your BBQ to-dos, stat.

1. Preheat a lightly oiled grill (or grill pan) over medium-high heat.
2. Remove the turkey cutlets from the fridge and let them come to room temperature while you prep the pineapple.
3. Prep the pineapple. Cut off the top and bottom of the pineapple using a sharp chef's knife. Stand the fruit upright and slice off the skin in strips, following the curve of the pineapple. Get rid of any remaining brown spots (aka "eyes") with a paring knife. Turn the pineapple on its side and slice it crosswise into ¾-inch-thick rounds. (You should have about 8 rounds.) Lightly brush both sides of each round with the oil and season with the salt and pepper. Place the pineapple rounds on the hot grill and cook for 3 minutes per side, or until grill marks appear and the fruit is very lightly softened. Transfer the rounds to a cutting board and let cool while you prep the turkey cutlets.
4. Combine the dry ingredients for the jerk seasoning in a small bowl, then stir in the oil to form a thick paste. Rub the turkey cutlets all over with the paste.
5. Place the turkey cutlets on the hot grill and cook for 4 to 5 minutes per side, until cooked through. Transfer to a cutting board or plate and cover with foil while you finish the pineapple relish.

6. Dice the cooled pineapple, discarding the hard core from each round. In a medium bowl, combine the lime juice, scallions, and cinnamon. Add the diced pineapple to the bowl and gently toss to combine. Season with extra salt and pepper if needed.

7. Serve the turkey cutlets warm or at room temperature topped with the relish.

¼ teaspoon ground cinnamon

1½ tablespoons liquid extra-virgin coconut oil (Olive oil also is fine.)

Spiced Lamb Lettuce Cups with Jalapeño–White Bean Spread

FOR THE SPREAD:

One 15-ounce can cannellini beans, drained and rinsed

1 small jalapeño, roughly chopped (If you're not into spice, seed the jalapeño first.)

2 garlic cloves, peeled and smashed

2 tablespoons fresh lemon juice

¼ teaspoon kosher salt

2 tablespoons extra-virgin olive oil

FOR THE LAMB:

1 tablespoon extra-virgin olive oil

½ medium yellow onion, minced

2 garlic cloves, minced

1 teaspoon ground cumin

½ teaspoon ground coriander

½ teaspoon kosher salt

¼ teaspoon ground cinnamon

I know the ingredient list for these lettuce cups seems long, but I promise it's mostly pantry staples. Once you're locked and loaded, this heady, and handsy, feast can be on the table in thirty minutes or less. If you're not feeling lettuce wraps or you want to stretch the recipe to feed four, serve the lamb and the spread on top of, or stuffed into, four whole-wheat pitas.

1. Start by making the spread. Combine the beans, jalapeño, garlic, lemon juice, and salt in the bowl of a food processor. Process for a minute or so, until very smooth, scraping down the sides of the bowl a few times if necessary. With the motor running, slowly drizzle in the oil and continue processing for 1 minute more, or until the mixture is silky smooth and fluffy. Transfer to a bowl and briefly set aside.

2. Make the lamb. Heat the oil in a large nonstick skillet over medium heat. When the oil is hot and shimmering, add the onion and garlic and cook for about 4 minutes, until the onion is translucent and the garlic is fragrant. Add the cumin, coriander, salt, cinnamon, and black pepper and cook for 1 minute to toast the spices. Add the lamb and cook for about 6 minutes, stirring the meat and breaking it up into small pieces, until no longer pink. (If there is a lot of excess fat in the pan, carefully pour it off.) Turn off the heat and stir in the parsley and mint.

3. Assembly time! Add a heaping spoonful of the white bean–jalapeño spread to each lettuce cup. (I like to double-layer each of my lettuce cups for stability, but you do you.) Add some spiced lamb and top with the cucumber. Serve garnished with a little extra parsley and lemon wedges, if you like.

¼ teaspoon freshly ground black pepper

1 pound ground lamb (Ground dark meat turkey, chicken, or 90% lean ground beef is also great.)

2 tablespoons finely chopped fresh flat-leaf parsley leaves (plus extra for serving)

1 tablespoon finely chopped fresh mint leaves

FOR SERVING:

Roughly half a head of iceberg lettuce leaves (Bibb lettuce also is great.)

½ medium English cucumber, cut into small dice

1 lemon, sliced into wedges (optional)

Nashville Hot Chicken Meatloaf Minis

Generously spiced with cayenne and black pepper, these portion-controlled meatloaves are a Dude Diet–friendly riff on Tennessee's finest fried chicken. Each cornflake-crusted bite of meatloaf is spicy, sure, but it's the honey-sweetened hot sauce drizzle that will truly set your taste buds (and soul) on fire. I'd give you instructions for how to make these bad boys a little milder, but this is one recipe that lives and dies by its hot, hot heat. Spice babies, you've been warned.

I recommend serving these meatloaf minis to a spice-loving group, but the fiery recipe is easily halved if you're cooking for one or two. For a true comfort food feast, whip up a side of Broccoli-Cheddar Mashed Potatoes (page 244).

1. Preheat the oven to 375°F. Line a large rimmed baking sheet with aluminum foil. Spray with nonstick cooking spray.

2. Place the cornflakes in a shallow baking dish and lightly crush them with your hands. Don't pulverize them completely—you just want to break them down into smaller flakes so they'll stick to the chicken better.

3. Transfer 1 cup of the crushed cornflakes to a medium bowl, then add the remaining ingredients for the meatloaf. Using your hands or a fork, gently mix everything together until combined. (Try not to overmix this stuff, or you'll end up with dry meatloaf.)

4. With damp hands, mold the meat into six roughly 3 × 4½-inch rectangular loaves. Carefully roll each loaf in the remaining crushed cornflakes, pressing gently to help them adhere, and place on the prepared baking sheet, leaving a little space around each one.

5. Bake for 35 minutes, or until the meatloaf is cooked through.

6. Meanwhile, combine the honey and hot sauce in a small saucepan and bring to a gentle simmer. Cook for about 4 minutes, until thickened slightly. Keep warm.

7. Serve the meatloaf minis warm, topped with pickle slices and drizzled with the sweetened hot sauce. (Be careful with the sauce, people. It's HOT.)

FOR THE MEATLOAF:

4 cups cornflakes cereal

2 pounds ground chicken breast

2 large eggs, lightly beaten

½ cup minced bread-and-butter pickles

2 teaspoons paprika

1½ teaspoons cayenne pepper

1½ teaspoons kosher salt

1 teaspoon freshly ground black pepper

1 teaspoon garlic powder

FOR SERVING:

3 tablespoons honey

⅔ cup Frank's Red Hot Cayenne Pepper Sauce

Sliced bread-and-butter pickles

Miso Flank Steak with Carrot-Ginger Dressing

FOR THE STEAK AND MARINADE:

2 tablespoons mellow white miso

1 large garlic clove, grated or finely minced

2½ tablespoons red wine vinegar

1½ teaspoons pure maple syrup

One 1½-pound flank steak

Freshly ground black pepper to taste

FOR THE DRESSING:

1 cup roughly chopped carrots

2 tablespoons minced shallot

1 garlic clove, peeled

1 tablespoon peeled and finely chopped ginger

Juice of 1 medium orange (¼ cup orange juice)

1 tablespoon fresh lime juice

1 tablespoon low-sodium soy sauce

2 tablespoons water, plus extra if needed

When it comes to svelte steak dinners, this umami-packed flank steak gets a gold star. Flank is an inexpensive and relatively lean cut of beef, and the bright gingery dressing is reminiscent of the Japanese restaurant staple but made without any oil(!!), saving you hundreds of calories without sacrificing flavor. Lucky for you, you'll likely have leftover dressing, which keeps for up to a week in the fridge. Use it to sauce up almost any meat or fish, toss it with greens or soba noodles, or serve it as a dip for veggies.

1. Make the marinade. In a small bowl, whisk the miso, garlic, vinegar, and maple syrup until smooth.

2. Pat the steak dry and place it in a shallow baking dish. Slather the marinade all over the steak with the back of a spoon (or with your hands) and cover the dish with plastic wrap. Marinate for 30 minutes at room temperature. (You can also marinate your steak in the fridge for several hours or overnight. Just make sure to bring it to room temperature before cooking.)

3. Meanwhile, place all the ingredients for the dressing in the bowl of a food processor. Process on high for a solid minute or two, until very smooth. (A mini food processor or the personal cup attachment for a high-speed blender is ideal.) The dressing should be thick but pourable. If it's too thick, add another tablespoon of water and blend again to thin. Transfer to a bowl and refrigerate until ready to use.

4. Preheat a lightly oiled grill (or grill pan) over medium-high heat. Remove the steak from the marinade, shaking off any excess, and season both sides generously with black pepper.

5. Grill the steak for 6 to 7 minutes per side for medium-rare. Transfer to a cutting board and let the steak rest for a full 10 minutes.

6. Using a sharp knife, thinly slice the steak across the grain. Serve with the carrot-ginger dressing.

> **JUST THE TIP:** White miso is a thick paste made from fermented soybeans and rice. Mild and slightly sweet, it's great for adding umami flavor to dressings, marinades, and soups. You can find it in the refrigerated or Asian section of most large markets and health food stores.

Cubano Stuffed Pork Chops

When creating Dude Diet cuisine, I often consult my muse for his input on flavor combinations. Logan's most common suggestion? An emphatic "DO IT CUBANO!!!" I've been forced to ignore many a Cubano proposition over the years (e.g., Cubano lasagna), but I have to hand it to the Dude on the Cubano stuffed pork chop tip. Stuffed with mustard and pickles, wrapped in prosciutto, and drizzled in a citrusy mojo sauce, these chops are absolute flavor bombs that still manage to fall into the cleanish category of meaty mains. After all, pork loin happens to be even leaner than chicken breast and contains more B vitamins—which boost metabolism and increase energy production—than most other types of meat.

1. Preheat the oven to 400°F. Line a large rimmed baking sheet with aluminum foil or parchment paper.

2. Using a sharp knife, carefully slice a deep pocket into each pork chop. (You want the pocket to be as deep as possible, while the chop still remains intact on one side. Do your best.) Spread the inside of each pocket with ½ tablespoon mustard, then add 2 pickle slices and half a slice of Swiss cheese. Pull the pockets closed, pushing the filling in as much as possible, and wrap each chop with 2 slices of prosciutto. It's okay if the wrapping job isn't perfect, but do try to cover the chops as securely as possible to keep the cheese from escaping during baking. Season each wrapped chop with a few cranks of black pepper.

3. Place the chops on the prepared baking sheet and bake for 20 minutes, or until cooked through.

4. Meanwhile, whisk the ingredients for the sauce in a small saucepan or skillet. Bring to a simmer over medium heat and cook for 5 to 6 minutes, until the liquid has reduced by about half. Briefly set aside.

5. Serve the stuffed pork chops warm, drizzled with the sauce.

FOR THE PORK:

4 boneless pork loin chops, about 1 inch thick

2 tablespoons whole-grain Dijon mustard

8 kosher dill pickle sandwich slices

Two 1-ounce slices Swiss cheese, sliced in half

8 slices prosciutto

Freshly ground black pepper to taste

FOR THE SAUCE:

⅔ cup fresh orange juice

2 tablespoons fresh lime juice

1 tablespoon whole-grain Dijon mustard

2 large garlic cloves, grated or finely minced

¾ teaspoon dried oregano

¾ teaspoon ground cumin

¼ teaspoon crushed red pepper flakes

Cincinnati Chili with Spaghetti Squash

SERVES 4

2 medium spaghetti squash

2 tablespoons extra-virgin olive oil, divided

½ teaspoon kosher salt, plus more for seasoning the squash

Freshly ground black pepper to taste

2 large garlic cloves, minced

1 large yellow onion, minced, divided

2 tablespoons chili powder

1 tablespoon unsweetened cocoa powder

¾ teaspoon ground allspice

¾ teaspoon ground cinnamon

¾ teaspoon ground cumin

¼ teaspoon cayenne pepper, plus extra as needed

1 tablespoon tomato paste

1 pound 90% lean ground beef (preferably grass-fed)

Outside of Texas, Cincinnati may be the most famous destination for a great bowl of chili. Saucier than most, Cincinnati chili gets its distinct flavor profile from a slightly unusual blend of spices, including cocoa, cinnamon, and allspice. If that sounds a little odd, don't knock it 'til you try it—it's famous for a reason. Keep things light by serving this "four-way" chili over spaghetti squash with a responsible amount of cheddar and onions.

To manage expectations, spaghetti squash tastes absolutely *nothing* like spaghetti, but it does have a pleasantly hearty texture and its slight sweetness complements the chili. You'll like it.

1. Preheat the oven to 400°F. Line a large baking sheet with parchment paper or aluminum foil.

2. Slice each spaghetti squash in half lengthwise with your sharpest chef's knife and scoop out the seeds and membrane. Lightly brush the interior of the squash halves with 1 tablespoon of the oil and season with salt and pepper. Place the squash cut side down on the prepared baking sheet and bake for 35 to 40 minutes, until soft. Let cool slightly.

3. Meanwhile, heat the remaining 1 tablespoon oil in a large skillet over medium heat. When the oil is hot and shimmering, add the garlic and half of the minced onion to the pan and cook for about 6 minutes, until the onion is soft and translucent and the garlic is fragrant. Add the chili powder, cocoa powder, allspice, cinnamon, cumin, salt, cayenne, and tomato paste to the pan and cook, stirring constantly, for 2 minutes to toast the spices and mellow the acidity of the tomato paste. Increase the heat to medium-high. Add the ground beef to the pan and cook for about 6 minutes, stirring the meat and breaking it up into small pieces with a spatula, until no longer pink. Stir in the tomato puree, water, and Worcestershire sauce and lower the heat to a simmer. Simmer for 10 minutes to allow the chili flavors to mingle. Stir in the spinach and cook for about 1 minute, just to wilt it. Taste and season with extra salt or cayenne if necessary.

4. Using a fork or tongs, rake the roasted squash flesh crosswise (not lengthwise) to create spaghetti-like strands.

5. Divide the squash among 4 bowls and smother with the chili. Top with the cheese and the remaining minced onion and serve immediately. (For a more festive presentation, you can serve the chili in the squash halves to make "boats.")

One 15-ounce can tomato puree

½ cup water

1 tablespoon Worcestershire sauce

3 packed cups baby spinach, finely chopped

¾ cup grated cheddar cheese

JUST THE TIP: Having trouble slicing your spaghetti squash? Pierce the shell a few times with a fork (to allow steam to escape) and microwave the whole squash for 3 to 4 minutes. This should soften a tough squash just enough to cut.

Cilantro-Lime Chicken under a "Brick"

SERVES 4

½ cup chopped fresh cilantro leaves, divided

4 garlic cloves, grated or finely minced

1 teaspoon ground cumin

1 teaspoon kosher salt, plus extra as needed

Freshly ground black pepper to taste

3 tablespoons extra-virgin olive oil, divided

One 4½- to 5-pound whole roasting chicken

2 limes, divided

STOP. Don't turn the page. This unbelievably moist, flavor-blasted, crispy-skinned chicken will rock your world, blow your mind, and possibly change your life!!!

All hyperbole aside, you really do need to experience this chicken ASAP. For that reason, I beg you not to panic when you see the length of the instructions below. I'm just walking you through how to spatchcock the chicken—i.e., remove the bird's backbone to split and flatten it—then it's an easy downhill coast from there. Rub a garlicky cilantro paste under the skin, sear the chicken under a weight (you don't need to use an actual brick) to ensure the skin achieves ultimate crispiness, then do a quick flip and finish it in the oven. It takes less time than a traditional roast chicken, and the result is undeniably bomb. You *can* do it. You must.

1. Start by prepping the delicious chicken rub. In a small bowl, combine ¼ cup of the cilantro, the garlic, cumin, salt, a few cranks of black pepper, and 2 tablespoons plus 1 teaspoon extra-virgin olive oil. (It should form a thick paste.) Briefly set aside.

2. Now, it's time to spatchcock the chicken. Remove any giblets from the cavity of the bird, then rinse the chicken thoroughly with cold water and dry it really, really well with paper towels. Place the chicken on a cutting board breast side down with the legs facing you. Using kitchen shears, cut up on either side of the spine all the way to the neck to fully remove the backbone. (This isn't nearly as terrifying as it sounds, I promise.) Once you've taken out the backbone, open the chicken up like a book and place it breast side up on the cutting board, flattening it as much as possible. Using your palms, press down hard on top of the breasts to reallllly flatten that bird out. You'll hear a crack, and that's a good thing. Last but not least, tuck the wing tips behind the breasts so they don't burn. CONGRATULATIONS, YOU SPATCHCOCKING MASTER!

3. Carefully run your fingers under the skin on the breasts and thighs of the bird to separate it from the meat. Rub the cilantro "paste" all over the chicken *underneath* the skin (not on top of it!). Rub the remaining 2 tea-

spoons oil on the chicken's skin and season with a little salt and plenty of black pepper.

4. Preheat the oven to 400°F.

5. Heat your largest (preferably 14-inch) ovenproof skillet over medium-high heat. When the skillet is piping hot, add the chicken skin side down. Immediately place a second heavy skillet of roughly the same size or two aluminum foil–wrapped bricks on top of the chicken to weigh it down. Reduce the heat to medium (you should still hear a crackling noise as the chicken cooks) and cook for 25 minutes, or until the skin is a deep golden brown and the chicken is cooked about halfway through. Carefully turn the chicken over. (The skin should release itself from the pan, but if it's sticking, let it cook for a few minutes more.) Slice 1 lime in half crosswise and add the halves to the pan cut-side down. Transfer the chicken to the oven. Roast for 20 to 25 minutes, until the chicken is cooked through. (An instant-read thermometer inserted into the deepest portion of the thigh should register 165°F.)

6. Let the chicken rest for 10 minutes.

7. Slice the remaining lime into wedges. Shower the chicken with the remaining cilantro and serve with the lime wedges.

Stuffed Poblano Bowls

If you appreciate the smoky deliciousness of a stuffed poblano, you'll dig this deconstructed version featuring the charred peppers, bison, brown rice, and a tangy Greek yogurt-based crema. Not familiar with bison? I'm thrilled to inform you that it's naturally leaner and cleaner than beef and gives this bowl a unique, subtly sweet flavor. I urge you to give it a try (variety is the spice of Dude Diet life!), but you can obviously sub your favorite lean ground meat if you're not big on buffalo.

1. Start by prepping the poblanos. Preheat the broiler on high and line a baking sheet with aluminum foil. Place the peppers on the prepared baking sheet and broil for 10-15 minutes, turning the peppers every few minutes, until softened and lightly charred in spots. Let the peppers cool to room temperature. Remove the skin from the peppers with your hands, then slice them in half lengthwise. Remove and discard the stems and seeds (I use the side of a knife to scrape the seeds away). Finely chop the peppers and briefly set aside.

2. Meanwhile, whisk all the ingredients for the crema in a medium bowl. It should have a drizzleable consistency. If it's too thick, add a little extra water. Cover and refrigerate until ready to use.

3. Heat a large nonstick skillet over medium heat. When hot, add the bison, paprika, and cumin and cook for about 5 minutes, stirring and breaking up the meat into small pieces with a spatula or until no longer pink. Add the broccoli and cook for 2 minutes or until just tender. Stir in the salsa, chopped poblanos, and beans and cook for two minutes more. Add the cooked brown rice and cilantro, folding everything together with a spatula. Cook for 1-2 minutes until piping hot. Taste and season with salt and pepper.

4. Divide this delicious skillet among four bowls. Top with avocado, drizzle generously with crema, and sprinkle with onion and cilantro.

4 poblano peppers

¾ pound ground bison

2½ teaspoons smoked paprika

1 teaspoon ground cumin

1½ cups very finely chopped broccoli florets (You can also use packaged "broccoli rice.")

1½ cups salsa of your choice

One 15-ounce can pinto beans, drained and rinsed

2 cups cooked brown rice (Quinoa or farro is also great.)

½ cup fresh cilantro leaves, chopped

FOR THE CREMA:

½ cup nonfat plain Greek yogurt

1 tablespoon fresh lime juice

1 tablespoon water (plus extra if needed to thin)

¼ teaspoon ground cumin

Pinch of kosher salt

FOR SERVING (OPTIONAL):

1 ripe avocado, pitted peeled, and sliced or diced

½ small red onion, minced

Fresh cilantro

JUST THE TIP: MSG (aka monosodium glutamate) is a flavor-enhancing additive that is known to cause the following symptoms: headache, flushing, sweating, facial pressure or tightness, heart palpitations, chest pain, nausea, and weakness. **Translation: MSG gives you the meat sweats.** Unacceptable.

Sweet and Sour Pork

Just in case there was any lingering doubt, the sweet and sour pork served at many Chinese restaurants in America is a Dude Diet disaster. Deep-fried chunks of fatty pork swimming in a sugary, MSG-laden sauce wreak havoc on your digestive system and your waistline, and no, an order of brown rice and a few rogue pieces of bell pepper in your take-out container don't do diddly to redeem it. Remember this fun fact the next time you're craving a sweet and sour fix, and whip up this slimming skillet version with lean pork tenderloin, juicy pineapple, and a crunchy combo of colorful veggies instead.

1. In a medium bowl, whisk all the ingredients for the sauce. Briefly set aside.
2. Season the pork cubes with the salt and pepper.
3. Heat 1½ tablespoons of the oil in your largest nonstick skillet over medium-high heat. When the oil is hot and shimmering, add the pork in an even layer. (You don't want the pan to be too crowded, so if your pan isn't that large, I recommend cooking the pork in two batches to get the best browning action.) Cook for 3 minutes, undisturbed, to let the pork get nice and brown on the underside. Cook for another 3 to 4 minutes, tossing occasionally, until the meat is light pink in the center. Transfer the pork to a plate or bowl and briefly set aside.
4. Wipe out the skillet and return it to medium-high heat. Add the remaining 1 tablespoon oil. When the oil is hot and shimmering, add the bell pepper, red onion, and snap peas and cook for 3 to 4 minutes, until the vegetables are just tender. (You want them to retain a little crunch!)
5. Give the sauce another whisk to smooth out any cornstarch clumps. Return the pork to the pan, add the pineapple, and pour in the sauce. Cook for about 90 seconds, tossing everything together, until the sauce has thickened. (If the sauce starts to thicken too quickly, don't freak out—just reduce the heat to medium and keep stirring.)
6. Serve warm over brown rice or quinoa if you like. Garnish with the scallions.

FOR THE SAUCE:
¼ cup pineapple juice

¼ cup unseasoned rice vinegar

¼ cup water

3 tablespoons low-sodium soy sauce

1½ tablespoons tomato paste

1½ tablespoons honey

1 tablespoon cornstarch

2 garlic cloves, grated or finely minced

½ teaspoon crushed red pepper flakes

FOR THE PORK:
1 pound pork tenderloin, trimmed of excess fat and cut into 1-inch cubes

½ teaspoon kosher salt

½ teaspoon freshly ground black pepper

2½ tablespoons light sesame oil (Coconut oil or olive oil also is fine.)

1 red bell pepper, seeded and diced

1 small red onion, diced

2 cups sugar snap peas, stem ends and strings removed

1 cup diced pineapple

2 whole scallions, thinly sliced

FOR SERVING (OPTIONAL):
2 cups brown rice or quinoa

CHAPTER 8

PLENTY OF FISH IN THE SEA

Grilled Salmon with California "Caviar"

FOR THE DRESSING AND SALMON:

¼ cup extra-virgin olive oil

¼ cup red wine vinegar

2 tablespoons fresh lime juice

2 garlic cloves, grated or finely minced

1 teaspoon honey

¼ teaspoon kosher salt, plus more for the fish

¼ teaspoon freshly ground black pepper, plus more for the fish

2 pounds salmon fillet with skin, about 1 inch thick (I like a single fillet, but you also can use four 8-ounce fillets if you prefer.)

FOR THE CAVIAR:

¼ cup finely chopped red onion

2 Roma tomatoes, seeded and diced

1 red bell pepper, seeded and diced

1 cup sweet corn kernels (fresh, canned, or thawed from frozen)

1 cup shelled edamame

1 small jalapeño, very thinly sliced (optional)

½ packed cup fresh cilantro leaves, finely chopped

1 ripe avocado, pitted, peeled, and diced

FOR SERVING (OPTIONAL):

1 lime, cut into wedges

While there are plenty of fish in the sea, salmon is one of the most nutritious. In addition to its sky-high omega-3 content, salmon is also a great source of B vitamins and antioxidants, especially astaxanthin, which protects the brain and nervous system against inflammation and has been shown to help prevent skin damage and reduce signs of aging. Hallelujah!

Lest I overwhelm you, I'll skip gushing over the nutritional perks of the zesty, veggie-packed "caviar" smothering this grilled salmon fillet, but trust that there are many, and they are awesome.

1. In a medium bowl, whisk all the ingredients for the dressing.

2. Pat the salmon dry with paper towels. Place it in a large zip-top food storage bag and pour in ⅓ cup of the dressing. Seal the bag, removing as much air as humanly possible, and gently squish the fish around to make sure it gets nicely coated. Refrigerate for 30 minutes (or longer if you have the time).

3. Meanwhile, make the caviar. Add the onion to the dressing remaining in the bowl. Let soak for 5 minutes just to mellow the onion's bite. Add the other ingredients for the caviar to the bowl and gently toss to combine. Cover and refrigerate while you grill the salmon.

4. Preheat a clean, well-oiled grill (or grill pan) over medium-high heat.

5. Remove the salmon from the bag, shaking off any excess marinade. Season both sides of the fillet with an extra pinch of salt and a few cranks of black pepper. Place the salmon skin side down on the hot grill and cook for 5 minutes undisturbed. Carefully turn the fish over and cook for 4 to 5 minutes on the opposite side, until just cooked through.

6. Serve the salmon alongside, on top of, or topped with the caviar. Garnish with lime wedges, if you like.

Grilled Fish Tacos with Street Corn Guacamole

I've always maintained that when it comes to incorporating healthier foods into your diet, "Make it a taco!" is the Dude Diet's version of "A spoonful of sugar helps the medicine go down." These marinated mahi mahi tacos stuffed with crunchy cabbage slaw and topped with game-changing guac have been known to cure many a fish phobia, and that's a beautiful thing.

1. Preheat a clean, lightly oiled grill (or grill pan) over medium-high heat.
2. In a small bowl, combine the lime zest and juice, oil, garlic, smoked paprika, salt, and cayenne. Pat the mahi mahi fillets dry and place them in a large zip-top food storage bag. Pour in the marinade and seal the bag, removing as much air as possible. Gently squish the fillets around in the bag, making sure they're well coated in marinade. Refrigerate for 30 minutes, turning the bag over once halfway through.
3. Meanwhile, get going on the street corn guacamole. Place the ear of corn directly on the hot grill. Cook for 8 to 10 minutes, rotating the corn every 2 to 3 minutes, until tender and lightly charred in spots. Let the corn cool to room temperature, then slice the kernels from the cob with a sharp knife. While the corn is cooling, slice the avocados in half lengthwise and remove the pits. Scoop the flesh into a medium bowl. Add the lime juice, salt, chili powder, and cayenne (if using) and mash with a fork until relatively smooth. (A few lumps are totally fine.) Fold in the cilantro and red onion, then fold in the corn and cheese. Season with a little extra salt if needed and some black pepper. Press plastic wrap onto the surface of the guacamole and refrigerate until ready to use.
4. Carefully remove the fillets from the bag and place each one on the grill with the more rounded side facing up. Cook for 5 minutes, undisturbed. (If you try to move the fish too early, it will stick to the grill! Don't do it.) Gently turn them over and cook them for 4 to 5 minutes on the opposite side, until firm to the touch. Transfer the fish to a cutting board and flake with a fork.
5. Quickly warm the tortillas. I like to do this directly on the grill for about 30 seconds per side, just until grill marks appear. (You can also wrap

FOR THE FISH:

Zest and juice of 1 large lime

1 tablespoon extra-virgin olive oil

2 garlic cloves, grated or finely minced

1 teaspoon smoked paprika

½ teaspoon kosher salt

¼ teaspoon cayenne pepper

Four 6-ounce mahi mahi fillets, skin removed (Cod and halibut are also great.)

FOR THE GUACAMOLE:

1 ear sweet corn, shucked

2 large ripe Haas avocados

Juice of 1 lime

¼ teaspoon kosher salt, plus extra as needed

¾ teaspoon chili powder

¼ teaspoon cayenne pepper (optional)

(continued)

3 tablespoons finely chopped fresh cilantro leaves

2 tablespoons minced red onion

¼ cup crumbled queso fresco or feta cheese

Freshly ground black pepper to taste

FOR SERVING:

8 medium flour tortillas (I also love grain-free tortillas by Siete Foods.)

2 cups very thinly sliced purple cabbage

1 jalapeño, thinly sliced (optional)

Lime wedges

4 tortillas at a time in damp paper towel and microwave in 30-second increments.)

6.   Assemble your tacos! Top each tortilla with a little cabbage, plenty of fish, a generous dollop of guac, and some sliced jalapeño (if using). Serve with lime wedges.

FISH COULD SAVE YOUR LIFE

Listen up, dudes! Fish is good for you, and you should be eating more of it. Not only is fish a low-fat, high-quality protein, it's also packed with omega-3 fatty acids, which have all kinds of important health benefits. Omega-3s help lower inflammation, decrease cholesterol and triglyceride levels, reduce blood clotting, and boost immunity. In short, your heart and brain need them to stay in tip-top shape.

Just so we're clear, your body does not produce omega-3 fatty acids on its own, which means that you need to consume them on the reg. Yes, there are foods besides fish that are high in omega-3s, but since I don't see many dudes regularly snacking on flaxseed, soybeans, and kale, fish is your best bet. According to the Mayo Clinic, eating one to two servings of fish a week could reduce your risk of dying of a heart attack by *more than a third*. This is great news for those of you who have consumed large quantities of pizza and cheeseburgers recently. I don't want to be melodramatic here, but FISH COULD SAVE YOUR LIFE.

If you're worried about potential contaminants in your fish, especially mercury, your concerns are valid but easily offset. First and foremost, always opt for wild-caught fish over farmed when possible and limit your consumption of fish known to contain high mercury levels, namely swordfish, sea bass, ahi/big-eye tuna, and shark. (I'm guessing most of you aren't crushing shark all too often anyway.) Unless you're pregnant, the benefits of omega-3s in fish outweigh the possible risk of contaminants, so stop making excuses and get on board.

Grilled Halibut with Sun-Dried Tomato Chimichurri

SERVES 4

Halibut happens to be one of the most versatile and least "fishy" fish, and its firm white flesh is ideal for grilling. The fillets need little more than a quick soak in citrusy marinade and a few minutes on the hot grate to elevate their mild, slightly sweet flavor, but the chimichurri is what takes things to the next level. Sun-dried tomatoes add dramatic depth and intensity to the traditional Argentinian garlic and herb sauce, and people tend to flip for it. If there was ever a time to rock a "Kiss the Cook" apron . . .

1. Marinate the fish. In a small bowl, combine the lemon juice, oil, garlic, salt, and black pepper. Pat the halibut fillets dry and place them in a large zip-top food storage bag. Pour in the marinade and seal the bag, removing as much air as humanly possible. Gently squish the fillets around in the bag, making sure each one gets lightly coated. Let the fish marinate at room temperature for 20 minutes, turning the bag over once halfway through.

2. Meanwhile, whip up the chimichurri. Put all the ingredients into a food processor and process until well combined, scraping down the sides of the bowl once or twice if necessary. Give it a taste and season with a little salt and pepper if needed. (The sun-dried tomatoes are salty, so you probably won't need extra salt.) Transfer the chimichurri to a bowl, cover with plastic wrap, and refrigerate until ready to use. The flavors in the sauce will have time to get nice and friendly with each other while you grill the fish.

3. Preheat an oiled grill (or grill pan) over medium heat. When hot, carefully remove the fillets from the bag and place each one on the grill. Cook for 5 minutes, undisturbed. (If you try to move the fish too early, it will stick to the grill!) Gently turn them over and cook for 4 to 5 minutes on the opposite side, until they are cooked through and flake easily with a fork.

4. Serve each fillet smothered with a generous amount of chimichurri.

> YOU DO YOU: Halibut can be pricy, so feel free to sub cod, mahi mahi, or salmon for a more frugal but equally fabulous feast.

FOR THE FISH:

Juice of 1 lemon

2 tablespoons extra-virgin olive oil

2 garlic cloves, grated or finely minced

½ teaspoon kosher salt

½ teaspoon freshly ground black pepper

Four 6-ounce halibut fillets, skin removed

FOR THE CHIMICHURRI:

½ cup fresh cilantro leaves

½ cup fresh flat-leaf parsley leaves

¼ cup sun-dried tomatoes packed in olive oil, patted dry with paper towels

4 garlic cloves, peeled and smashed

½ small shallot, roughly chopped

¼ cup plus 2 tablespoons extra-virgin olive oil

2 tablespoons red wine vinegar

½ teaspoon crushed red pepper flakes

Kosher salt to taste

Freshly ground black pepper to taste

Summer Fried Rice with Shrimp

4 garlic cloves, grated or finely minced

¼ cup low-sodium soy sauce

1½ tablespoons unseasoned rice vinegar

1½ tablespoons sriracha sauce

1 tablespoon plus 1 teaspoon light sesame oil, divided

1 pound large shrimp, peeled (including tail shells), deveined, and chopped into ½-inch pieces

Pinch of kosher salt

Freshly ground black pepper to taste

1 medium zucchini, cut into ½-inch dice

1 cup chopped snap peas

1 cup sweet corn kernels (from 1 ear of corn)

½ medium yellow onion, minced

2 large eggs

2 cups cooked brown rice

1 dry pint cherry tomatoes, halved crosswise

½ packed cup fresh basil leaves, chopped

2 whole scallions, thinly sliced

Cherry tomatoes, corn, and basil may not be the usual fried rice suspects, but they add addictive pops of crunch and sweetness to this show-stopping skillet that you'll want to crush on repeat all summer long. And you should. Thanks to the combo of fiber-rich brown rice and vegetables and high-protein (but low-cal) shrimp, this smart stir-fry is ideal for naked season. The recipe is even better with day-old rice, so if you have the foresight, whip up a batch the night before.

1. In a small bowl, combine the garlic, soy sauce, vinegar, and sriracha sauce. Set this mixture by the stove.

2. Heat 1 teaspoon of the oil in a large skillet or wok over medium-high heat. Place a bowl or plate by the stove. When the oil is hot and shimmering, add the shrimp to the pan in an even layer. Season with a generous pinch of salt and a few cranks of black pepper. Cook for about 1 minute, shaking the pan regularly, until the shrimp are just pink and barely opaque (they're going to cook more later on, so do not overcook!!!), then transfer them to the waiting bowl/plate.

3. Add the remaining 1 tablespoon oil to the pan. When the oil is shimmering, add the zucchini, snap peas, corn, and onion and cook for about 4 minutes, until just tender. Push the veggies to one half of the pan. Crack the eggs into the empty half of the pan and scramble with a spatula until set. (This should take less than 1 minute.) Fold the eggs into the vegetables.

4. Add the cooked shrimp, brown rice, cherry tomatoes, and soy sauce mixture to the pan, folding everything together with a spatula. Cook for 1 to 2 minutes, until piping hot, then fold in half of the basil.

5. Divide the rice among 4 bowls and serve garnished with the remaining basil and the scallions.

JUST THE TIP: Deveining shrimp sound scary? Don't worry. When you purchase peeled shrimp, it's usually already peeled and deveined. All you have to do is remove the tail shells.

Crispy Cod with Lemon-Dill Sauce

SERVES 2

There's something to be said for a perfectly cooked piece of flaky fried fish, which is why you need this recipe in your seafood arsenal. Yes, the cod technically is baked, but a crispy panko shell makes it a rather convincing stand-in for your favorite deep-fried fish. Smothered in a luscious lemon-dill sauce, each clean bite tastes deceptively dirty. Serve the cod alongside Herb Potato Coins (page 245) for a fancy fish-and-chips vibe.

1. Preheat the oven to 450°F. Line a baking sheet with parchment paper.
2. Heat a large skillet over medium heat. When hot, add the bread crumbs and cook for 2 to 3 minutes, stirring regularly, until they're a deep golden brown. Immediately transfer them to a shallow baking dish (they will burn if you don't get them out of the pan!). Add the dill, garlic powder, salt, and black pepper and stir to combine.
3. Pat the cod fillets dry with paper towels.
4. Lightly beat the egg in a shallow bowl.
5. Time to coat the fish. Set up a little assembly line with fish, beaten egg, bread crumb mixture, and the prepared baking sheet. Dip each piece of fish into the egg, shake off any excess, and dredge it in the bread crumbs. Dip in the egg again (some bread crumbs will fall off, and that's okay), then dredge a second time, pressing gently with your fingers to help the crumbs adhere. Place the breaded fillets on the prepared baking sheet. Bake for 12 minutes, carefully turning once halfway through the cooking time, or until the fish is cooked through.
6. Meanwhile, stir together all the ingredients for the sauce in a small bowl.
7. Serve the fish warm, topped with the lemon-dill sauce. Garnish with lemon wedges if you like extra zip.

FOR THE FISH:

¾ cup whole-wheat panko bread crumbs

2 teaspoons finely chopped fresh dill (or ¾ teaspoon dried dill weed)

½ teaspoon garlic powder

¼ teaspoon kosher salt

¼ teaspoon freshly ground black pepper

Two 6-ounce wild cod fillets (about 1 inch thick), skin removed

1 large egg

Lemon wedges for serving (optional)

FOR THE SAUCE:

⅓ cup nonfat plain Greek yogurt

2 tablespoons mayonnaise

1 large garlic clove, grated or finely minced

½ teaspoon freshly grated lemon zest

1 teaspoon fresh lemon juice

1 tablespoon finely chopped fresh dill (or 1 teaspoon dried dill weed)

Pinch of kosher salt

Thai Seafood Curry with Zucchini Noodles

1 tablespoon extra-virgin coconut oil

3 tablespoons Thai red curry paste (I dig Thai Kitchen brand.)

3 garlic cloves, grated or finely minced

1 tablespoon peeled and grated fresh ginger

1 small white onion, thinly sliced

1 red bell pepper, seeded and thinly sliced

¼ teaspoon crushed red pepper flakes

2 cups low-sodium vegetable broth, divided

One 13.5-ounce can full-fat coconut milk

1 tablespoon granulated sugar (Cane, brown, and coconut palm sugar all are great.)

2 tablespoons low-sodium soy sauce

2 teaspoons Thai fish sauce

Zest of 1 lime

3 cups zucchini noodles (purchased packaged or made

This curry looks and tastes exotic, but it couldn't be easier to pull off. The entire process boils down to: "Add things to pot. Stir," and it shouldn't run you more than forty minutes from start to finish. I know curry paste and fish sauce aren't exactly pantry staples, but they can be found front and center in the Asian section of most markets, and when it comes to the zucchini noodles, you can easily get by without a spiralizer. Pick up some pre-packaged "zoodles" (they're widely available these days), or serve your curry over regular rice noodles or a little brown rice and call it a day.

Thinly sliced red onion

Chopped peanuts

1. Heat the oil in a medium sauté pan or Dutch oven over medium heat. When the oil is hot and shimmering, add the curry paste, garlic, and ginger and cook for 3 minutes to unlock the curry's badass flavors. Add the onion, bell pepper, red pepper flakes, and ¼ cup of the vegetable broth and cook for about 4 minutes, just until the vegetables have softened slightly.

2. Add the remaining 1¾ cups vegetable broth, the coconut milk (don't panic if the coconut milk has separated in the can—just go ahead and scrape everything into the pan), sugar, soy sauce, fish sauce, and lime zest. Bring the curry to a simmer and cook for 10 minutes to allow the flavors to combine.

3. Meanwhile, if you're making your own noodles, spiralize the zucchini using whatever setting on your spiralizer creates spaghetti-size noodles. Trim the noodles with a knife or scissors (just so that they're not crazy long) and pat them dry with paper towels. Briefly set aside.

4. Add the cod and shrimp to the curry and simmer for 5 minutes, or until both are opaque and just cooked through. Remove from the heat and stir in the lime juice and zucchini noodles. Taste and season with a little

YOU DO YOU: This recipe also is great with boneless, skinless chicken breast instead of seafood. Simply dice the chicken into 1-inch cubes and add it to the pan in step 4. It will cook through in 10 minutes.

from roughly 1 large
zucchini, spiralized)

12 ounces cod fillet, cut
into 1½-inch cubes

8 ounces large shrimp
(fresh or frozen),
peeled, deveined, and
tail shells removed

Juice of ½ lime

FOR SERVING (OPTIONAL):
Lime wedges

Chopped fresh cilantro

Crab Cakes with Green God Sauce

FOR THE CRAB CAKES:

1 large egg, lightly beaten

3 whole scallions, finely chopped

1½ tablespoons mayonnaise

2 teaspoons fresh lemon juice

1 teaspoon Dijon mustard

1 teaspoon Worcestershire sauce

1 teaspoon hot sauce of your choice

½ teaspoon smoked paprika

¼ teaspoon kosher salt

1 pound backfin lump crab meat

½ cup almond meal (See tip on almond meal in the sidebar on page 15.)

⅓ cup whole-wheat panko bread crumbs

2 tablespoons extra-virgin olive oil

Lemon wedges for serving (optional)

I have good news, dudes. You don't actually need a boatload of bread crumbs or canola oil to make crispy golden crab cakes in your own kitchen. (You also don't need to be scared of cooking them, I swear.) A little bit of almond meal and whole-wheat panko bind and crust these kickass cakes, and just 2 tablespoons of olive oil are plenty to give the patties the necessary crunch. Make sure you're generous with the Greek yogurt–based sauce—it's cooling and tangy with an herbal sweetness that perfectly complements the crab-meat's delicate flavor.

1. Make the crab cakes. In a medium bowl, combine the egg, scallions, mayonnaise, lemon juice, mustard, Worcestershire sauce, hot sauce, smoked paprika, and salt. Add half of the crab meat and the almond meal and mix to combine. Gently fold the remaining crabmeat into the mixture. Cover the bowl with plastic wrap and refrigerate.

2. Put all the ingredients for the sauce in a small food processor (or blender with a personal cup attachment). Process until smooth, scraping down the sides of the bowl a few times if necessary. Transfer the sauce to a bowl, cover with plastic wrap, and refrigerate until ready to use. (No food processor/blender? Finely chop the herbs, grate the garlic, and mix everything together by hand.)

3. Place the panko in a shallow bowl or on a plate. Remove the crab mixture from the refrigerator and form into 8 balls. Lightly roll each ball in the panko. Gently flatten the balls into patties, roughly 1 inch in thickness.

4. Heat the oil in your largest nonstick skillet over medium heat. When the oil is hot and shimmering (but not smoking!), add the crab cakes to the pan. (Depending on the size of your pan, you may need to do this in two batches.) Let them cook, undisturbed, for 4 to 5 minutes, until you can see that they are golden brown around the edges. Using a thin metal spatula,

carefully flip the crab cakes over and cook for another 4 to 5 minutes, until browned and crispy on the opposite sides. Transfer to a platter or plates.

5. Serve the crab cakes warm with the Green God Sauce and lemon wedges (if using).

> YOU DO YOU: Green God Sauce not up your alley? Lemon-Dill Sauce (page 177), Chipotle Romesco (page 26), Street Corn Guacamole (page 171), Mango and Cherry Tomato Salsa (page 15), or Peach-Jalapeño Salsa (page 183) for the fruit fans would all make killer additions to these cakes.

FOR THE SAUCE:

1 cup nonfat plain Greek yogurt

⅓ packed cup fresh basil leaves

⅓ packed cup fresh flat-leaf parsley leaves

¼ cup thinly sliced whole scallions

1 small garlic clove, peeled and smashed

1 teaspoon chopped fresh tarragon leaves

1 tablespoon fresh lemon juice

¼ teaspoon honey

¼ teaspoon kosher salt

¼ teaspoon freshly ground black pepper

YOU DO YOU: The seasoning on this fish is pretty mild given the salsa's kick, but feel free to add more black pepper or a pinch of cayenne to the spice rub if you can handle more heat.

Blackened Grouper with Peach-Jalapeño Salsa

Back in The Dude Diet's early days, I was the private chef for a couple of players on the New York Giants. One was particularly down with fish, and having grown up in Florida, he requested that I make him blackened catfish on the reg. I obliged, but since most catfish in the United States is imported from places that do not adhere to American health standards, I would often blacken other white fish for him instead. Grouper, with its mild flavor and large, moist flakes, was always a winner, especially topped with a generous amount of fresh and spicy fruit salsa.

This recipe couldn't be easier, and the "choose your own adventure" aspect is clutch. Feel free to use your favorite fish (halibut, cod, and salmon are particularly good), and play with fruits depending on what's in season.

1. Preheat the oven to 400°F.
2. Combine all the ingredients for the salsa in a medium bowl. Cover tightly with plastic wrap and refrigerate until ready to use.
3. In a small bowl, combine the chili powder, smoked paprika, black pepper, cumin, garlic powder, and salt. Pat the fish fillets dry with paper towels. Brush the fillets all over with 2 teaspoons of the oil and season with the spice mixture.
4. Heat a large ovenproof skillet (preferably cast-iron) over medium-high heat. When the pan is piping hot, add the remaining 1 tablespoon oil and swirl to coat the bottom of the pan. Add the fillets to the pan, skinned side up, and cook for 1 minute, or until lightly "blackened" (read: deep reddish-brown) on their undersides. The spices and oil will smoke!! That's part of the "blackening" process—crack open a window or turn on the vent fan and don't panic. Carefully flip the fillets and cook for 1 minute more, or until equally blackened on the opposite side. Pour the lime juice over the fish and transfer the skillet to the oven. Bake for 6 to 8 minutes, until the fish is just opaque in the center and flakes easily with a fork.
5. Serve your blackened fish warm, topped with plenty of salsa.

FOR THE SALSA:

- 2 medium yellow peaches, cut into small dice (or 2 cups seasonal fruit of your choice)
- 1 small jalapeño, very thinly sliced or minced (If you're sensitive to heat, seed the pepper first.)
- ¼ cup minced red onion
- ½ cup fresh cilantro leaves, finely chopped
- Juice of 1 large lime
- Pinch of kosher salt

FOR THE FISH:

- 1 tablespoon chili powder
- 2 teaspoons smoked paprika
- 1 teaspoon freshly ground black pepper
- 1 teaspoon ground cumin
- ½ teaspoon garlic powder
- ½ teaspoon kosher salt
- Four 6-ounce grouper fillets, 1 inch thick, skin removed
- 1 tablespoon plus 2 teaspoons extra-virgin olive oil, divided
- Juice of ½ lime

Sesame-Crusted Ahi with Citrus Soy Sauce

SERVES 2

2 tablespoons sesame seeds (I like "tuxedo," aka black and white sesame seeds, but you do you.)

12 ounces sushi-grade ahi tuna steak (You can use 1 large steak or 2 smaller steaks.)

Kosher salt to taste

Freshly ground black pepper to taste

2 tablespoons light sesame oil

2 tablespoons thinly sliced whole scallions (optional)

FOR THE CITRUS SOY DRESSING:

3 tablespoons low-sodium soy sauce

1½ tablespoons fresh lemon juice

1 tablespoon fresh lime juice

1 teaspoon toasted (aka dark) sesame oil

1 teaspoon honey

The great thing about seared tuna is that it looks restaurant-level impressive, when in reality, it couldn't be easier to execute. This sesame-crusted tuna steak drizzled with a five-ingredient citrus soy dressing is particularly impossible to screw up, making it the perfect starter recipe for nervous seafood chefs. Just season the fish with a little salt and pepper, dredge it in sesame seeds, and throw it into a hot pan for about a minute and a half per side. Done and done. The entire process takes five minutes total and requires next to no culinary skill. Don't tell your friends and family that, though—gotta capitalize on those compliments.

You can serve this tuna alongside your favorite whole grain or seasonal roasted vegetables, or over salad, but I stand by Greens and Grains (page 226) as its side dish soul mate.

1. Pour the sesame seeds onto a plate. Pat the tuna steak(s) dry with paper towels and season both sides with salt and black pepper. Press both sides of the steak(s) into the sesame seeds, using your hands to help the seeds adhere.

2. Heat the oil in a large nonstick skillet over medium-high heat. When the oil is hot and shimmering (but not smoking!), add the tuna steaks. Cook for 1 to 1½ minutes per side for rare (depending on the thickness of your fish). Transfer the steaks to a cutting board and let them rest while you whip up the sauce.

3. Place all the ingredients for the citrus soy dressing in a bowl and whisk to combine.

4. Thinly slice the tuna steak against the grain and serve drizzled with the citrus soy. Garnish with the sliced scallions, if you like.

Striped Bass with Cherry Tomato Sauce, Bacon, and Garlicky Bread Crumbs

SERVES 2

2 slices thick-cut bacon (preferably with no added nitrates), sliced crosswise into ½-inch strips

¼ cup minced shallot (about 1 medium shallot)

1 dry pint cherry tomatoes, halved crosswise

Pinch of kosher salt

¼ to ½ teaspoon crushed red pepper flakes (depending on how much heat you like)

¼ cup dry white wine, such as Sauvignon Blanc

Two 6- to 8-ounce striped bass fillets, skin removed

Freshly ground black pepper

1 teaspoon extra-virgin olive oil

1 garlic clove, minced

1 tablespoon whole-wheat panko bread crumbs

1½ tablespoons chopped fresh chives

Whenever you're in need of a culinary confidence boost, this recipe has your back. Perfectly poached fish in a fresh cherry tomato sauce screams domestic god/dess and happens to be a foolproof thirty-minute meal. Striped bass has a deliciously delicate flavor and texture, but sometimes it can be tricky to find, so feel free to sub your favorite white fish—cod and halibut are personal go-tos.

p.s. The garlicky bread crumbs might seem a little precious, but they make the dish. Don't cheat yourself.

1. Heat a medium nonstick skillet over medium heat. When hot, add the bacon and cook for 6 minutes or until lightly browned and crisp. Using a slotted spoon, transfer the bacon to a paper towel–lined plate.

2. Add the shallot to the pan with the bacon grease and cook for 2 minutes, or until softened and translucent. (If it starts to brown, reduce the heat slightly.) Add the cherry tomatoes, a large pinch of salt, and the crushed red pepper and cook for 2 minutes, or until the tomatoes are just beginning to soften (they're going to get a good long cooking time, so don't overdo it here), then add the wine.

3. Season the bass generously on both sides with salt and pepper. Add the fish to the pan and reduce the heat to medium-low. Cover the skillet with a lid and cook for 8 to 10 minutes, until the fish is opaque and flakes easily.

4. Meanwhile, heat the oil in a small skillet over medium heat. When the oil is hot and shimmering, add the garlic and cook until golden brown, 1½ to 2 minutes. (Be very careful not to burn the garlic! If it looks like it's browning too much, turn down the heat.) Stir in the bread crumbs and a tiny pinch of salt and cook for 2 minutes, or until the bread crumbs are nicely toasted and have darkened a shade in color. Transfer to a small bowl and briefly set aside.

5. Remove the fish from the skillet and turn up the heat to high. Cook the sauce for about 1 minute just to thicken it slightly.

6. Spoon the cherry tomato sauce over each piece of fish and top with the cooked bacon, garlicky bread crumbs, and chives. Serve immediately.

YOU DO YOU: The fish is great on its own or with a side of roasted broccoli or potatoes, but you can also serve it over a little quinoa, brown rice, or whole-grain pasta for added heft.

JUST THE TIP: You can cook these skewers on a grill pan or griddle in an emergency, but you'll need to use short skewers to make sure that they fit in the pan. You'll likely also need an extra minute or so for the shrimp to cook through.

Cajun Shrimp and Sausage Skewers

Lean andouille chicken sausage adds heartiness and extra heat to these kickin' Cajun-spiced shrimp skewers, and a squeeze of lightly charred lemon will keep you coming back for more. I like to round out the meal with a summery side of Grilled Corn, Asparagus, and White Bean Salad (page 227), and let the good times roll.

1. If you're using bamboo skewers, make sure to soak them in a shallow baking dish filled with water for at least 30 minutes to prevent them from catching fire on the grill. Do NOT skip this step.

2. In a small bowl, combine all the ingredients for the Cajun seasoning.

3. Place the shrimp in a medium bowl and drizzle with the oil. Add the Cajun seasoning and toss to combine, making sure all the shrimpies are good and coated. Cover the bowl tightly with plastic wrap and refrigerate for 20 minutes.

4. Meanwhile, slice the chicken sausage links into ¾-inch rounds. (You should get roughly 6 rounds per link.)

5. Preheat a lightly oiled grill over medium-high heat.

6. Depending on the size of your skewers, thread 2 or 3 shrimp and 2 or 3 sausage rounds onto each skewer, alternating between shrimp and sausage. (FYI, you want the skewer to pierce each shrimp twice, once just above the tail shell and once near the head, to form a tight C shape.)

7. Place the skewers on the hot grill along with the lemon halves, cut side down. Cook the skewers for 2 to 3 minutes per side, until the shrimp are pink and just opaque throughout and the sausage is lightly charred in spots. (Please don't overcook the shrimp! Remember, it's going to continue cooking once you remove it from the heat.) Let the lemon halves cook undisturbed for a full 4 minutes.

8. Transfer the skewers to a large serving plate. Squeeze the juice from the charred lemon halves over the skewers. Garnish with the scallions and hot sauce if you're crazy like that.

FOR THE SKEWERS:

8 to 12 metal or bamboo skewers

1 pound large shrimp (about 24 shrimp), peeled and deveined with the tail shells still on

1 tablespoon extra-virgin olive oil

12 ounces (4 links) fully cooked andouille chicken sausage (or spicy sausage of your choice)

1 large lemon, sliced in half crosswise

FOR THE CAJUN SEASONING:

1 tablespoon paprika

¾ teaspoon dried oregano

¾ teaspoon garlic powder

½ teaspoon kosher salt

½ teaspoon freshly ground black pepper

¼ teaspoon cayenne pepper

FOR SERVING (OPTIONAL):

4 whole scallions, thinly sliced

Hot sauce of your choice

Salmon and Soba Bowls

This bowl is a smorgasbord of flavor and texture, and the foolproof baked salmon practically melts in your mouth, but it's the dressing that's the real star here—semi-sweet with a gingery kick. It's hard not to obsess over the umami-flavored awesomeness. It does double duty as fish marinade and soba dressing in this recipe, but it's also fantastic on everything from steak to roasted vegetables and plain old mixed greens.

1. Whisk all the ingredients for the dressing in a medium bowl.
2. Pat the salmon fillets dry with paper towels. Place them in a large zip-top food storage bag and pour in ¼ cup of the dressing. Seal the bag, removing as much air as possible, and very gently squish the salmon around to make sure each fillet is well coated. Allow the fish to marinate in the fridge for 25 to 30 minutes.
3. Meanwhile, bring a medium pot of water to a boil. When boiling, add the soba noodles and cook for about 4 minutes, until just tender. (Be careful—most packages will tell you to cook the noodles for 6 minutes, which will turn them into sticky mush!) Immediately drain the noodles and rinse them well with cold water to keep them from sticking together. Transfer to a medium bowl, add half of the remaining dressing, and toss to coat. Add the basil and sesame seeds and toss again. Briefly set aside or cover and refrigerate for chilled noodles. (Personally, I'm a fan of cold noodles with warm salmon, but you do you.)
4. Preheat the oven to 375°F. Line a baking sheet with parchment paper or aluminum foil.
5. Remove the salmon fillets from the marinade and place them on the prepared baking sheet skinned side down. Season with a little black pepper if you like. Bake for 15 minutes or until the salmon is just cooked through and flakes easily with a fork.
6. Assembly time! Divide the soba noodles between 2 bowls. Add the sliced cucumber and avocado (if using) to the bowls and top each with a salmon fillet. Drizzle with the remaining dressing and garnish with some extra sesame seeds if you're feeling wild.

FOR THE DRESSING:

⅓ cup finely chopped scallions (white and light green parts only)

¼ cup low-sodium soy sauce

3 garlic cloves, grated or finely minced

1½ tablespoons unseasoned rice vinegar

1½ tablespoons dark (aka toasted) sesame oil

1 tablespoon peeled and grated fresh ginger

1 tablespoon honey

FOR THE SALMON AND SOBA:

Two 6-ounce center-cut salmon fillets, about 1¼ inches thick, skin removed

4 ounces buckwheat soba noodles

¼ cup fresh basil leaves, finely chopped

1½ tablespoons sesame seeds (black, white, or mixed—all are great), plus more for topping if you like

Freshly ground black pepper (optional)

⅓ medium English cucumber (aka seedless cucumber), thinly sliced into half-moons

½ ripe avocado, pitted, peeled, and thinly sliced (optional)

CHAPTER

9

BLACK TIE OPTIONAL

Friday Night Pasta

SERVES 4

FOR THE PASTA:

Kosher salt to taste

Florets from 1 medium head cauliflower (about 6 cups florets)

1½ tablespoons extra-virgin olive oil

Freshly ground black pepper to taste

8 ounces brown rice fusilli pasta (I like Jovial brand) or whole-grain/grain-free pasta of your choice

1 recipe Idiotproof Chicken Breasts (page 136), diced (You also can use 2 heaping cups diced or shredded store-bought rotisserie chicken.)

4 ounces goat cheese, crumbled

FOR THE PESTO:

3 packed cups baby spinach

½ packed cup fresh basil leaves

3 garlic cloves, peeled and smashed

½ cup raw walnuts

Juice of 1 lemon

¾ teaspoon kosher salt, plus extra as needed

½ teaspoon crushed red pepper flakes, plus extra as needed

¼ cup extra-virgin olive oil

Some people hit the town on Friday nights. Logan and I stay in. We don our finest sweat suits and retire to the couch to eat oversize bowls of this perfect pasta with roasted cauliflower, chicken breast, creamy goat cheese, and OG Dude Diet spinach pesto. I don't remember exactly how or when this tradition started, but it's become the highlight of my week, and the extreme joy the Dude radiates for "the pasta" is a beautiful thing.

p.s. Apologies to anyone who has ever invited us anywhere on a Friday night. These are the plans we couldn't get out of.

1. Preheat the oven to 450°F. Line a large baking sheet with parchment paper. Bring a large pot of salted water to a boil.

2. Place the cauliflower florets on the prepared baking sheet. Drizzle with the oil, season generously with salt and black pepper, and toss to coat. Arrange the cauliflower in an even layer, leaving a little space around each floret. Roast for 20 to 25 minutes, until the cauliflower is tender and nicely browned.

3. Meanwhile, whip up the pesto. Place the spinach and basil in the bowl of a food processor (or high-speed blender) and pulse a few times, until coarsely chopped. Add the garlic, walnuts, lemon juice, salt, and red pepper flakes and process until the mixture forms a relatively smooth paste, scraping down the sides of the bowl a few times if necessary. With the motor running, slowly pour in the oil and process until the pesto looks uniform. Taste and season with a little extra salt and crushed red pepper if necessary.

4. Cook the pasta al dente according to the package directions. Drain, reserving about ¾ cup of the pasta's cooking water, and rinse with tepid water to prevent the pasta from sticking. (If you're using wheat pasta, no need to rinse.)

5. Return the pasta to the pot over medium-low heat. Add the pesto, cauliflower, diced chicken, and ¼ cup of the reserved pasta water and toss to coat. (If the pesto is too thick, add more cooking water until you achieve the perfect consistency.) Cook for a minute or so, until everything is warmed through.

6. Transfer the pasta to bowls. Top with the crumbled goat cheese and serve warm.

Slow-Roasted Beef Tenderloin with Rosemary Red Wine Sauce

SERVES **6**

FOR THE BEEF:

One 3-pound center-cut beef tenderloin, trimmed and tied (A butcher can do this for you.)

2½ tablespoons extra-virgin olive oil

2½ teaspoons kosher salt

1½ teaspoons freshly ground black pepper

6 to 8 sprigs fresh rosemary

FOR THE SAUCE:

1 tablespoon extra-virgin olive oil

½ cup minced shallots

1 large garlic clove, peeled and smashed

1 cup Cabernet Sauvignon (or dry red wine of your choice)

2 tablespoons balsamic vinegar

2 cups low-sodium beef broth

4 sprigs fresh rosemary

1 tablespoon unsalted butter, at room temperature

1 tablespoon all-purpose flour

Freshly ground black pepper to taste

Trust me when I say that eating this outrageously tender beef is a truly transcendent experience. Instead of the traditional 400°F for 35 minutes, the tenderloin is cooked at 275°F for about an hour, and the result is slap-yourself-in-the-face amazing. Served with a decadent red wine sauce, it makes an unforgettable centerpiece for any and all special occasions. Try it with a simply dressed arugula salad and some crusty bread if you're keeping things light, or go full feast mode with a side of cauliflower puree and Boss Brussels Sprout Salad (page 240) or Kickass Carrots (page 239).

One important note: **You must use an instant-read thermometer for this recipe.** Beef tenderloin is an insanely expensive cut of meat, and it's straight-up sacrilege for it to be anything less than perfect!

1. Preheat the oven to 275°F. Line a large rimmed baking sheet with aluminum foil or parchment paper.

2. Pat the tenderloin dry with paper towels and place it on the prepared baking sheet. Rub the beef all over with 2 tablespoons of the oil and season with the salt and black pepper. Really make sure the entire surface of the tenderloin gets some seasoning love. Secure the rosemary sprigs to your tenderloin by threading them through the kitchen string (that should be tying your beef) at regular intervals. Brush the rosemary with the remaining ½ tablespoon oil.

3. Roast the tenderloin for 1 hour to 1 hour and 10 minutes, until an instant-read thermometer inserted into the thickest part of the meat registers an internal temperature of 125°F for medium-rare. (The temperature will continue to rise to 130°F to 135°F while the meat rests.) Transfer the beef to a cutting board, tent it loosely with aluminum foil, and let it rest for 20 minutes.

4. Meanwhile, whip up the sauce. Heat the oil in a large skillet over medium heat. When the oil is hot and shimmering, add the shallots and cook for 2 to 3 minutes, until soft and translucent. Add the garlic, red wine, and vinegar. Bring to a vigorous simmer and cook until the liquid is reduced by half, 6 to 8 minutes. Add the broth and rosemary and bring to a vigorous simmer once again. Simmer until the total liquid is reduced by half

(leaving a little more than a cup of liquid in the pan), about 12 minutes. Strain the sauce through a fine-mesh strainer into a small saucepan, pressing gently on the solids (aka the shallots, rosemary, and garlic) to release any remaining liquid. Mix the butter and flour in a small bowl. Return the sauce to a simmer over medium heat. Once simmering, whisk in the flour mixture and cook for about 2 minutes, until the sauce has thickened enough to coat the back of a spoon. Season with black pepper.

5. Remove the kitchen string from the roast and discard the rosemary. Slice the beef crosswise into 1-inch-thick rounds. Serve with the red wine sauce.

YOU DO YOU: Not into red wine sauce? Try this beef with Arugula and Goat Cheese Pistou (page 206), Sun-Dried Tomato Chimichurri (page 173), or a double batch of Pistachio-Mint Gremolata (page 202).

JUST THE TIP: Harissa is a deliciously spicy North African sauce made from chiles, spices, and olive oil. You can find it in the international section of most major markets or make your own if you're feeling adventurous. I like Mina brand.

Parchment Halibut with Chickpeas and Spicy Harissa

If you're looking to up your entertaining game, this halibut will give your seafood street cred a major boost. It tastes intimidatingly exotic but couldn't be easier, mostly because cooking fish "en papillote" (aka in parchment paper) is one of the greatest cooking hacks of all time. Just wrap the ingredients up in paper packages, pop them in the oven for twenty minutes, and . . . that's it. Rip open the paper to reveal perfectly flaky fish over tender chickpeas, veggies, and plump raisins. Garnish with a little extra lemon and fresh cilantro, and go to town. No muss, no fuss.

Cooking for one or two? Love it. Make only as many fish packets as you need and roast the remaining vegetable mixture on a separate parchment-lined baking sheet while the packets cook. You can eat the roasted veggies as a side or add them to salads, bowls, or wraps throughout the week.

1. Preheat the oven to 375°F. Fold four 15 × 16-inch pieces of parchment paper in half. Open each paper back up and place them on the counter.
2. In a medium bowl, combine the chickpeas, carrots, onion, oil, ¼ cup of the harissa sauce, half of the lemon juice, and a good pinch of salt.
3. Pat the halibut dry and season generously on both sides with salt and pepper. (The harissa is spicy, so if you're sensitive, go easy on the black pepper or skip it altogether.)
4. To assemble each parchment packet: Place a quarter of the chickpea mixture on one side of the parchment paper near the fold and sprinkle with 1 tablespoon of the raisins (if using). Place a halibut fillet on top and spread the fish with 1 tablespoon of the remaining harissa sauce. Fold the parchment paper over the fish. Starting at the top crease, make small overlapping folds to seal the edges of your "package" in a half-moon shape. (It doesn't have to be perfect, but please make sure it's tightly sealed.)
5. Place the prepared packages on 2 large baking sheets. Bake for 20 minutes, or until the halibut is cooked through.
6. Transfer the packets to four plates, open them up (careful, there will be some steam!!), and drizzle with the remaining lemon juice. Serve garnished with cilantro.

One 15-ounce can chickpeas, drained and rinsed

1 cup ¼-inch-thick carrot rounds (about 3 medium carrots)

1 small red onion, diced

1½ tablespoons extra-virgin olive oil

½ cup green harissa sauce, divided

Juice of 1 large lemon, divided

Kosher salt to taste

Four 6- to 8-ounce halibut fillets, 1 inch thick, skin removed (Cod, hake, or any other firm white fish will also work.)

Freshly ground black pepper to taste

¼ cup golden raisins (optional)

¼ packed cup fresh cilantro leaves, finely chopped

Pork Tenderloin "Steaks" with Warm Shallot Vinaigrette

FOR THE PORK:

1 pound pork tenderloin, trimmed of excess fat

½ teaspoon kosher salt

½ teaspoon freshly ground black pepper

2 teaspoons extra-virgin olive oil

FOR THE VINAIGRETTE:

2 tablespoons extra-virgin olive oil

2 tablespoons minced shallots

1 tablespoon plus 2 teaspoons red wine vinegar

1 teaspoon Dijon mustard

1 teaspoon Worcestershire sauce

½ teaspoon maple syrup

2 tablespoons chopped fresh flat-leaf parsley leaves

For most meat lovers, a good steak is the quintessential special occasion meal. I fully support going caveman on a giant rib eye every once in a while—God knows I'd never dream of asking you to walk into your favorite steak house and pass on beef—but on nights when you're craving a steak dinner in the comfort of your own home, I beg you to consider this pork tenderloin stand-in.

Dividing a pork tenderloin in half and pounding the pieces to a uniform thickness produces two "steaks" with a much leaner and cleaner nutritional profile than their beefy counterparts. Pan-sear the pork until golden brown on the outside and lightly pink on the inside, slice it thinly across the grain, and serve it with warm shallot vinaigrette and your favorite sexy side for the ultimate fake steak feast.

1. Slice the pork tenderloin in half crosswise so that you have two pieces of the same size. Using a meat mallet (or the bottom of a heavy skillet), pound each piece of tenderloin to an even 1-inch thickness. Season the "steaks" on both sides with the salt and pepper.

2. Heat the oil in a large skillet over medium-high heat. When the oil is hot and shimmering, add the steaks to the pan. Cook for 6 minutes, then flip the steaks and cook for another 4 to 5 minutes on the second side, until the meat registers 140°F on an instant-read thermometer. The steaks should have nicely browned exteriors and lightly pink interiors. (Heads up—the pork will generate some smoke while it cooks. Don't panic.) Transfer the steaks to a cutting board and let rest for 5 to 10 minutes.

3. While the pork rests, make the vinaigrette. Warm the oil in the skillet used to cook the pork over medium heat. When the oil is hot and shimmering, add the shallots and reduce the heat to low. Cook gently for 5 minutes (you don't want them to brown at all!), or until the shallots are very soft and translucent. Add the vinegar, mustard, Worcestershire sauce, and maple syrup and whisk until emulsified (aka completely combined). Turn off the heat and stir in the parsley.

4. Thinly slice the steaks across the grain and serve topped with the warm vinaigrette.

Pan-Seared Lamb Chops with Pistachio-Mint Gremolata

FOR THE LAMB:

Four 1-inch-thick loin lamb chops (roughly 6 ounces each)

¾ teaspoon ground cumin

½ teaspoon kosher salt

¼ teaspoon freshly ground black pepper

⅛ teaspoon ground cinnamon

2 teaspoons extra-virgin olive oil

FOR THE GREMOLATA:

¼ cup finely chopped shelled pistachios (Chop them by hand or pulse them a few times in a mini food processor.)

½ cup fresh cilantro leaves, finely chopped

¼ cup fresh mint leaves, finely chopped

1 large garlic clove, grated or finely minced

Finely grated zest of 1 lemon

1 teaspoon fresh lemon juice

Pinch of crushed red pepper flakes (optional)

Pinch of kosher salt

Despite its highbrow title and flavors, this recipe happens to be one of the quickest and easiest in the book. Searing the seasoned chops takes all of ten minutes, and you can throw together the gremolata while they rest. In addition to being a fun word to say, gremolata is a classic condiment typically made with parsley, garlic, and lemon zest that's ideal for adding a little extra oomph to a variety of dishes. I went slightly rogue here by replacing parsley with a mix of cilantro and mint and adding some toasted pistachios into the mix, and the effect is bright and herby with a soft crunch.

1. Remove the lamb chops from the fridge and let them come to room temperature. (This should take about 20 minutes.)

2. Meanwhile, get going on the gremolata. Heat a small skillet (with no oil) over medium heat. When hot, add the pistachios to the pan and cook, shaking the pan occasionally, for about 3 minutes, until toasted and fragrant. Transfer the nuts to a medium bowl and let cool.

3. In a small bowl, combine the cumin, salt, pepper, and cinnamon. Pat the lamb chops dry and season all over with the spice mix.

4. Heat the oil in a large skillet over medium-high heat. When the oil is hot and shimmering, add the chops to the pan. Cook for about 6 minutes per side, until the chops reach an internal temperature of 130°F for medium-rare. (Add an extra minute per side if you like your lamb medium.) Transfer the chops to a plate or cutting board, cover loosely with aluminum foil, and let them rest for 5 minutes.

5. While the chops rest, finish up the gremolata. Add the remaining ingredients for the gremolata to the bowl with the pistachios and toss to combine.

6. Serve the lamb chops warm, topped with the gremolata.

YOU DO YOU: If you can't find large chops, 6 smaller chops will do. Just reduce the cooking time by about a minute per side.

Penne with Sausage, Cherry Tomatoes, and Arugula

SERVES 4

I firmly believe in having a signature pasta dish in your arsenal, and this one's a triple threat. On top of being unbelievably tasty, it also happens to be good for you (high-fiber pasta, lean chicken sausage, and antioxidant-rich tomatoes for the win!) and pretty damn sexy to look at. If you're planning to entertain, go ahead and do all of the chopping, slicing, and mincing ahead of time. Once you're prepped, the recipe comes together in about twenty minutes.

1. Bring a large pot of salted water to a boil.

2. Cook the penne al dente according to the package directions. Drain, reserving ½ cup of the pasta's cooking water. If you're using gluten-free pasta, rinse it thoroughly to prevent sticking.

3. Meanwhile, heat the oil in a large sauté pan over medium-high heat. When the oil is hot and shimmering, add the sausage and cook for 5 to 6 minutes, until lightly browned. Reduce the heat to medium. Add the shallot and garlic and cook until the shallot is soft, about 3 minutes, then add the cherry tomatoes, salt, and crushed red pepper. Cook for 3 to 4 minutes, just until the tomatoes have softened slightly. Add ¼ cup of the reserved pasta water, scraping up any browned bits from the bottom of the pan, and simmer for 1 minute, or until the liquid is slightly thickened. (If your sauce needs a little more liquid, add the remaining ¼ cup reserved pasta water.) Stir in ½ cup of the basil.

4. Add the pasta to the pan and toss to combine. Add the arugula and toss again. Taste and season with extra salt if needed.

5. Transfer the pasta to a serving dish or individual bowls and top with the cheese and the remaining basil. Serve immediately.

½ teaspoon kosher salt, plus extra for cooking the pasta

8 ounces grain-free or whole-grain penne (I like Banza chickpea flour penne or Jovial brown rice penne for this.)

1 tablespoon extra-virgin olive oil

12 ounces fully cooked spicy Italian chicken sausage links (4 to 5 links), thinly sliced at a slight angle

1 large shallot, minced

4 garlic cloves, minced

4 cups cherry tomatoes, halved crosswise

¼ to ½ teaspoon crushed red pepper flakes (depending on how much heat you like)

¾ cup fresh basil leaves, chopped

3 packed cups baby arugula

½ cup shaved Parmesan cheese

Steak and Asparagus Roll-ups with Arugula and Goat Cheese Pistou

FOR THE STEAK:

- 3 tablespoons balsamic vinegar
- 1½ tablespoons extra-virgin olive oil, divided
- 1 large garlic clove, grated or finely minced
- Two 8-ounce top sirloin steaks
- 1 bunch (approximately 12 ounces) medium-thick asparagus, woody ends removed
- Kosher salt to taste
- Freshly ground black pepper to taste

FOR THE PISTOU:

- 2 packed cups baby arugula
- 1 cup fresh basil leaves
- 2 garlic cloves, peeled and smashed
- 4 ounces goat cheese
- 1 tablespoon balsamic vinegar
- Freshly ground black pepper to taste
- 2 tablespoons extra-virgin olive oil
- Kosher salt to taste

Would it be easier to just cook a few steaks and serve them alongside asparagus with this gloriously creamy pistou on the side? Obviously. But does a piece of steak with a side of asparagus look as cool as these steak-wrapped bundles? NOPE. Sometimes you just gotta hike up your fancypants and go the extra mile in the name of presentation, and on those days, I hope you'll consider some steak roll-ups. They'll serve two or three as a fancy meal with a side of Herb Potato Coins (page 245) or your favorite whole grain, but they also make quite the fetching first course at a dinner party.

Oh, and if you're wondering WTF pistou is, it's essentially nut-free pesto, and it's delightful. You will have a decent amount left over from this recipe, which you can use to sauce up everything from roasted vegetables and pasta to crab cakes (page 180).

1. Marinate the steak. In a large shallow baking dish, whisk the vinegar, ½ tablespoon of the oil, and the garlic. Briefly set aside.

2. Holding your knife parallel to the cutting board, slice each steak in half horizontally to create 2 thinner steaks. Using a meat mallet or the bottom of a heavy skillet, pound the steaks to ¼-inch thickness. (That's really thin, people.) Slice each pounded steak in half crosswise. At this point you should have 8 thin slices of steak. Add the steaks to the baking dish in an even layer, turning each one over to ensure it's coated in marinade. Marinate for 30 minutes at room temperature while you prep the pistou and asparagus.

3. Make the pistou. Place the arugula, basil, and garlic in the bowl of a food processor and pulse a few times, until coarsely chopped. Add the goat cheese, vinegar, and a few cranks of black pepper and process until the mixture is relatively smooth, scraping down the sides of the bowl once or twice if necessary. With the motor running, slowly pour in the oil and process until the pistou looks uniform. Taste and season with a little salt or extra pepper if needed. Transfer to a bowl, cover with plastic wrap, and briefly set aside.

4. Preheat the broiler to high. Line a large baking sheet with aluminum foil.

5. Place the asparagus on the prepared baking sheet. Drizzle with the remaining 1 tablespoon oil. Season with salt and black pepper and toss to coat. Broil the asparagus for about 4 minutes, until crisp-tender. (You don't want to overcook the asparagus here—it's going to keep cooking with the steak!)

6. Remove the steak from the marinade and season each piece on both sides with salt and black pepper.

7. Place 3 or 4 asparagus spears on each piece of steak and roll them up in the meat. Place the rolls on the same foil-lined baking sheet you used for the asparagus, seam side down. Broil for 4 to 5 minutes for meat that's just shy of medium.

8. Serve the rolls warm with plenty of pistou.

JUST THE TIP: To save time, you can buy a pound of thinly sliced steak from your grocery market or local butcher and skip pounding your own. It's usually labeled "sandwich steak" or "pepper steak."

Crispy Duck Breasts with Balsamic Cherry Sauce

FOR THE DUCK:

Two 6- to 8-ounce duck breasts, about 1 inch thick

Kosher salt to taste

FOR THE SAUCE:

2 tablespoons minced shallot

1 cup dark sweet cherries, halved and pitted

¼ cup full-bodied red wine, such as Cabernet Sauvignon (You can then drink the remainder of this wine with your duck.)

3 tablespoons balsamic vinegar

Tiny pinch of kosher salt

Freshly ground black pepper (optional)

Cooking duck might seem a little daunting, but a few simple tips and tricks make it a total breeze. First, scoring the skin and fat is key. It helps the fat render and the skin develop a glorious golden brown exterior. Second, starting the duck in a cold pan and cooking it low and slow allows plenty of time for the fat to render and the skin to crisp while keeping the meat tender and succulent. Last but not least, using a meat thermometer allows you to pull off perfectly cooked breasts with zero stress.

This recipe is an awesome date night meal with a side of roasted vegetables, arugula salad, or cauliflower puree, but if you're looking to dress it down or stretch the duck (which can be pricy) to serve more people, I highly recommend making the dankest of duck tacos. Warm some tortillas; add a little arugula, duck breast, and sweet-tart cherry pan sauce to each; and sprinkle with goat cheese. You won't regret it.

1. Start by scoring the duck breasts. Place the breasts on a cutting board skin side up. Run a sharp knife across the skin diagonally at ¼-inch intervals. (You want to cut *almost* through the layer of fat between the skin and flesh, being careful not to cut the flesh itself.) Turn the breast 90 degrees and slice in the opposite direction to create a crosshatch/diamond pattern. Season the duck on both sides with salt.

2. Place the breasts skin side down in a large skillet. (Do NOT preheat the skillet!) Place the pan over medium-low heat and cook for 14 to 15 minutes, until most of the fat has rendered, the skin is nicely browned, and the duck breasts have an internal temperature of 125°F. (After about 3 minutes of the cook time, the fat will start bubbling gently in the pan. You want to maintain this gentle bubbling throughout. If the fat isn't bubbling, increase the heat slightly, and if it's spitting, reduce the heat.) Flip the breasts and cook for about 2 minutes, until they reach an internal temperature of 130°F for medium-rare meat. Transfer the breasts to a cutting board and let rest for 10 minutes.

3. Meanwhile, pour off all but 2 teaspoons of fat from the skillet and return the pan to the stove over medium heat. (Feel free to save the fat in an airtight container in the refrigerator for future use.) Add the shallot and

cook for 30 seconds, or just until softened. Add the cherries and wine, scraping up any browned bits from the bottom of the pan, and cook for 3 minutes, or until the cherries are beginning to soften and the wine has reduced by about half. Add the vinegar, salt, and a few cranks of black pepper (if using) and cook for another 3 minutes, until the cherries are soft but still holding their shape and the sauce has a slightly syrupy consistency.

4. Cut the duck breasts crosswise into thin slices. Serve warm topped with the balsamic cherry sauce.

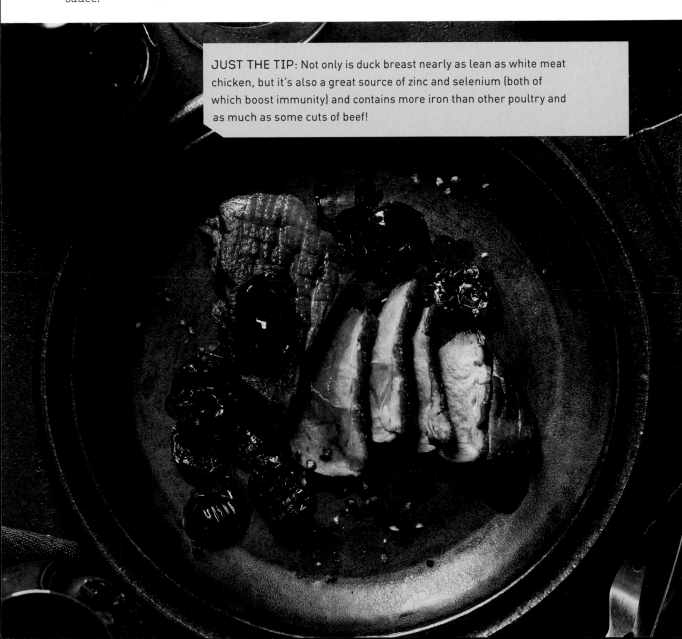

JUST THE TIP: Not only is duck breast nearly as lean as white meat chicken, but it's also a great source of zinc and selenium (both of which boost immunity) and contains more iron than other poultry and as much as some cuts of beef!

Seared Scallops and Couscous with Cucumber, Orange, and Pistachios

quick + DIRTY

SERVES 4

FOR THE SCALLOPS:

1½ pounds dry scallops (also called diver or day boat scallops)

Kosher salt to taste

Freshly ground black pepper to taste

1 tablespoon unsalted butter

1 tablespoon extra-virgin olive oil

FOR THE COUSCOUS:

1 cup water

2 tablespoons extra-virgin olive oil, divided

¾ teaspoon kosher salt, divided

1 cup whole-wheat couscous

⅓ cup shelled pistachios, roughly chopped

1 large orange (Blood orange or ruby red grapefruit is also great.)

½ English cucumber (aka seedless cucumber), halved lengthwise and

(continued)

This deceptively impressive meal is the epitome of fresh. Simply seasoned and quickly seared until they develop a beautiful golden crust, the scallops are poised to steal the show, but I'm here to tell you that the citrus-studded whole-wheat couscous gives them a run for their money. And since you can prep the couscous up to a full day in advance, and the scallops take roughly four minutes total to cook, this is an ideal recipe for relaxed entertaining. Open a bottle of chilled white wine and you're good to go.

One quick warning before you hit the kitchen. Your pan is going to smoke while you cook the scallops. It shouldn't be too scary, but if you have a sensitive smoke alarm, make sure you've got a vent fan on, windows open, or a sous chef to stand on a chair and fan the device while you sear. Forewarned is forearmed.

1. Prep the scallops. Pat the scallops dry and season on both sides with salt. Place them on a paper towel–lined plate and refrigerate while you prep the couscous.
2. Make the couscous. Combine the water, 1 tablespoon of the oil, and ½ teaspoon of the salt in a medium saucepan and bring to a boil. Remove from the heat and stir in the couscous. Cover the pan with a lid and let stand for 5 minutes, then fluff with a fork. Transfer the couscous to a medium bowl and let cool to room temperature.
3. Meanwhile, heat a medium skillet over medium heat. When the pan is hot, add the pistachios and cook for about 3 minutes, shaking the pan occasionally, until the nuts are toasted and fragrant. Add them to the bowl with the couscous.
4. Segment the orange. Using a sharp knife, carefully slice the top and bottom from the orange. Slice the peel and white pith from all around the fruit. (It doesn't need to be perfect!) Cut between the membranes to release the orange segments, then slice each segment crosswise into roughly ½-inch pieces.

very thinly sliced
crosswise

½ small red onion,
very thinly sliced

1 cup fresh flat-leaf
parsley leaves, finely
chopped, plus extra
as needed

Juice of 1 large lemon

Freshly ground black
pepper to taste

5. Add the orange, cucumber, red onion, parsley, lemon juice, the remaining 1 tablespoon oil, and the remaining ¼ teaspoon salt to the cooled couscous. Toss to combine and season with black pepper. Briefly set aside while you cook the scallops. (You also can cover the couscous with plastic wrap and refrigerate for up to 1 day.)

6. Time to cook the scallops! Gently pat the scallops dry with paper towels—yes, you need to pat them dry twice—and season on both sides with black pepper.

7. Heat your largest skillet (I like cast iron) over high heat. When hot, add ½ tablespoon each of the butter and oil. When the butter is melted and bubbling and the oil is smoking slightly, add half of the scallops to the skillet, leaving plenty of space around each one. Cook, undisturbed, for 2 minutes, or until golden brown on the underside. DO NOT MOVE THE SCALLOPS. Turn the scallops over (careful, the fat may spit a little!) and cook undisturbed on the opposite side for another 1 to 2 minutes, until golden brown. (If your scallops are particularly large, you may need to cook them for a minute or two longer.) Transfer the scallops to a paper towel–lined plate. Wipe out the skillet and return it to the heat. Add the remaining ½ tablespoon each of butter and oil to the skillet. Repeat the cooking process with the remaining scallops.

8. Divide the couscous among 4 plates or shallow bowls. Top with the scallops and garnish with a little extra parsley if you're feeling fancy.

JUST THE TIP: Make sure you purchase *dry* scallops for this recipe! Dry scallops are harvested directly from the sea. Off-white and translucent, they taste and smell like the ocean and develop a beautiful crust when seared. Wet scallops (also labeled "soaked" or "treated") are treated with a chemical brine to extend their shelf life, and they appear whiter, plumper, and glossier than their dry counterparts. They simply don't taste as good and are nearly impossible to brown because of the amount of water they release.

Farrotto "Carbonara"

When someone asks me what to cook for a new love interest, I immediately send along this dreamy one-pot recipe for two. And while I'm not saying that this carbonara-inspired farroto—aka risotto made with whole-grain farro instead of Arborio rice—will secure you lasting love and a lifetime of happiness . . . it might. (You can thank me later.) If for some crazy reason you don't eat the whole batch, reheat leftovers the next day in a small skillet with a splash of chicken broth.

p.s. *Farrotto* would be a lovely name for a Dude Diet offspring. Just saying.

1. Heat a medium Dutch oven or sauté pan over medium heat. When hot, add the bacon and cook for 6 to 8 minutes, until browned and crisp. Using a slotted spoon, transfer the bacon to a paper towel–lined plate.

2. Pour off all but about 1 tablespoon of the bacon grease from the skillet and return the pan to the heat. Add the onion and garlic and cook for 3 minutes, or until the onion is translucent and the garlic is fragrant. (Be careful not to burn the garlic! If it starts to brown, reduce the heat slightly.) Add the farro and cook for 2 minutes, stirring regularly to toast the grains. Add the wine and cook for 1 to 2 minutes, until the liquid has been completely absorbed, scraping up any delicious browned bits from the bottom of the pan. Add the chicken broth and bring to a boil over high heat. Reduce the heat until the liquid is gently simmering and cook for about 25 minutes, stirring periodically, until the farro is al dente (aka just tender). There should still be a good ½ cup or so of liquid in the pan.

3. Meanwhile, whisk the egg, cheese, a pinch of salt, and plenty of black pepper in a small bowl.

4. Add the peas to the pan and cook for about 2 minutes, until thawed, then stir in the bacon. Turn off the heat and stir in the egg mixture. Taste and season with a little extra salt and black pepper if needed.

5. Divide the farrotto between 2 bowls and serve immediately, garnished with the parsley.

4 slices thick-cut bacon (preferably with no added nitrates), diced

¼ cup minced yellow onion

2 garlic cloves, minced

¾ cup pearled or semi-pearled farro, rinsed

¼ cup dry white wine, such as Sauvignon Blanc

2½ cups low-sodium chicken broth

1 large egg

¼ cup freshly grated Parmesan cheese

Pinch of kosher salt

Freshly ground black pepper to taste

¾ cup frozen sweet peas

¼ cup fresh flat-leaf parsley leaves, chopped

Pork Chops with Shaved Brussels Sprout and Apple Slaw

SERVES 2

FOR THE PORK CHOPS:

Two 8-ounce bone-in center-cut pork chops, 1 inch thick

½ tablespoon extra-virgin olive oil

1 teaspoon pure maple syrup

½ teaspoon kosher salt

½ teaspoon dried thyme

¼ teaspoon freshly ground black pepper

FOR THE SLAW:

¼ cup raw walnuts, chopped

2 tablespoons Dijon mustard

1½ tablespoons apple cider vinegar

1½ teaspoons pure maple syrup

1 teaspoon extra-virgin olive oil

2 cups shaved Brussels sprouts

1 small Pink Lady apple, peeled, cored, and sliced into matchsticks

¼ cup golden raisins (optional)

Kosher salt to taste

Freshly ground black pepper to taste

When it comes to juicy pork chops, technique is key, and this is one of very few times I'll ask you to flip your meat often while it cooks. Turning the chops every minute or so until they hit an internal temp of 140 degrees helps them cook evenly and stay moist while slowly building a glorious golden-brown crust. I know hovering over the stovetop for ten minutes isn't ideal, but it's a small price to pay for perfect pork chops, so please suck it up. Round out the meal with a mountain of crunchy, mustardy slaw for a date-worthy dinner in thirty minutes flat.

1. Remove the pork chops from the fridge and let them rest on the counter while you prepare the slaw. You want them to be as close to room temperature as possible when you cook them.

2. Get going on the slaw! First, toast the walnuts. Heat a large skillet over medium heat. (Use the skillet you're planning to use for the pork.) When the pan is hot, add the walnuts. Cook for about 3 minutes, shaking the pan occasionally, until the nuts are toasted and fragrant. Transfer to a bowl to cool slightly.

3. In a medium bowl, whisk the mustard, vinegar, maple syrup, and oil. Add the Brussels sprouts, apple, raisins (if using), and toasted walnuts to the bowl and toss to combine. Taste and season with a little salt and black pepper if needed. Briefly set aside while you cook the pork.

4. Make the pork chops. Preheat a large skillet over medium-high heat until it's good and hot.

5. While the pan is heating, combine the oil and maple syrup in a small bowl. Pat the pork chops dry with paper towels, brush them with the oil mixture, and season all over with the salt, thyme, and black pepper.

6. Add the chops to the hot pan, leaving a little space between them, and sear for 1 minute, or until the underside is nicely browned. Flip the chops and cook for 1 minute on the opposite side. Flip the chops again and reduce the heat to medium. Continue cooking for 8 to 9 minutes, turning the chops every minute, until the pork registers 140°F on an instant-read thermometer. Transfer the chops to a cutting board and let rest for a full 5 minutes.

7. Serve the pork chops warm alongside or on top of the slaw.

Slow-Cooker Brisket with Carrots and Onions

SERVES 6

- 2½ pounds lean brisket
- 1 teaspoon kosher salt
- ¾ teaspoon freshly ground black pepper
- 2 teaspoons extra-virgin olive oil, divided
- 2 large yellow onions, thinly sliced
- 2 teaspoons smoked paprika
- 3 large garlic cloves, minced
- 1½ tablespoons tomato paste
- 1 cup low-sodium beef broth
- 2 tablespoons Dijon mustard
- 2 tablespoons pure maple syrup
- 1 tablespoon apple cider vinegar
- 2 teaspoons Worcestershire sauce
- 2 bunches rainbow carrots (about 2 pounds), peeled and sliced into 2-inch pieces
- 2 sprigs fresh rosemary
- Chopped fresh flat-leaf parsley or your favorite fresh herb for serving (optional)

This recipe is a long-overdue homage to Logan's all-consuming love for brisket (he was personally offended that I failed to include a recipe for it in the first cookbook), and it's become a cold-weather staple. In fact, anytime Logan comes home and sees the slow cooker on, he screams, "IS THE DANK BRISKET IN THERE?!" His enthusiasm for this super-tender beef warms my heart. Even when I'm not making the dank brisket.

1. Pat the brisket dry with paper towels and season on both sides with the salt and pepper.

2. Preheat a large skillet (I recommend cast iron for this) over medium-high heat. When the pan is good and hot, add 1 teaspoon of the oil, swirling to coat the bottom of the pan. Add the brisket and sear for about 6 minutes per side, until nicely browned. Transfer the beef to the slow cooker.

3. Return the skillet to the stovetop over medium heat. Add the remaining 1 teaspoon oil to the pan, then add the onions. Cook for 12 to 15 minutes, until the onions are soft and beginning to caramelize. Stir in the smoked paprika and garlic. Cook for 1 minute, then stir in the tomato paste and cook for 1 additional minute to mellow the acidity. Stir in the beef broth, mustard, maple syrup, vinegar, and Worcestershire sauce, using a spatula to loosen any browned bits from the bottom of the pan.

4. Pour the onion mixture over the brisket and nestle the carrots and rosemary around the beef. Cover and cook on low for 8 hours or until the meat is very tender.

5. Half an hour before the timer goes off, remove the brisket from the slow cooker and transfer it to a cutting board. Thinly slice the meat against the grain (aim for ¼-inch slices). Return the meat to the slow cooker, submerging it in the braising liquid and onions, and cook for 30 minutes more.

6. Serve the brisket with the onions, carrots, and plenty of braising liquid. Garnish with parsley, if you like.

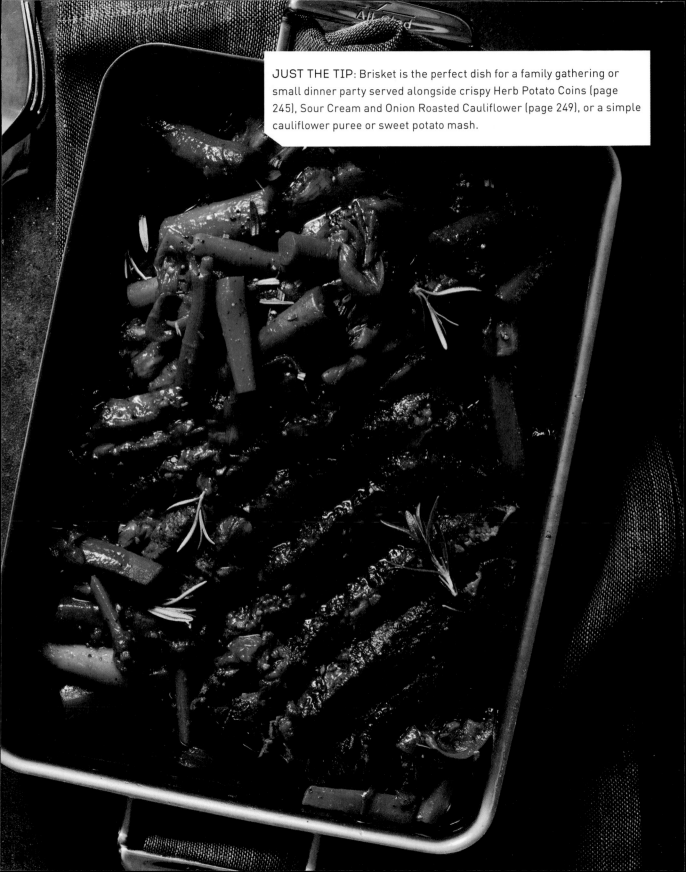

JUST THE TIP: Brisket is the perfect dish for a family gathering or small dinner party served alongside crispy Herb Potato Coins (page 245), Sour Cream and Onion Roasted Cauliflower (page 249), or a simple cauliflower puree or sweet potato mash.

Herb Turkey Breast with Cider Gravy

SERVES 4 to 6

FOR THE TURKEY:

4 garlic cloves, grated or finely minced

1½ tablespoons chopped fresh thyme leaves (or 1½ teaspoons dried thyme)

1 tablespoon finely chopped fresh rosemary leaves (or 1 teaspoon dried rosemary)

1½ teaspoons kosher salt

½ teaspoon freshly ground black pepper

2 tablespoons extra-virgin olive oil

1 boneless turkey breast half with skin on (2 to 2½ pounds)

1 small apple, peeled, cored, and diced small (I like Gala or Honeycrisp.)

1 cup low-sodium chicken broth

FOR THE GRAVY:

½ cup low-sodium chicken broth

½ cup apple cider

2 tablespoons all-purpose flour

(continued)

Turkey breast gets a bad rap for being bland and dry, but that's because it's often, and all too easily, overcooked. Roasting the herb-rubbed breast at a low temperature (300°F vs. 350°F/375°F) helps keep the meat nice and juicy and despite the "slow-cooking," it needs only about an hour and a half in the oven. Whip up the lip-smacking apple cider–spiked gravy while the meat rests, and brace yourself for the cozy flavor fireworks.

A 2½- to 3-pound boneless breast will comfortably serve four to six, so it's ideal for tinier T-Day dinners and Friendsgivings that don't require the fanfare of a whole bird centerpiece, as well as for year-round dinner parties. But don't limit this turkey to special occasion meals! It's definitely doable on a weeknight and happens to make an awesome meal prep option, as the meat can be added to sandwiches, salads, and casseroles throughout the week. Heads up, you'll need kitchen twine for this recipe.

1. Preheat the oven to 300°F.
2. Prep the turkey. In a small bowl, combine the garlic, thyme, rosemary, salt, pepper, and oil to form a thick paste. Gently loosen the skin on the turkey breast with your fingers. Rub the breast all over with the garlic and herb paste, including underneath the skin. Arrange the turkey breast neatly with your hands, tucking the edges under. You're aiming for your "roast" to be as cylindrical as possible. Tie the breast with a few loops of kitchen twine, making sure to tie it once lengthwise to help keep its compact shape.
3. Place the turkey skin side up in a small shallow roasting pan or large cast-iron skillet. Scatter the apple around the breast, then pour the chicken broth into the base of the pan. (You want the turkey to fit snugly in its roasting vessel here. If you use something too large, the liquid will evaporate and the apple will dry out, which is bad news for the gravy.)
4. Roast the turkey breast for 1 hour and 15 minutes to 1½ hours (depending on its size), until an instant-read thermometer inserted into the thickest part of the breast reads 160°F and the juices run mostly clear with a little pink, basting once at the 45-minute mark. (I just use a spoon to drizzle the pan juices over the breast. No need for a baster.) The internal

218   THE DUDE DIET DINNERTIME

1 teaspoon fresh
thyme leaves

Kosher salt to taste

Freshly ground
black pepper to
taste

temperature of the breast will continue to rise to about 165°F after you re-move it from the oven, so be very careful not to overcook it!

5. Turn the broiler to high. Place the turkey beneath the broiler for 1 to 2 minutes, until the skin is browned and crisp. Transfer the turkey breast to a cutting board. Tent it loosely with foil and let it rest for 15 minutes while you make the gravy.

6. Make the gravy. Transfer the liquid and apple from the roasting pan to a small saucepan and bring to a simmer over medium-low heat. Mean-while, whisk the chicken broth, cider, and flour in a small bowl. Add this mixture to the saucepan and cook for 3 to 5 minutes, whisking occasion-ally, until the gravy has thickened. Stir in the thyme. Season with salt and black pepper to taste.

7. Remove the strings from the turkey breast and slice crosswise into ¼-inch slices. Serve warm with the cider gravy.

JUST THE TIP: A boneless turkey breast half with skin on is NOT a "boneless turkey roast." The latter is typically a combination of brined light and dark meat, and it's not what you want for this recipe. If you can't find a boneless tur-key breast half, simply buy one with the bone in, and either ask your butcher to remove the breastbone or remove it yourself at home—it's pretty easy.

Grilled Chicken Paillard with Peach Caprese Relish

For the uninitiated, *paillard* is a fancy French word describing one of the simplest techniques for making tender, juicy chicken. Just place the chicken breasts between two pieces of plastic wrap, pound the shit out of them with the bottom of a skillet (or a meat mallet if you fancy like that), season with plenty of salt and pepper, and grill for a few minutes on each side. That's it.

You can do all manner of delicious things with your chicken paillard, but I'd make smothering it in a fresh and fruity caprese relish a priority come peach season. The recipe comes together in under thirty minutes, and the chicken can be served at room temperature, so you'll want to whip it up for all your summer shindigs. It's a crowd-pleaser.

1. Make the relish. Place the tomatoes, peach, cheese, basil, oil, vinegar, and pepper in a medium bowl and gently mix to combine. Season with salt. Cover and refrigerate while you grill the chicken.

2. Make the chicken. Preheat a lightly oiled grill (or grill pan) over medium-high heat.

3. One at a time, place each chicken breast between two pieces of plastic wrap. Using the bottom of a skillet, pound the chicken to a ¼-inch thickness. (Don't get too crazy here, you don't want to tear the meat!) Season the breasts very generously on both sides with salt and black pepper.

4. Place the chicken on the hot grill and cook for 3 to 4 minutes per side, until cooked through.

5. Serve the chicken warm or at room temperature, topped with relish.

> YOU DO YOU: If you don't like peaches, or can't get your hands on a good one, try subbing 1½ cups diced watermelon or using all tomatoes. You can also play with cheese here—goat and feta are both great options.

FOR THE RELISH:

- 1 dry pint cherry tomatoes, sliced into quarters
- 1 large yellow peach, pitted and diced
- 1 cup ciliegine fresh mozzarella cheese (mozzarella cheese balls), sliced into quarters
- ½ packed cup fresh basil leaves, stacked, rolled, and thinly sliced (aka chiffonade)
- 1½ tablespoons extra-virgin olive oil
- 1 tablespoon balsamic vinegar
- ¼ teaspoon freshly ground black pepper
- Kosher salt to taste

FOR THE CHICKEN:

- Four 8-ounce boneless, skinless chicken breasts
- Kosher salt to taste
- Freshly ground black pepper to taste

SEXY SIDES

Squash Casserole

1½ tablespoons unsalted butter

1 small yellow onion, finely chopped

2 pounds summer squash (about 4 medium squash), sliced into ½-inch-thick half-moons

½ teaspoon kosher salt

½ teaspoon freshly ground black pepper

3 tablespoons whole-wheat panko bread crumbs

¼ teaspoon garlic powder

1 cup full-fat plain Greek yogurt, at room temperature

¼ cup grated Pecorino Romano cheese

¼ cup finely chopped fresh chives, plus extra for serving

¼ cup grated sharp cheddar cheese

Dude Dieters, rejoice! By popular demand, I finally perfected a significantly healthier version of this celebrated Southern side. Ditching the dirty duo of mayo and sour cream, this bomb (and beautiful!) bake relies on moderate amounts of sharp cheeses and a little full-fat Greek yogurt to achieve its seemingly indulgent flavor profile, while seasoned whole-wheat panko provides a significantly less caloric crunch than the typical sleeve of Ritz crackers. I'm all about an aesthetically pleasing mix of zucchini and yellow squash for this, but feel free to go monochromatic if you like.

1. Heat the butter in a large ovenproof skillet over medium heat. When the butter is melted and foamy, add the onion and cook for about 4 minutes, until soft and translucent. Add the squash, salt, and pepper to the skillet. Cover the pan with a lid and cook for about 8 minutes, until lightly softened. Remove the lid and cook for another 6 minutes, or until the squash is very tender. Turn off the heat. (There shouldn't be much excess liquid in the pan at this point, but if there is, carefully pour it off.)

2. Meanwhile, preheat the broiler to high.

3. Combine the bread crumbs and garlic powder in a small bowl.

4. Add the yogurt, Pecorino Romano cheese, and chives to the pan with the squash and gently fold everything together until well combined. Gently smooth the top of the squash with a spatula. Sprinkle with the cheddar cheese and top with the bread crumb mixture.

5. Place the skillet under the broiler for 2 to 3 minutes, until the cheese is melted and bubbling and the bread crumbs are nicely browned. (Broilers are fickle, so keep a close eye on your casserole!) Serve warm, garnished with extra chives.

> JUST THE TIP: When you broil the bake, the Greek yogurt will curdle slightly and take on a ricotta cheese–like texture. It's a good thing, but I feel the need to point it out lest you think you did something wrong when you go to dig in.

Greens and Grains

1 cup pearled or semi-pearled farro, rinsed and drained

3 cups low-sodium chicken or vegetable broth (Water will also do.)

Juice of 1 lemon

Juice of 1 lime

1 tablespoon dark (aka toasted) sesame oil

2 teaspoons pure maple syrup

½ teaspoon kosher salt, plus extra as needed

2 cups baby arugula

1 cup shelled edamame

½ cup thinly sliced whole scallions

½ packed cup fresh cilantro leaves, roughly chopped

¼ cup fresh mint leaves, roughly chopped

1 small jalapeño, thinly sliced (Seed the pepper before slicing if you're sensitive to heat.)

⅓ cup chopped almonds or peanuts

Freshly ground black pepper (optional)

Logan is a big farro guy. I first introduced him to the nutrient-dense whole grain back in the Dude Diet's early days, and nobody was more surprised than me when he fell head over heels for the nutty grain's "boss chewiness." I've kept a stash of semi-pearled farro on hand ever since, and while I use it in everything from baked eggs to risotto (e.g., Farrotto "Carbonara"; page 213), it gets the most action in hearty grain salads. This particular recipe has converted many a whole-grain- and green-fearing dude thanks to its citrusy freshness (the combo of lemon and lime is key), crunch factor, and gentle kick. It's an awesome year-round side for almost any meat or fish and travels extremely well, so keep it in mind for potlucks, picnics, and BBQs.

1. Combine the farro and broth in a medium saucepan and bring to a boil. Lower to a simmer and cook for 15 to 30 minutes (depending on whether you use pearled or semi-pearled farro—see note below), until just tender. Drain the farro and let it cool to room temperature.

2. In a large bowl, whisk the lemon and lime juices, the oil, maple syrup, and salt. Add the cooled farro and toss to coat. Add the arugula, edamame, scallions, cilantro, mint, jalapeño, and nuts and toss again.

3. Taste and season with a little extra salt and pepper if needed. Serve at room temperature or chilled.

JUST THE TIP: Heads up, there are multiple varieties of farro. It can be whole/unpearled, semi-pearled, or pearled based on how much of the exterior bran and germ have been removed from the grain itself. Trickier still is the fact that some farro labeled "whole" is actually semi-pearled. The best way to distinguish between types of farro is simply to look at the cooking time stated on the package: 15 minutes or less = pearled, 30 minutes = semi-pearled, and 50+ = whole. Any variety will work in this recipe, but I assume you're busy and important, so I suggest going the pearled or semi-pearled route.

Grilled Corn, Asparagus, and White Bean Salad

When it comes to sexy summer sides, a protein- and fiber-packed salad is always an excellent choice, and this one featuring smoky grilled sweet corn, asparagus, and cannellini beans is poised to become a fan favorite. Its bright, clean flavors pair well with everything from burgers to grilled fish, and since said flavors only intensify after a day in the fridge, this recipe crushes as a make-ahead option for BBQs and picnics. Tarragon is responsible for the salad's unique flair, but if you don't dig the herb's somewhat strong, anise (aka licorice-like) taste, you can skip it or add a handful of chopped basil or flat-leaf parsley instead.

1. Preheat a lightly oiled grill (or grill pan) over medium-high heat.

2. In a small bowl, combine 2 tablespoons of the oil, the smoked paprika, and ½ teaspoon of the salt.

3. Brush the corn and asparagus all over with the oil mixture.

4. Place the corn and asparagus on the hot grill. (Feel free to use a grill basket for the asparagus!) Cook the asparagus for about 5 minutes, turning every 1 to 2 minutes, until crisp-tender and lightly charred in spots. Cook the corn for about 10 minutes, turning every 2 to 3 minutes, until tender and lightly charred in spots. Transfer the vegetables to a cutting board and let cool slightly. Slice the asparagus on the diagonal into 1-inch pieces, leaving the tips whole. Using a sharp knife, slice the corn kernels from the cob.

5. Place the asparagus and corn in a large bowl. Add the beans, shallot, chives, tarragon, lemon juice, and the remaining 1 tablespoon oil and ¼ teaspoon salt. Toss to combine. Season with black pepper and extra salt to taste. Serve warm, at room temperature, or chilled. (Dealer's choice!)

3 tablespoons extra-virgin olive oil, divided

1 teaspoon smoked paprika

¾ teaspoon kosher salt, divided, plus extra as needed

4 ears sweet corn, shucked

1 bunch medium-thick asparagus, woody ends removed

One 15-ounce can cannellini beans, drained and rinsed

1 medium shallot, minced

3 tablespoons finely chopped fresh chives

1 to 2 teaspoons finely chopped fresh tarragon leaves (Start small and add more to taste.)

Juice of 1 large lemon

Freshly ground black pepper to taste

Summery Pasta Salad

FOR THE PASTA SALAD:

¾ teaspoon kosher salt, plus extra for cooking the pasta

8 ounces whole-wheat fusilli or farfalle (I like Trader Joe's or Barilla.)

2 tablespoons extra-virgin olive oil, divided

2 medium zucchini, cut into roughly ¾-inch dice

1 red bell pepper, seeded and diced

¼ teaspoon crushed red pepper flakes

1½ cups sweet corn kernels (from 2 ears of corn)

⅓ packed cup fresh basil leaves, chopped

⅓ cup sun-dried tomatoes packed in olive oil, patted dry with paper towels and sliced into ribbons

4 ounces feta cheese, crumbled

FOR THE DRESSING:

2 tablespoons minced shallot

1 large garlic clove, grated or finely minced

1 teaspoon dried oregano

3 tablespoons red wine vinegar

1 tablespoon extra-virgin olive oil

¼ teaspoon kosher salt

We're flipping the script on pasta salad! Made with whole-wheat fusilli and the best of summer veggies tossed in a simple red wine vinaigrette, this is one satisfying summer side that won't bang up your beach bod. The party-ready recipe keeps fabulously in the fridge but tastes best at room temperature, so if you're whipping it up in advance, be sure to pull it out a good twenty minutes before serving.

1. Bring a large pot of salted water to a boil. Cook the pasta al dente according to the package directions. Drain and place in a large bowl. Drizzle with ½ tablespoon of the oil to prevent the pasta from sticking and let cool to room temperature.

2. Meanwhile, heat a large skillet over medium-high heat. (I like cast iron for this.) When hot, add the remaining 1½ tablespoons oil to the pan. Add the zucchini, bell pepper, ½ teaspoon of the salt, and the crushed red pepper. Cook for 5 to 6 minutes, stirring only occasionally—you want to allow some browning action, so resist the urge to stir constantly—until the vegetables are tender (not mushy!) and lightly browned in spots. Add the corn kernels to the pan and cook for about 2 minutes, just until bright yellow and tender. Transfer the veggies to a shallow bowl or a baking sheet and let cool to room temperature.

3. Combine the ingredients for the dressing in a small bowl.

4. Once the veggies have cooled, add them to the bowl with the pasta along with the basil and sun-dried tomatoes. Drizzle with the dressing and toss to combine. Gently fold in the cheese. Serve at room temperature.

YOU DO YOU: This pasta can also be served warm as a meal if that's more your style. (It will make enough for 3 large or 4 moderate entrée portions.) Without the cooling time, it falls into the Quick + Dirty dinner category.

Crispy Zucchini Fries

Needless to say, I didn't invent zucchini "fries," but I'm venturing boldly into the oversaturated veggie fry market because this addictively crunchy (and low-maintenance) version is an excellent addition to your Dude Diet dinner plate. The secret to truly crispy zucchini fries? A mix of cornmeal and whole-wheat panko bread crumbs. Trust.

These babies are simply seasoned—just a little salt, crushed red pepper, and garlic powder—for maximum versatility. You can serve them as is or dress them up with your favorite garnishes (fresh herbs, lemon, grated Pecorino Romano, etc.) and/or sauces. You'll also want to keep them in mind for game day snacking. Set them out with a few different dipping options, such as Creamy-Spicy Sauce (page 232), Lemon-Dill Sauce (page 177), Secret Sauce (page 101), or good old marinara, and watch the crowd go wild.

2 medium zucchini (roughly 8 inches long)

1 large egg

1 large egg white

½ cup whole-wheat panko bread crumbs

⅓ cup yellow cornmeal

1 teaspoon kosher salt

½ teaspoon garlic powder

¼ teaspoon crushed red pepper flakes

1. Preheat the oven to 400°F. Line a baking sheet with aluminum foil (or a silicone baking mat). Spray with cooking spray and briefly set aside.

2. Slice each zucchini in half crosswise, then slice each half lengthwise into three planks. Slice each plank lengthwise into roughly ½-inch "fries."

3. Beat the egg and egg white in a shallow bowl. In a separate shallow bowl, combine the panko, cornmeal, salt, garlic powder, and crushed red pepper.

4. Time to coat your fries! Set up a little assembly line with the sliced zucchini, egg, panko mix, and prepared baking sheet. Dip each piece of zucchini into the egg mix, shake off any excess, and lightly coat it in the panko mix. Place the breaded zucchini fries on the baking sheet, leaving a tiny bit of space around each one. Spray the fries with cooking spray.

5. Bake for 30 to 35 minutes, turning once at the 20-minute mark, until the zucchini is lightly browned and crispy on the outside and tender on the inside. Serve immediately.

Roasted Sweet Potatoes with Creamy-Spicy Sauce

FOR THE SWEET POTATOES:

- 2 large sweet potatoes (about 1 pound each), scrubbed, dried well, and cut into roughly 1½-inch cubes
- 1½ tablespoons extra-virgin olive oil
- ¼ teaspoon kosher salt

FOR THE SAUCE:

- ½ cup nonfat plain Greek yogurt
- 1 tablespoon fresh lime juice
- 2 teaspoons sriracha sauce
- 1 teaspoon low-sodium soy sauce
- 1 teaspoon honey
- 1 tablespoon water

FOR SERVING:

- ½ cup fresh cilantro leaves, finely chopped
- ¼ cup chopped peanuts

Plain old roasted sweet potatoes are delicious, nutritious, and idiotproof, but drizzling them with a fiery sriracha-lime yogurt sauce is a genius move that will give you a whole new appreciation for the caramelized spuds. Don't skimp on the cilantro and peanuts here—the added freshness and crunch are what really puts this drool-worthy side over the edge. Plus, cilantro is actually quite the superfood garnish. It's known to protect against oxidative stress, lower blood sugar levels and anxiety, and support digestion, so if you dig the taste, use it liberally in this dish and others to boost your overall health.

1. Preheat the oven to 425°F. Line a large baking sheet with parchment paper. (The paper may brown a little in the oven, but it won't burn, I promise.)

2. Arrange the sweet potatoes on the prepared baking sheet in an even layer. Drizzle with the oil, sprinkle with the salt, and toss to coat. (Try to leave a teeny bit of space between the sweet potatoes so they can brown and caramelize.) Roast for 20 minutes. Carefully flip the sweet potatoes and roast for about 15 minutes more, until lightly browned and tender.

3. Meanwhile, whisk all the ingredients for the creamy-spicy sauce in a medium bowl.

4. Transfer the sweet potatoes to a serving plate/platter. Drizzle the sauce generously on top. (I like to add about half of the sauce and pass the rest in a small bowl at the table.) Top with the cilantro and peanuts and serve immediately.

Damn Good Green Beans

SERVES 4

Green beans don't get a lot of love. Trust me, I get it. The two most common preparations for the humble green bean are (1) douse it in canned soup and top it with french-fried onions, or (2) boil it to death. The former doesn't do wonders for your health, and the latter doesn't exactly inspire vegetable eating morale.

But the truth is, green beans are incredibly versatile and shockingly delicious when given a little TLC. They're great sautéed, but in order to cook them just right, it's best to blanch them (aka boil them for a few minutes and then shock them in ice-cold water) beforehand. This isn't difficult, but when you're feeling lazy and don't want to dirty any dishes, I recommend popping the beans under the broiler. They get a little charred without completely losing their crisp, and tossing the beans with mustardy vinaigrette and plenty of chives really ups the flavor (and fancy) factor. Plus, the entire recipe takes ten minutes from start to finish, and employing a foil-lined baking sheet means minimal cleanup. Pretty damn good, if I do say so myself.

1. Preheat the broiler to high.

2. Place the green beans on a large rimmed baking sheet. Drizzle with 2 teaspoons of the oil and season with the salt and few cranks of black pepper. Toss to coat.

3. Broil for 7 to 8 minutes, until tender (but not mushy!) and lightly charred in spots.

4. Meanwhile, whisk the remaining 1 tablespoon oil, 1 tablespoon of the chives, the mustard, vinegar, and honey in a large bowl.

5. Add the green beans to the bowl with the dressing and toss to combine.

6. Serve the green beans warm or at room temperature topped with the remaining 1 tablespoon chives.

---

1 pound green beans, washed well, ends trimmed

1 tablespoon plus 2 teaspoons extra-virgin olive oil, divided

Pinch of kosher salt

Freshly ground black pepper to taste

2 tablespoons finely chopped fresh chives, divided

1½ tablespoons whole-grain mustard

1 tablespoon plus 1 teaspoon red wine vinegar

¼ teaspoon honey

"Pad Thai" Quinoa

¾ cup quinoa, rinsed and drained

1 cup water

Juice of 1 lime, divided

3 tablespoons low-sodium soy sauce (or tamari)

1 tablespoon honey

1 teaspoon Thai fish sauce

½ teaspoon crushed red pepper flakes

1 tablespoon extra-virgin coconut oil

1½ cups very finely chopped broccoli florets (Think "broccoli rice.")

1 large red bell pepper, seeded and cut into small dice

1 cup grated carrots

3 whole scallions, finely chopped

2 garlic cloves, minced

2 large eggs

FOR SERVING:

½ cup fresh cilantro leaves

⅓ cup chopped cashews or peanuts

Lime wedges

At this point, you're probably familiar with my feelings on the awesome health benefits of quinoa, so I'll spare you another fetishist rant on its superfood magic and focus instead on the top-notch pad Thai–inspired flavors in this epic whole-grain side. Studded with a rainbow-colored assortment of fresh veggies, this savory stir-fried quinoa tastes super fresh and just a little bit funky thanks to a splash of fish sauce (which you can find in the Asian section of your supermarket). It pairs perfectly with marinated or simply grilled meats and fish, but that's not to say you can't crush it as a meal when you're in the mood for something light.

1. Combine the quinoa, water, and the juice of ½ lime in a small saucepan and bring to a boil. Lower to a simmer, cover the saucepan with a lid, and cook for 14 minutes, or until all of the liquid has been absorbed. Let the quinoa rest, covered, for 5 minutes, then fluff with a fork.

2. In a small bowl, combine the juice of the remaining ½ lime, the soy sauce, honey, fish sauce, and crushed red pepper. Place this mixture by the stove.

3. Heat the oil in your largest nonstick pan over medium-high heat. When the oil is hot and shimmering, add the broccoli, bell pepper, carrots, scallions, and garlic and cook for 4 to 5 minutes, just until tender. Push the veggies to one half of the pan. Crack the eggs into the empty half of the pan and scramble with a spatula until set. (This should take a minute or two, tops!) Mix the eggs into the vegetables.

4. Add the cooked quinoa and the soy sauce mixture to the pan, folding everything together with a spatula. Cook for about 1 minute, until piping hot.

5. Transfer the quinoa to a serving bowl and top with the cilantro and nuts. Serve with lime wedges.

Kickass Carrots

SERVES 4

On top of their signature sweetness and versatility, carrots are celebrated for their high antioxidant content, particularly beta-carotene, which offers a laundry list of health benefits. Long story short, you should eat more carrots, and this recipe is the most kickass way to do it.

Roasting carrots at high heat transforms the vegetable, caramelizing the exterior and softening the interior to the point where it actually melts in your mouth. And while roasted carrots are addictive on their own, I urge you to embrace a "more is more" mentality here and shower them with garlicky toasted walnuts, plenty of fresh parsley, creamy feta, and a squeeze of fresh lemon juice for extra zip. Rainbow carrots make this side look particularly sexy, but standard orange will serve you just as well.

1. Preheat the oven to 450°F. Line a large baking sheet with parchment paper (it will brown in the oven, but I promise it won't burn).
2. Arrange the carrots in an even layer and drizzle with 1½ tablespoons of the oil. Sprinkle with the smoked paprika, salt, and pepper and toss to coat. Roast for about 30 minutes, shaking the pan every 10 minutes, until tender and lightly charred in spots.
3. While the carrots are roasting, heat the remaining ½ tablespoon oil in a small skillet over medium heat. When the oil is hot and shimmering, add the walnuts, garlic, and a small pinch of salt and cook for about 5 minutes, until the nuts have darkened slightly in color and the garlic is fragrant. (Be very careful not to burn yo' garlicky nuts! If they start to brown, turn down the heat immediately.) Transfer the nuts to a bowl and briefly set aside.
4. Transfer the carrots to a serving plate. (You also can garnish them directly on the baking sheet if you're doing a more casual thing.) Top with the garlicky walnuts, parsley, and cheese. Drizzle the whole shebang with lemon juice and serve warm or at room temperature.

2 bunches medium rainbow carrots (about 16 carrots), tops removed, scrubbed clean (No need to peel them!)

2 tablespoons extra-virgin olive oil, divided

½ teaspoon smoked paprika

¼ teaspoon plus a small pinch of kosher salt

¼ teaspoon freshly ground black pepper

½ cup finely chopped walnuts

3 garlic cloves, minced

½ cup fresh flat-leaf parsley leaves, chopped

½ cup crumbled feta cheese

Juice of ½ lemon

Boss Brussels Sprout Salad

1½ pounds Brussels sprouts, washed well, stems and any ugly outer leaves removed, divided

2½ tablespoons extra-virgin olive oil, divided

¼ teaspoon kosher salt, plus extra as needed

¼ teaspoon freshly ground black pepper, plus extra as needed

One 4-ounce chunk pancetta, cut into small dice (Thick-cut bacon will also do.)

2 tablespoons balsamic vinegar

2 teaspoons Dijon mustard

1 teaspoon pure maple syrup

1 garlic clove, grated or finely minced

Brussels sprouts have enjoyed quite the renaissance in recent years. They're the MVPs of almost every restaurant's side dish menu, and endless recipes have flooded the Interwebs, magazines, and cookbooks alike. On the one hand, increased consumption of the cruciferous veggie is great news—Brussels are wildly nutritious. On the other hand, they're not always handled in the healthiest of ways, and the amount of fat and sugar used to cook the tiny cabbages often negates the aforementioned health benefits. Sad, but true.

With that said, I'd never suggest you go back to boiling your sprouts. That's how they got a bad rap in the first place. Instead, try this boss, and nutritionally balanced, recipe starring a combo of roasted and raw sprouts tossed with a reasonable amount of crispy pancetta and tangy, maple-sweetened balsamic vinaigrette.

1. Preheat the oven to 425°F. Line a large rimmed baking sheet with aluminum foil or parchment paper.

2. Slice 1 pound of the Brussels sprouts in half lengthwise (if any of the sprouts are particularly huge, slice them into quarters) and place them in a large bowl. Drizzle with 1½ tablespoons of the oil, sprinkle with the salt and pepper, and toss to coat. Transfer to the prepared baking sheet and roast, stirring at the 10- and 20-minute marks, until tender and caramelized, about 25 minutes.

3. Meanwhile, slice the remaining ½ pound of Brussels sprouts in half lengthwise, then slice them very thinly crosswise. Briefly set aside.

4. Heat a small skillet over medium heat. When hot, add the pancetta and cook until lightly browned and crispy, about 5 minutes. Transfer the pancetta along with any grease from the pan to a large bowl. Add the remaining 1 tablespoon oil, the vinegar, mustard, maple syrup, and garlic to the bowl and whisk to combine.

5. Add the roasted and raw Brussels sprouts to the bowl with the dressing and toss to combine. Taste and season with a little extra salt and pepper if needed. Serve warm or at room temperature.

YOU DO YOU: While this is both a great everyday and holiday side, you may also dig it as a sandwich or quesadilla filling
or served with an egg on top as a breakfast bowl.

Wild Rice with Roasted Butternut Squash, Walnuts, and Cranberries

1 cup wild rice

1 medium butternut
squash, peeled,
seeded, and cut into
1-inch cubes (about
6 cups cubed squash)

2½ tablespoons extra-
virgin olive oil

½ teaspoon ground
cinnamon

½ teaspoon kosher
salt, plus extra as
needed

¼ teaspoon cayenne
pepper (optional)

2 tablespoons fresh
lemon juice

2 teaspoons low-
sodium soy sauce

2 teaspoons pure
maple syrup

½ cup coarsely
chopped walnuts

⅓ cup dried
cranberries

3 whole scallions,
thinly sliced

Freshly ground black
pepper to taste

Need a healthy holiday side? Looking to jazz up a basic piece of meat or fish? In the market for a sassy Dude Diet desk lunch? You came to the right place, you smart, sexy beast. I'm very excited to introduce you to your new cool-weather go-to. Whether served alongside Thanksgiving turkey or eaten as a plant-based midday meal, this crowd-pleasing recipe crushes the seasonal competition when it comes to both flavor and keeping the "winter layer" at bay.

1. Cook the wild rice according to the package directions.

2. Preheat the oven to 425°F. Line a baking sheet with aluminum foil or parchment paper.

3. Place the butternut squash cubes in a large bowl. Drizzle with 1½ tablespoons of the oil and sprinkle with the cinnamon, salt, and cayenne pepper (if using). Toss to combine, making sure each cube is coated. Transfer the squash to the prepared baking sheet, leaving a little space around each cube.

4. Roast the squash for 25 to 30 minutes, turning once halfway through the cooking time, until it is tender but not too soft (you don't want it to fall apart when mixing it with the other ingredients) and lightly browned. Set aside and let cool slightly.

5. In a large bowl, whisk the remaining 1 tablespoon oil, the lemon juice, soy sauce, and maple syrup. Add the cooked wild rice to the bowl with the dressing and toss to combine. Add the roasted butternut squash, walnuts, cranberries, and scallions and gently fold all the ingredients together. Taste and season with black pepper and a little extra salt (if needed). Serve warm or at room temperature.

242 THE DUDE DIET DINNERTIME

Broccoli-Cheddar Mashed Potatoes

1½ pounds baby red potatoes, scrubbed and sliced in half (If you have any particularly large potatoes, slice them into quarters.)

2 cups finely chopped broccoli florets

½ cup nonfat buttermilk (See homemade buttermilk tip in the sidebar on page 100.)

½ ripe avocado, pitted, peeled, and mashed until very smooth

¼ teaspoon garlic powder

¾ cup extra-sharp cheddar cheese

Kosher salt to taste

Freshly ground black pepper to taste

Here's the deal with potatoes, people. Spuds themselves aren't inherently bad for you. In fact, they have some pretty impressive health benefits. Potatoes are high in vitamin C, vitamin B_6, and iron, and a medium potato actually packs more potassium than a banana. (FYI, potassium helps regulate blood sugar and blood pressure, improves bone health, and can even reduce stress and anxiety. You could probably use some.) The problem is that most potatoes are consumed in french fry form or smothered in less healthy accoutrements like butter, sour cream, and cheese. Mashed potatoes are particularly dangerous, as most recipes call for a truly terrifying amount of butter and cream to achieve their luscious flavor and texture. Not on my watch.

These taters get their crave-worthy creaminess from mashed avocado and nonfat buttermilk, and the beloved childhood combo of broccoli and cheddar provides a tasty and nutritious boost. As one enthusiastic tester noted, "Holy shit! These taste like broccoli-cheddar soup and mashed potatoes had a beautiful baby!" I concur.

1. Put the potatoes in a medium Dutch oven or saucepan and add enough cold water to cover by at least 2 inches. Bring to a rolling boil over high heat. Once boiling, reduce the heat slightly so that the water is gently boiling and cook for about 20 minutes, until the potatoes can be easily pierced with the tip of a sharp knife. Add the broccoli and cook for 5 minutes more, or until the florets are bright green and very tender.

2. Meanwhile, heat the buttermilk in a small saucepan over low heat just until warm, about 2 minutes. (Do not let it boil!)

3. Drain the potatoes and broccoli and return them to the Dutch oven over low heat. Cook for 1 minute, stirring to help any excess water evaporate. (The potatoes will start to break down, and that's fine.)

4. Turn off the heat and add the buttermilk, mashed avocado, and garlic powder. Mash everything together with a potato masher (or a large fork if that's all you have) until well combined and relatively smooth. Fold in the cheese and season generously with salt and black pepper. Serve warm.

Herb Potato Coins

This one goes out to the crispy-potato lovers. So . . . everyone? These potatoes fall somewhere between roasted potatoes and potato chips, boasting the best qualities of both; think a little bit of fluffy potato interior encased in an herby, golden brown shell with just the right amount of crunch. Equally at home alongside scrambled eggs as they are as part of a holiday spread, potato coins are the ultimate go-with-anything side, and you'll want to cash in on their deliciousness as often as possible.

1. Preheat the oven to 400°F. Spray a large baking sheet with cooking spray.
2. Scrub the potatoes and slice them into thin coins roughly ⅛ inch thick. If you have a mandoline, you'll want to use it. (Carefully! Mandolines are sharp, and I want you to keep all your digits.)
3. Place the potatoes in a large bowl. Add the oil, rosemary, thyme, salt, and garlic powder and season with black pepper. Toss well, making sure all the potatoes are coated with oil and spices.
4. Spread the potatoes on the prepared baking sheet in an even layer. (If your potatoes are overlapping, divide them between 2 baking sheets so that they crisp instead of steam.) Roast for 35 to 40 minutes, stirring every 10 minutes, until the potatoes are tender, golden brown, and lightly crisped.
5. Sprinkle the parsley over the potatoes and stir to combine. Serve warm.

1½ pounds baby potatoes (red or white)

2 tablespoons extra-virgin olive oil

1 teaspoon dried rosemary

1 teaspoon dried thyme

¾ teaspoon kosher salt

½ teaspoon garlic powder

Freshly ground black pepper to taste

2 tablespoons finely chopped fresh flat-leaf parsley leaves

Crowd-Pleasing Kale Salad

quick + DIRTY

SERVES 4

FOR THE DRESSING:

1 large garlic clove, grated or finely minced

1 small shallot, minced

Juice of 1 lemon

2 tablespoons extra-virgin olive oil

1 teaspoon pure maple syrup

Kosher salt to taste

Freshly ground black pepper to taste

FOR THE SALAD:

1 bunch lacinato kale, center ribs removed, leaves finely chopped

¼ cup sliced almonds

1 cup cooked quinoa

¼ cup dried cranberries

2 tablespoons grated or shaved Parmesan cheese

Unless you live under a rock, you know that kale is good for you. It's loaded with calcium, fiber, and mass quantities of vitamins A, C, and K, as well as a boatload of essential minerals. It fights cancer. It helps prevent heart disease and promotes detoxification and brain health. I could go on, but you get the point. As far as superfoods go, kale is the GOAT.

If you've already embraced kale as your personal salad savior, awesome. You'll dig the killer textures in this hearty recipe and appreciate the perfectly balanced lemon dressing. And if you hate kale, I'm Kanye-level confident this salad will be the one that helps you see the leafy green light. It's incredibly versatile as a side salad, but it also makes two large entrée-size salads that you can top with Idiotproof Chicken Breasts (page 136), sliced steak, or your favorite fish. . . .

1. Combine all the ingredients for the dressing in a large bowl and set aside while you prep the kale. (This will soften the shallots and allow the flavors to get friendly.)

2. Add the chopped kale to the bowl with the dressing. Massage the kale in handfuls—literally rub the leaves between your fingers—for a minute or two, until the leaves soften and darken in color. (Yes, I know giving your salad a rubdown is a little weird, but it's worth it. DO NOT SKIP THIS STEP.) Briefly set aside.

3. Toast the almonds. Heat a small skillet over medium heat. (Do not put any oil in the pan!) When hot, add the almonds to the pan and cook for 2 to 3 minutes, shaking the pan regularly, until golden brown and fragrant. Immediately transfer to a small bowl.

4. Add the quinoa, along with half of the almonds and half of the cranberries, to the kale and toss to combine.

5. Transfer your salad to a serving platter or plates, top with the remaining almonds and cranberries, and sprinkle with the cheese.

YOU DO YOU: This recipe is meant to be a road map for creating your perfect kale salad, so play with your favorite nuts, dried fruits, cheeses, and whole grains. You can also try curly kale, although it tastes slightly more grassy than lacinato.

Sour Cream & Onion Roasted Cauliflower

I'm guessing it has something to do with the crazy-delicious sour cream sauce, but this roasted cauliflower with caramelized red onion and chives was the sleeper hit among the Dude Diet recipe-testing squad. Everyone from Logan to five-year-old children felt comically passionate about this crucifer-ous, cancer-fighting side, and I'm now moderately concerned that I have mis-judged Buffalo as the Dude Diet's flavor mascot all these years when it's truly Sour Cream and Onion.

A standout choice alongside everything from California Burgers (page 16) to Herb Turkey Breast (page 218), this cauliflower can be your sexy side for all seasons. Double the recipe for holiday gatherings, and keep it in mind as a healthier alternative to potato salad when it comes time for summer cookouts.

1. Preheat the oven to 425°F. Line a large baking sheet with parchment paper.

2. Add the cauliflower florets and onion to the prepared baking sheet. Drizzle with olive oil, season with kosher salt and a few cranks of freshly ground black pepper, and toss to coat.

3. Roast for 25 to 30 minutes, stirring once halfway through the cook-ing time, or until the cauliflower is tender (but not mushy!) and lightly browned in spots and the onion has softened.

4. Meanwhile, combine the sour cream, garlic, vinegar, mustard, chives, and a few cranks of black pepper in a medium mixing bowl.

5. Add the roasted cauliflower and onion to the mixing bowl and toss to coat with the sour cream mixture. Serve warm or at room temperature, sprinkled with extra chives.

---

1 medium head of cauliflower, cored and broken into florets (about 6 heaping cups florets)

1 small red onion, cut into ½-inch slices

1½ tablespoons extra-virgin olive oil

½ teaspoon kosher salt, plus extra to taste

Freshly ground black pepper to taste

¼ cup sour cream

1 garlic clove, grated or finely minced

1 tablespoon distilled white vinegar (Apple cider vinegar works too.)

1 tablespoon grainy mustard

2 tablespoons finely chopped fresh chives, plus extra for serving

---

YOU DO YOU: A little bit of full-fat sour cream goes a long way in this recipe, but you can always sub Greek yogurt if you're looking to lighten things up even further. And feel free to try this recipe with broccoli if you prefer, but note that the florets will cook in about 15 to 20 minutes.

CHAPTER

11

BREAKFAST FOR DINNER

Elvis Panini

4 slices turkey bacon

1 tablespoon extra-virgin coconut oil in liquid form, divided

2 small ripe but firm bananas, sliced into ½-inch rounds

½ teaspoon ground cinnamon

4 slices whole-grain sandwich bread

¼ cup plus 2 tablespoons peanut butter (crunchy or smooth, your choice)

YOU DO YOU:
If you're short on time and/or dig a softer sandwich, feel free to skip the final cooking step. You could also just assemble the sandwiches on toasted bread if you prefer.

Not gonna lie, the King was clearly on to something with his signature sandwich. With that said, buttered white bread loaded with half a jar of peanut butter, a slab of pork bacon, and bananas will likely leave you feeling like . . . Elvis (the '70s version).

Because I firmly believe in treating yourself to the sweet-savory-nutty thrill of this unexpected culinary masterpiece on occasion, I took the liberty of re-creating it with a few tweaks. Whole-grain bread helps get a handle on the refined carb content, while ditching the half stick of butter and swapping pork for turkey bacon cut a significant amount of calories and fat. Don't worry, I guarantee this portion-controlled panini will still have you all shook up. (Had to.)

1. Heat a large nonstick skillet over medium heat. When hot, add the turkey bacon and cook for 4 to 5 minutes per side, until browned and crisp. Let cool slightly, then chop into small pieces.

2. Wipe out the skillet and return it to the stovetop over medium-high heat. Add 1 teaspoon of the oil and swirl to coat the bottom of the pan. When the oil is hot and shimmering, add the bananas and cinnamon and cook for 1½ to 2 minutes, shaking the pan occasionally, until the bananas are softened and slightly caramelized. Transfer to a small plate.

3. Sandwich assembly time! Spread one side of each slice of bread with peanut butter. (If your peanut butter is very thick, microwave it in a small bowl for 10 to 15 seconds.) Sprinkle 2 slices of bread with the chopped bacon and top with the caramelized banana. Close the sandwiches with the remaining 2 slices of bread. Lightly brush the outside of each sandwich with the remaining 2 teaspoons coconut oil.

4. Wipe out the skillet a second time and return it to the stovetop over medium heat. When hot, add the sandwiches to the pan and place a sandwich press (or another skillet) on top of them to weigh them down. Cook for about 3 minutes per side, until they are golden brown and crisp on both sides.

5. Slice each sandwich in half and serve warm.

Skillet Eggs with Roasted Cauliflower and Pepperoncini

When it comes to easy and convenient anytime meals, skillet eggs are a home run. They're made with basic ingredients, require minimal prep, and if you eat them straight out of the skillet (no judgment), you have to clean only a single dish. Once you nail the simple technique, skillet eggs become the ultimate "choose your own adventure" meal in terms of sauces and mix-ins, but this marinara-based combo of roasted cauliflower, tangy pepperoncini, and salty feta is a foolproof starting point.

The recipe makes a badass healthy meal for two, but the quantities can easily be halved to serve one or doubled to serve four. Just adjust skillet size accordingly. (Duh.) I highly recommend getting a big green side salad involved, but some crusty whole-grain bread also is acceptable. The latter is sometimes necessary to sop up the liquid gold #yolkporn remains.

1. Preheat the oven to 450°F.
2. Place the cauliflower florets in a 10-inch ovenproof skillet. Drizzle with the oil and season with a pinch of salt and a little black pepper. Toss to coat. Transfer the skillet to the oven and roast the cauliflower for 20 minutes, until tender and lightly browned.
3. Carefully remove the skillet from the oven (it will be scary hot!!) and place it on the stovetop over medium-low heat. Add the marinara sauce and pepperoncini to the skillet and bring to a gentle simmer.
4. Once simmering, make 4 wells in the sauce with a spatula and crack an egg into each of the wells. Sprinkle the cheese over everything. Cook for 8 to 10 minutes, until the egg whites are just set but the yolks are still runny. If your whites are having trouble setting, pop a lid onto the pan to help them along.
5. Sprinkle the skillet with some parsley or chives if you've got them and serve immediately.

2 cups cauliflower florets

2 teaspoons extra-virgin olive oil

Pinch of kosher salt

Freshly ground black pepper to taste

1½ cups marinara sauce (See "Just the Tip.")

3 tablespoons chopped pepperoncini (Cherry peppers or pickled jalapeños are also great.)

4 large eggs

¼ cup crumbled feta cheese

Chopped fresh flat-leaf parsley or chives for serving (optional)

> JUST THE TIP: The marinara sauce matters, so please use a good one with minimal added sugar! I recommend Rao's brand or the marinara on page 20 if you're going the homemade route.

BEC Frittata

4 slices turkey bacon

6 large eggs

1 tablespoon plus 1 teaspoon everything bagel spice/seasoning, divided (Trader Joe's makes a great one.)

1 teaspoon extra-virgin olive oil

1 cup cherry tomatoes, halved crosswise

⅓ cup grated sharp cheddar cheese

2 whole scallions, thinly sliced

Hot sauce for serving (optional)

*B*acon. Egg. And. Cheese.

Say these four simple words in that specific order to any dude and you're 99 percent guaranteed a Pavlovian response of puppy-like excitement (and occasional drooling). I worried said excitement could only be sustained by the traditional gut-busting breakfast sandwich, but after some field experiments, I concluded it's apparently linked to any dish containing the three key ingredients, including a feel-good frittata. Made with turkey bacon, sharp cheddar, cherry tomatoes, and a sprinkling of everything bagel seasoning, this twenty-minute meal is a responsible go-to when a BEC craving strikes.

1. Heat a large skillet over medium heat. When hot, add the turkey bacon and cook for 4 to 5 minutes per side, until browned and crisp. Transfer the bacon to a paper towel–lined plate and let cool slightly. Chop into small pieces.

2. In a medium bowl, whisk the eggs and 1 tablespoon of the everything bagel spice.

3. Preheat the broiler to high.

4. Heat the oil in a 10-inch nonstick ovenproof skillet over medium heat. When the oil is hot and shimmering, add the tomatoes and turkey bacon to the pan. Give them a little toss, then pour in the eggs and cook for about 3 minutes, until the eggs are beginning to set. Sprinkle with the cheese and cook for another 2 minutes or so, until your frittata is almost set but the top is still a little runny.

5. Place the skillet under the broiler. Broil for about 2 minutes, until the cheese has melted and the top of the frittata is puffed up and very lightly browned. (Keep a close eye on it!)

6. Loosen the frittata from the pan with a spatula and slide it onto a cutting board. Sprinkle with the remaining 1 teaspoon everything bagel spice. Slice the frittata in half (or into quarters), transfer to 2 plates, and garnish with the scallions and your favorite hot sauce if you're feeling spicy.

BBQ Sweet Potato Hash with Chicken Sausage

SERVES 4

When it comes to brinner, nothing hits the spot quite like a fully loaded hash. Sadly, most hashes are heavy on fat and light on nutrients, but this sheet pan version breaks the moob-inducing mold. Each satisfying serving provides plenty of lean protein, fiber, and essential vitamins and minerals, and the entire recipe calls for only a single tablespoon of heart-healthy olive oil. This hash serves four hungry humans as written, but you could easily stretch it to serve six by adding a couple of extra eggs. And as great as it is for a weeknight dinner, it absolutely slays the weekend brunch game, especially when you're feeling a little the worse for wear.

1. Preheat the oven to 425°F. Line a large rimmed baking sheet with aluminum foil and spray it with cooking spray.
2. Place the sweet potatoes, bell peppers, onion, and corn on the prepared baking sheet. Drizzle with the oil; sprinkle with the paprika, chipotle chile powder, salt, and pepper; and toss to coat. Add the sausage and toss again. Spread everything out in an even layer on the baking sheet.
3. Transfer the baking sheet to the oven and cook for 25 minutes, stirring once halfway through the cooking time, until the sweet potatoes are tender.
4. Using a spatula or a spoon, create 4 small holes in the hash. Crack the eggs into the holes. Return the hash to the oven and cook for 6 to 7 minutes, until the whites have set but the yolks are still runny. (Keep a close eye on the eggs—they go from perfect to overcooked *fast*!)
5. Drizzle the whole shebang with barbecue sauce and sprinkle with the scallions. Serve immediately.

> YOU DO YOU: Chipotle chile powder gives this sweet and savory hash a serious kick, but if you're sensitive to spice or don't have it on hand, chili powder (the spice mix) will do you right.

2 medium sweet potatoes, peeled and cut into ½-inch cubes

2 bell peppers (I prefer red and yellow), seeded and diced

1 medium red onion, diced

1 cup sweet corn kernels (from 1 ear of corn)

1 tablespoon extra-virgin olive oil

2 teaspoons smoked paprika

1½ teaspoons chipotle chile powder

¾ teaspoon kosher salt

¼ teaspoon freshly ground black pepper

12 ounces fully cooked chicken sausage links (4 to 5 links), sliced in half lengthwise, then sliced crosswise into ½-inch pieces

4 large eggs

¼ cup barbecue sauce

2 whole scallions, thinly sliced

"Green Eggs and Ham" Avocado Toast

MAKES 2 TOASTS

All I have to say to those who think avocado toast is basic is . . . *bitch, please.* Sliced avocado on bread is one thing, but this nutritious toast piled high with prosciutto and herbed scrambled eggs exists on a higher plane. I'd go so far as to call it "decadent." Or "dank." (Depends on who I'm talking to.) The recipe makes two toasts, which will serve two moderately hungry humans with a side of vegetables or salad, but if you're starving, it's acceptable to double down and crush them both yourself.

1. Crack the eggs into a medium bowl. Add the crushed red pepper and a tiny pinch of salt and whisk vigorously until pale yellow and slightly frothy. (The prosciutto is salty, so be careful not to add too much salt to the eggs!) Add the basil and chives and whisk once or twice to combine.
2. Go ahead and toast your bread.
3. While the bread is toasting, heat the oil in a medium nonstick skillet over medium heat. (True nonstick is key here, people.) When the oil is hot and shimmering, add the spinach and cook for 1 to 2 minutes, just until wilted. Reduce the heat to medium-low and add the egg mixture. Cook, stirring in big sweeping motions to form large curds, until the eggs are just set. This will take 1 to 2 minutes max, so please have your plates handy.
4. Rub the top of each piece of toast with the cut side of the garlic halves. Add half of the sliced avocado to each piece of toast and sprinkle with a little salt and pepper. Top with the prosciutto and eggs and serve immediately.

> **YOU DO YOU:** There is much debate surrounding slicing versus mashing the avocado for this toast. Sliced avocado is more visually appealing, while mashed is easier to eat. Do what feels right.

Ingredients

2 large eggs

¼ teaspoon crushed red pepper flakes

Tiny pinch of kosher salt

4 fresh basil leaves, finely chopped

1 tablespoon finely chopped fresh chives

2 large slices whole-grain bread (I love a whole-grain sourdough or seeded loaf for this.)

1 teaspoon extra-virgin olive oil

3 packed cups baby spinach, very finely chopped

1 garlic clove, sliced in half crosswise

1 ripe avocado, pitted, peeled, and thinly sliced

Freshly ground black pepper to taste

2 ounces sliced prosciutto (4 slices), torn into large pieces

Blueberry Oatmeal Pancakes

SERVES 2 to 3

1½ cups old-fashioned rolled oats (not the quick-cooking kind!)

1 large egg

¾ cup unsweetened almond milk (or milk of your choice)

2 tablespoons pure maple syrup, plus extra for serving

½ teaspoon ground cinnamon

½ teaspoon freshly grated lemon zest (optional)

½ teaspoon pure vanilla extract

Pinch of sea salt

2 teaspoons baking powder

Coconut oil or butter for cooking

⅔ cup blueberries

Pancakes for dinner!!!!" is music to most people's ears, and I firmly support getting down with the occasional evening short stack. These simple blueberry cakes are made with rolled oats, which are an excellent source of fiber and help balance your blood sugar. They're slightly denser than their white flour counterparts, but the stick-to-your-ribs quality is a big part of oatmeal pancakes' hearty charm. Drizzled with a little pure maple syrup, this is one pancake that you can party with on the reg.

1. Put the oats, egg, almond milk, maple syrup, cinnamon, lemon zest (if using), vanilla, salt, and baking powder in a blender. Blend until smooth. Let the batter rest for 5 minutes. The batter will be pretty thick, but it should still be pourable. (If it's not pourable, add an extra splash of almond milk and blend again to thin it slightly.)

2. Heat a large nonstick skillet or griddle over medium heat. When hot, add a little coconut oil and swirl to coat the bottom of the pan. Pour scant ¼-cup measures of batter into the pan—you can eyeball it, but if you do use a measuring cup, grease it with a little coconut oil so that the batter will slide right out—and sprinkle each pancake with a few blueberries. (I recommend cooking 2 to 3 pancakes at a time, so you don't crowd the pan or get overwhelmed.) Cook until you see small bubbles appear on the top surface of each pancake, about 1 minute. Carefully flip the pancakes with a thin spatula and cook until the undersides are lightly browned, another minute or so.

3. Transfer the pancakes to a plate, add a little more oil to the skillet, and repeat the cooking process with the remaining batter.

4. Serve the pancakes warm, drizzled with a little maple syrup.

JUST THE TIP: These pancakes keep for a couple of days in the fridge and reheat well. They're also sturdy enough to be used as a sub for bread or toast. Try spreading them with a little nut butter and/or chia jam.

Steak and Egg Tacos

SERVES 2 to 3

I'm not against rolling up some eggs and salsa in a tortilla and calling it a breakfast taco in the a.m., but that doesn't really cut it come dinnertime, when most need a more substantial (read: meatier) meal. That's where spiced skirt steak comes in. This lean (and cheap!) cut cooks in less than five minutes and plays very well with fluffy scrambled eggs and your favorite fiesta-style toppings. If you're more of a breakfast burrito type, feel free to ditch the corn tortillas in favor of a large whole-grain wrap.

1. Preheat a grill pan or large skillet over medium-high heat.

2. In a small bowl, combine the paprika, cumin, garlic powder, black pepper, and salt. Rub the steak all over with the spice mixture.

3. Place the steak in the hot pan and cook for about 2 minutes per side for medium-rare. Transfer the steak to a cutting board and let rest for at least 5 minutes, then cut it into ½-inch cubes.

4. Meanwhile, crack the eggs into a medium bowl. Add a pinch of salt and a few cranks of black pepper and whisk vigorously until pale yellow and slightly frothy. Heat the oil in a large skillet over medium heat. When the oil is hot and shimmering, reduce the heat to medium-low and add the beaten eggs. Cook, stirring in big, sweeping motions to form large curds, until the eggs are just set, 2 to 3 minutes. Transfer the eggs to a plate.

5. Warm each tortilla in a skillet or directly on a gas burner for 10 to 15 seconds per side.

6. Add some scrambled eggs and steak to each tortilla. Top with the avocado, red onion, cilantro, and hot sauce. Serve with lime wedges if you like a citrusy kick.

FOR THE TACOS:

¼ teaspoon smoked paprika

¼ teaspoon ground cumin

¼ teaspoon garlic powder

¼ teaspoon freshly ground black pepper, plus extra for the eggs

¼ teaspoon kosher salt, plus extra for the eggs

½ pound skirt steak

6 large eggs

1 tablespoon extra-virgin olive oil (You can use butter if you prefer.)

6 corn tortillas

FOR SERVING:

1 ripe avocado, pitted, peeled, and thinly sliced

3 tablespoons minced red onion

¼ cup fresh cilantro leaves, chopped

Hot sauce of your choice

Lime wedges (optional)

Turkey & Apple Sausage Sandwiches with Fried Eggs

1 pound 93% lean ground turkey (99% lean will be too dry!!)

1 small sweet apple (I like Fuji), peeled and grated on the large holes of a box grater (about ½ cup grated apple)

1 tablespoon finely chopped fresh sage leaves

1 teaspoon kosher salt

1 teaspoon freshly ground black pepper

¾ teaspoon fennel seed

½ teaspoon garlic powder

¼ teaspoon ground allspice

1½ tablespoons extra-virgin olive oil, divided

¾ cup grated sharp cheddar cheese

6 large eggs

6 whole-grain English muffins, split in half

3 tablespoons Dijon mustard

1½ packed cups baby arugula or spinach (optional)

Several years ago, Logan was recognized at a local bagel shop. The Dude had just ordered three breakfast sandwiches when a woman in line behind him commented, "That's not Dude Diet approved, you know." Logan laughed good-naturedly, before reminding her that it was No-Calorie Sunday and asking how she knew me. She simply responded, "Oh, I don't know Serena. Just a fan of yours." Overwhelmed by his newfound stardom, Logan came running home, waving his sandos in the air and screaming, "Daddy is FAMOUS!!!" (Logan started referring to himself as "Daddy" years ago. No explanation.)

You'd think that being recognized as the face of a sexy lifestyle brand would motivate the Dude to keep it tight, but unfortunately, it had exactly the opposite effect for a few weeks. According to my famous roommate, "Celebrities do what they want! Look at Leo and his dad bod!" Terrified that this sausage, egg, and cheese indulgence may become the new norm, I introduced a significantly less artery-clogging alternative with homemade turkey sausage into the rotation. It's remained a favorite over the years and hits the spot day or night. Don't be alarmed by the thought of making your own sausage here. It's nothing more than a spiced-up burger with some grated apple thrown in for sweetness and flair.

1. Place the ground turkey in a mixing bowl. Pat the grated apple dry with a paper towel (no need to get crazy, you just want to get rid of some of the excess moisture) and add it to the bowl along with the sage, salt, pepper, fennel seed, garlic powder, and allspice. Mix until well combined. (I recommend using your hands for this, but a fork will do if you're squeamish.)

2. With damp hands, mold the turkey mixture into 6 patties, about ¾ inch thick, and place them on a piece of parchment or wax paper.

3. Heat ½ tablespoon of the olive oil in a large nonstick skillet over medium heat. When the oil is hot and shimmering, carefully add 3 patties to the pan. (They will be pretty soft, so I like to grease a thin metal spatula and use it to transfer each patty to the pan.) Cook undisturbed for 5 minutes or until lightly browned on the undersides and beginning to firm, then flip with a spatula and cook for another 5 minutes on the opposite

sides. During the last 2 minutes of the cook time, sprinkle each patty with 2 tablespoons of cheddar cheese and cover the skillet with a lid to melt the cheese. Transfer the sausage patties to a plate and cover with aluminum foil to keep warm. Add another ½ tablespoon of olive oil to the pan and repeat the cooking process with the remaining patties.

4. Wipe out the skillet used for the sausage and return it to the stove over medium heat. Add the remaining ½ tablespoon of olive oil to the pan. When the oil is hot and shimmering, crack 3 eggs into the pan (leaving a little space around each one) and cook for 3 to 4 minutes or until the whites are set but the yolks are still runny. (If your whites are having trouble setting, pop a lid onto the pan for a minute or so.) Repeat this process with the remaining eggs.

5. Meanwhile, toast the English muffins.

6. Spread the bottom half of each muffin with ½ tablespoon of Dijon. (Feel free to use more if you're a mustard lover.) Top with ¼ cup arugula or spinach (if using), a sausage patty, and a fried egg, and sandwich everything together. Go to town.

Potato and Brussels Sprout Rosti with Prosciutto

Also known as "Swiss hash browns," potato rosti is made from coarsely grated potatoes that are pressed and then panfried. In layman's terms, it's a big-ass potato pancake (sans eggs and flour!) with a crisp golden-brown exterior and a tender, almost fluffy interior. A straight-up potato rosti is pretty great, but getting some shaved Brussels sprouts, salty prosciutto, and nutty Gruyère involved ups the ante in a big way. Hash browns have never been hotter, dudes. Get some.

1. Start by prepping the potatoes. Wrap the grated potatoes in a clean dish towel and twist the towel tightly, wringing out as much moisture from the potatoes as humanly possible. (I find it's easiest to do this in two or three batches.) Place the dried potatoes in a large bowl. Add the Brussels sprouts, salt, and a few cranks of black pepper and toss to combine. Briefly set aside.

2. Heat 1 tablespoon of the oil in a 10-inch skillet over medium-high heat until hot and shimmering. (Test the oil with one strand of potato—if it sizzles enthusiastically, you're good to go.) Add half of the potato mixture to the pan in an even layer. Add the cheese in an even layer and then the prosciutto. Top with the remaining potatoes in an even layer and smooth the top with a spatula.

3. Cook the rosti for 3 minutes, then lower the heat to medium-low. (You should still hear the potatoes sizzling.) Cook for about 12 minutes, until the underside of the potatoes is golden brown and crisp.

4. Time to flip the rosti. To do this, place a large plate over the skillet and carefully turn the skillet over, flipping the rosti onto the plate.

5. Add the remaining 1 tablespoon oil to the skillet. When hot, carefully slide the rosti from the plate back into the skillet. Cook for another 10 to 12 minutes, until the underside is browned and the center is tender. Remove the rosti from the pan and allow it to cool slightly.

6. Slice the rosti in half (or into quarters) and serve warm. Top each serving with an egg or two if you like.

1 pound Yukon gold potatoes, peeled and grated on the large holes of a box grater (about 3 cups grated potato)

1½ cups thinly sliced Brussels sprouts

¼ teaspoon kosher salt

Freshly ground black pepper to taste

2 tablespoons extra-virgin olive oil

½ cup grated Gruyère cheese (I also love Fontina, Gouda, and goat cheese in this.)

2 ounces sliced prosciutto, torn into small pieces

FOR SERVING (OPTIONAL):

2 to 4 fried, poached, or scrambled eggs

B.L.A.T. Breakfast Caesar

Basically a deconstructed B.L.A.T. sandwich tossed with slimming Caesar dressing and topped with a fried egg, this salad packs an explosion of creamy, crunchy, savory awesomeness in each bite. You can skip the egg if you like, or replace it with a small chicken breast or salmon fillet, but I feel obligated to stress the magic of a runny yolk mingling with the Greek yogurt–based dressing here. The added layer of richness is downright epic.

1. Heat a large skillet or sauté pan over medium-low heat. When hot, add the bacon and cook, turning occasionally, until browned and crispy, 12 to 15 minutes. Transfer the bacon to a paper towel–lined plate to cool slightly, then break into bite-size pieces. Reserve 2 teaspoons bacon grease from the skillet.

2. Meanwhile, preheat the broiler to high. Line a baking sheet with aluminum foil.

3. Add the English muffin pieces to the prepared baking sheet. Drizzle with the reserved bacon grease, sprinkle with a tiny pinch of salt and a little black pepper, and toss to combine. Spread the English muffin pieces in an even layer. Broil for 3 to 4 minutes, shaking the pan every minute or so, until the bread is browned and crisp. (Keep a close eye on it!) Briefly set aside.

4. In a large bowl, whisk all the ingredients for the dressing. Add the romaine hearts and toss to coat. Add the bacon, English muffin pieces, tomato, and avocado and gently toss again. Briefly set aside while you cook the eggs.

5. Heat a large nonstick skillet over medium heat. (If you do not have a true nonstick skillet, add 1 teaspoon extra-virgin olive oil to the pan.) When hot, add the eggs. Cook for 3 to 4 minutes, until the whites are just set but the yolks are still runny. (If your eggs aren't setting, cover the skillet with a lid for a minute or so to help them along.)

6. Divide the salad between 2 plates or bowls. Top each with an egg and serve immediately.

4 slices thick-cut bacon (preferably with no added nitrates)

1 whole-grain English muffin, split and cut into ¾-inch pieces

Tiny pinch of kosher salt

Freshly ground black pepper to taste

6 cups roughly chopped romaine hearts

1 medium heirloom tomato, diced (or ¾ cup cherry tomatoes, sliced in half)

½ ripe avocado, pitted, peeled, and diced

2 large eggs

FOR THE DRESSING:

⅓ cup nonfat plain Greek yogurt

3 tablespoons grated Parmesan cheese

1 garlic clove, grated or finely minced

1 tablespoon plus 1 teaspoon extra-virgin olive oil

1 teaspoon fresh lemon juice

¾ teaspoon anchovy paste

½ teaspoon Dijon mustard

Freshly ground black pepper to taste

ACKNOWLEDGMENTS

Writing a cookbook is both amazing and terrible, and this one would never have been possible without the expertise, dedication, patience, and support of so many. I'm endlessly grateful to the following wonderful people for helping make *The Dude Diet Dinnertime* a reality. I sincerely hope my computer keyboard survives the river of tears that's about to be shed acknowledging them....

Julie Will, thank you for "getting" The Dude Diet, believing in me, and helping me become the best version of myself as an author. I loved working on this book (and the last) with you. Milan Bozic and Bonni Leon-Berman, thank you for designing my fantasy cookbook—you nailed it from cover to cover. And to the entire team of hardworking folks at Harper Wave who helped bring this book to life, thank you so much for your time, effort, and creativity.

Matt Armendariz and Marian Cooper Cairns, where do I start? I'm not saying I wrote this book just so I could spend twelve straight days with the two of you, but I'm not *not* saying that, either. Matt, your photography, passion, and dance skills consistently blow my mind, and I couldn't be more obsessed with you as a photographer or as a human. Marian, I don't know how you manage to make my food look so insanely beautiful, but I am forever in your debt. You're the best in the biz, and I'm so grateful for your food-styling wizardry, life wisdom, and friendship. The Dude Diet series (!!) wouldn't be the same without the magic from both of you. Thank you. And to Diana, Byron, and Laura, shoot team extraordinaire, thank you for your help in executing these glorious photos and for making the experience infinitely more fun. I'm counting down the days until our next shoot. Bye.

To my agent, Eve Attermann, I appreciate you more than you know. Thank you for championing The Dude Diet and me since 2014. I'm so lucky to have you in my corner (and watching all my Instagram Stories).

Pam Golum, Katie Fuchs, Jeanne O'Keefe, and the entire team at the Lippin Group, thank you for tirelessly pitching me and The Dude Diet concept for the past three years. You all have had my back like no one else, and this book would never have been possible without your help.

Patty Ehinger, thank you for being my stage mom, tour manager, camera lady, human spreadsheet, and personal hype girl. Fingies crossed this book is my big break so I can start paying you more to run my life. In the meantime, please don't leave me.

Thank you a million times over to my DDD recipe-testing family. The recipes in this book are so much better thanks to your selfless culinary commitment and honest feedback. It still baffles me that so many of you were willing to sacrifice your precious time and hard-earned money to help a stranger with her cookbook, and I'm eternally grateful for your service. An especially enormous thank-you to my star testers: Carly Cloud, Emily Ballard, Brian Leary and co., Jan Lehmann-Shaw, Kay Cochran, and Alex Morris. The number of recipes each of you tackled was almost unfathomable, and I can only hope there will still be a few fun surprises for you in this book. You're my heroes.

To my online community, you all are the smartest, funniest, most badass people on the Internet, and your messages and pictures light me up on the daily. I'm humbled that you choose to spend your time virtually hanging out with me and that my recipes have made their way into so many of your kitchens. Thank you for supporting your weird blog/book lady in countless ways over the years. It means everything to me.

I never would have survived the book process in one piece without my people. Thank you to my family—Mom, Dad, Olivia, Will, Elliot, John, Linda, and Tyler—for your unconditional love and support. Each of you has opened doors, lifted me up, and kept me motivated in your own way throughout this process. I hope you know how much I love and appreciate you. To Fifi, Annie Blaine, and my girls (Annabel, Daphne, Lara, and Starr), thank you for putting up with my crazy ass the past two years (/forever), for talking me off many a ledge, shamelessly pimping The Dude Diet, and always, always being there. Special thanks to Sydney Gaybrick and Cabot Barry for making regular food pickups and providing free recipe feedback. To *all* my friends, old and new, thank you for filling my life with absurd happiness. I love you.

Lastly, I want to thank my muse. Logan, thank you for providing me with endless inspiration, for allowing me to share your nutritional "journey" and stories in print, for being my number one recipe tester and brand ambassador, and for supporting me through the many highs and lows of my batshit creative process. Thank you for making me laugh every single day (and for being willing to laugh at yourself) and for loving me as hard as you do. Being married to you has been the single greatest pleasure of my life, and I never take that for granted. You're my favorite. I love you.

INDEX

Page references in *italics* refer to illustrations.

ABOUT THE AUTHOR

After graduating from Harvard, Serena fell in love with food at Le Cordon Bleu Paris, earning her cuisine diploma in 2011. Since then, she has put her culinary skills (and sense of humor) to work as a private chef, culinary instructor, recipe developer, author, and blogger at Domesticate-Me.com. Serena is the author of *The Dude Diet* and has appeared on the *Today* show, *Dr. Oz*, *The Chew*, and many other shows. Her writing and recipes have been featured in print and online in outlets such as FoodandWine.com, People.com, the *New York Post*, *Self*, *Women's Day*, Elle.com, Parade.com, TheKitchn, and *Real Simple*. She lives in New York City with her dude.